# INTERESTS

To Frank -
Happy Christmas -
Mam & Dad

# INTERESTS

T. K. Whitaker

Institute of Public Administration

First Published 1983

Institute of Public Administration
57-61 Lansdowne Road, Dublin 4, Ireland

Designed by Della Varilly.


Acknowledgment for photographs to Bord Fáilte,
Irish Press, Office of Public Works and Irish Times.

Whitaker, T. K.
Interests.
I.   Title
082          PR6073.H/

ISBN 0-906980-24-0
ISBN 0-906980-25-9   Pbk

Typeset 11pt. Baskerville and Printed by Cahills, Dublin.

# Contents

# Foreword

Banking and academic friends have persuaded me that students and perhaps others would be facilitated if some of my lectures and articles were gathered into one volume.

During my period as Governor of the Central Bank (1969-76) most of what I wrote in Irish and English – attributed and non-attributed – appeared in the *Quarterly Bulletins* or *Annual Reports* of the Bank and is thus reasonably accessible. I have written a confidential memoir of the Central Bank – government relationship in that period which is in the archives of the Central Bank and will be available to future historians. What I said in Seanad Éireann on various topics over the years 1977 to 1982 appears in Volumes 87-97 (as indexed) of the *Official Report*.

Two previous books stand on their own: *Financing by credit creation* Clonmore & Reynolds, Dublin, 1947; and *Economic Development* (written with the collaboration of various colleagues) which was published by the Stationery Office in November 1958.

Other writings have appeared mainly in the *Journal of the Statistical and Social Inquiry Society of Ireland, Studies,* and in the hospitable pages of *Administration,* which celebrated its silver jubilee in 1982.

It seemed too lazy merely to insert within the covers of this book scripta and dicta already on record so I have indirectly expressed my gratitude to publisher and sponsor by writing some fresh pieces for this publication, of which the most substantial is 'Financial Turning-Points'. I have also gone outside the boundaries of economics and finance to include a piece (with postscript) on Northern Ireland as well as notes and essays on the Irish language and other cultural matters in which I have long had an interest. As an act of *pietas,* there is a commemoration of some friends who gave distinguished service to Ireland. To end on a lighter note, and justify the generic title 'Interests', I include the story of my first salmon. Professor Louden Ryan very kindly read and commented on a number of the financial papers when they were in draft; any errors of fact or judgement, however, remain solely mine.

Notes in Appendix 1 indicate when and where items were originally published and the background to those which appear here for the first time. Appendix 2 contains a fairly complete list of publications over the past forty years.

I am grateful to the Bank of Ireland for the encouragement, and the financial sponsorship, to which this volume owes its appearance.

T.K.W.

# I  Economics and Finance

# 1  Ireland's Development Experience

It is part of the mythology – perhaps I should say martyrology – of Irish nationalism that the country's development, at least outside the north-east corner, suffered malign neglect during the union with Great Britain which lasted from 1800 to 1922. The active promotion of infrastructural and industrial development, financed from ample revenue, which was undertaken by the Irish Parliament for some decades even before Grattan secured its independence from Westminster in 1782, is often contrasted with the post-Union decline of the no-longer-protected Irish cotton and woollen industries. The popular perception of Ireland as a neglected colonial appendage of Britain does not, however, give sufficient recognition to the inevitable effects of the depression which hit Britain and Ireland alike in the wake of the Napoleonic Wars, nor to Ireland's disadvantages as a peripheral and mainly agricultural entity, outside the mainstream of the industrial revolution and without indigenous resources of the coal and iron then so important. Ireland's social and economic vulnerability increased in the early decades of the nineteenth century according as the rural population grew, its dependence on the potato crop increased, and the supplementary income provided by spinning and weaving in the home dried up with the spread of factory-based production in the major industrial centres of the United Kingdom. The abject poverty of Ireland's large rural population, the absence of cheap fuel and power and the tragic social and psychological disruption caused by the Great Famine in the 1840s were amongst the principal causes of the slow growth of the Irish economy in the nineteenth century. Professor L. M. Cullen has drawn attention also to the 'dramatic reduction in transport costs' during that century, another factor which left

1

Ireland's 'small-scale and domestic industries vulnerable in a more fiercely competitive age.'[1]

To counter Ireland's economic, no less than its political, subservience to Britain was one of the strongest motivations of the Home Rule and independence movements. An independent Irish parliament was looked to as a renewed source of the stimulus to development and the protective benevolence with which memory invested Grattan's parliament. The foremost exponent of economic nationalism was Arthur Griffith, who was to be President of the Republic for a few months before his death, and the emergence of the Irish Free State, in 1922. As early as 1905, in his book *The Resurrection of Hungary*, Griffith had espoused the protectionist doctrine of Friedrich List and made it part of Sinn Féin policy. Ireland's 'manufacturing arm' was to be developed with the aid of tariff protection, particularly for infant industries, but the interdependence of agriculture and industry was recognised.

The new twenty-six county Irish Free State which came into being in 1922 was predominantly agricultural; its population of $3\frac{1}{4}$ million included a workforce of $1\frac{1}{4}$ million, over half of whom were on the land. I use this neutral phrase deliberately. Of the 670,000 persons described for statistical purposes as being 'engaged in agriculture' many were so-called 'relatives assisting' on farms too small to afford them gainful employment. They lived at a miserable subsistence level without regular or adequate cash incomes, as indeed did many old and unmarried proprietors of farms. These 'relatives assisting' formed the reservoir of hopeless underemployment which filled the emigrant ships for many years, dwarfing the gains in industrial employment which began to be made from the late 1920s onwards.

The development problem which faced the government of the new state – and which, indeed, has been of concern to every Irish government since – was to try to ensure, in a small economy with a large agricultural sector, the availability of employment at an acceptable income for everyone who wished to stay at home. Involuntary emigration was to be brought to an end.

In brief, the policies tried have ranged from tentative interference with free trade, to extensive and indiscriminate protectionism, to a more consciously planned development oriented towards free trade, and finally to the mixture of industrial competition and agricultural support which is the special mark of the European Economic Community. I shall review and assess the development experience of the Irish state in these four policy phases.

## Phase 1 – 1922-32, Modified Free Trade

The new state of only 26,000 square miles and $3\frac{1}{4}$ million people which emerged from the United Kingdom in 1922 was in touch with the rest of the world through emigration rather than through exports. All but 2 per cent of exports went to the UK and nearly 80 per cent of imports came from the UK. The more industrial north-eastern part of the island of Ireland had remained on a partly self-governing basis within the UK and, in consequence, there was in the new state, as I have already remarked, a heavy concentration on agriculture, much of it of a merely subsistence character. Only one person was employed in transportable goods industries for every eleven 'engaged' in agriculture. The relative importance of industry in Northern Ireland can be judged from the fact that in 1921 textiles represented a larger proportion of total all-Ireland exports than agricultural produce.

The continuing high level of emigration gave rise to a high dependency ratio. Industrialisation was clearly desirable but was unlikely to develop quickly in such an agriculturally-oriented state with little manufacturing tradition and not many skilled workers. Private enterprise would be slow to set up industry in the state without special incentives because of the small market size, the falling population, the assumed absence of mineral resources and deficiencies of infrastructure.

On the other hand, the new state had taken over a well-organised administrative system and a sound banking and financial framework. It was also the inheritor and sponsor of a Sinn Féin philosophy which might have been expected to result in an active policy of protection of infant industries, considering the obvious scope for replacement of finished imports by home products. Unfortunately, the early years of the new state were marred by a civil war and most of the efforts and resources of government were engaged in quelling this threat to the life of the state and later in repairing the infrastructural damage consequent on long years of disturbed conditions. Friedrich List, as relayed by Arthur Griffith, was not forgotten but securing the foundations of independent government had to take precedence. A few moderate tariffs were introduced after careful inquiry but they were far from making any significant progress on the road to self-sufficiency.

Apart from the deflection of their energies to the suppression of violence and to economic reconstruction, the reluctance to embrace an outright protectionist policy can be explained by the first Irish government's desire to establish, in face of widespread doubt, the respectability and viability of the state. Orthodoxy in economic and financial matters seemed a more reliable prop than adventurousness. The new Irish currency was established at parity with sterling; budgetary policy was extremely conservative. Free trade was the accepted commercial philosophy of the day. Moreover, agriculture was by far the stronger arm of the economy and it seemed vital to sustain it so that farmers would have more to spend on the products of new domestic industry and agricultural exports would expand to pay for the imports of machinery and raw materials necessary for industrialisation. It was hoped that the benefits of agricultural prosperity would percolate to other sectors and lead progressively to an expansion of home industries.

Two major moves were, however, made in this period to reduce dependency on imports. The establishment of the Electricity Supply Board in 1927 was a bold step in this direction, providing the power infrastructure for a developing economy. The introduction of a beet sugar industry was intended to improve husbandry and promote self-sufficiency. On a broad view, however, this whole period was marked less by active industrial promotion than by careful concentration on restoring and strengthening the foundations for development. Much of the energy of government was spent on repair of the damage caused by the 'Troubles' and the civil war and on the establishment of law and order, an efficient administration and a sound monetary and financial system.

Because of emigration the population continued to fall, though at a slower rate; there was a gain of only 5,000 new jobs in transportable goods industries between 1926 and 1931.

## Phase 2 – Protectionism – 1932-58

The 1930s saw a much more active interventionism. The advent of a new government to power in 1932 set the stage for a vigorous policy of protection and industrialisation. A financial dispute with the UK invited retaliatory recourse by both parties to tariffs and quotas. Internationally also, the trend of events was running against free trade and in favour of resort to national protectionism. The new government's protectionist policy was geared primarily towards self-sufficiency rather than the encouragement of new industry from outside. There was concern that industry should be Irish-controlled, a policy reflected in the Control of Manufactures Acts and the setting up of state-controlled monopolies in sugar and cement and a state-owned airline. In agriculture, self-sufficiency in wheat and beet and tillage generally were encouraged in preference to beef and milk production.

Protection was granted rather freely and with little scientific measurement of what was needed in individual cases. The heated atmosphere of retaliation was not conducive to any careful adjustment of aid to need. A few figures will give an idea of the zeal with which what Professor Meenan has called 'the last surviving example of a predominantly free-trading state' was transformed into one of the most highly protected in the world.[2] At the end of 1931 – before the Fianna Fáil administration came to power – the list of tariffs covered 68 articles. In 1932 alone successive rounds of tariff increases brought in 67 new classes of goods at ad valorem duties ranging from 15 per cent to 75 per cent. Every year from then to 1938 saw high and wide-ranging duties, ad valorem or specific, imposed on previously free imports. Tariffs on intermediate products piled up to create a pyramid of protection for some final products.

Professor Louden Ryan's measurement of the mounting height of the tariff wall shows that, for a representative list of commodities which bore no duty in 1924, the tariff level index in 1931 was 9 per cent but had risen to 45 per cent by 1936, the year which marked the high-water mark of protection. In that year a Coal–Cattle Pact eased the Anglo-Irish dispute,

which was finally settled by the Trade Agreement of 1938, the
provisions of which included machinery for review of protective
duties and other import restrictions. Some tariffs were reduced
or abolished in the 1936-38 period with the result that Professor
Ryan's index for 1938 is down to 35 per cent. It is to be noted,
however, that the index does not measure the protective effect
of the numerous quota restrictions. *The Economist* calculated in
1938 that 1,947 articles were subject to restriction or control
in the state.

We should remind ourselves that protectionism was not an
Irish aberration of the 1930s. The world at large was in the
grip of depression; the prices of primary products had plummeted, the demand for goods had fallen catastrophically,
unemployment was severe and widespread. In 1931 the new
government in England announced its intention of imposing
a tariff – the first general British tariff since the 1850s – and of
protecting British agriculture. The practical and theoretical
considerations supporting free trade were thus undermined
and no inhibition lay in the way of a policy of protection aimed
at securing self-sufficiency. No less an economist than Keynes
spoke out in favour of such a move at University College,
Dublin, in April 1933 declaring that 'if I were an Irishman I
should find much to attract me in the economic outlook of your
present government towards self-sufficiency'.[4] The extent to
which free trade had been abandoned before World War II is
indicated by a table in Professor Ryan's paper which shows
that, taking Ireland's tariff level as 100, the level for Britain
was 65, for the United States 55, for Switzerland 70 and for
Germany 152.

The indiscriminate granting of protection did encourage a
rapid development of industry catering almost exclusively for
the home market. By 1936 there were 101,000 people employed
in transportable goods industries, nearly twice as many as a
decade before. Even during the 1930s, however, there were
signs that protected industries catering only for the home
market were no long-term solution for Ireland's employment
problem. Gaining the wider openings in export markets on
which any significant expansion of Irish industry depended
would require a high level of productivity to be achieved in
order to offset the cost handicap involved in both importing

raw materials and re-exporting the final products. The industries which had been set up under protection required a substantial import content and this, without corresponding export buoyancy, could cause trouble on the external payments front. This difficulty, indeed, proved to be one of the great constraints on development policy so long as agriculture was the main source of exports and agricultural produce had to be consigned to the British market where prices were deliberately held at a low level and even access at times was not assured.

The Second World War caused scarcities and postponed any widening of the Irish industrial base. Tariffs were largely suspended during the war, industrial output fell and net output in agriculture rose. For a time after the war emigration fell slightly below the rate of natural increase but this tendency towards a rise in population was sharply reversed in the 1950s. In 1946 there were 116,000 people employed in transportable goods industries and the numbers engaged in agriculture had fallen from the 670,000 of 1926 to 594,000. Entering the 1950s exports of manufactured goods were, however, only 6 per cent of total exports, a long way short of the contribution of agriculture.

As supplies became more freely available in the post-war period protective duties were gradually revived but with less conviction as to their efficacy as an instrument of development. In this respect, the focus was shifting to public capital expenditure as the mainspring of economic expansion. The shortcomings of an uncritical protectionist policy were being recognised, particularly its cost and price effects and the complacency and inefficiency it induced. The chief protagonist of protection, Seán Lemass, who was for many years Minister for Industry and Commerce and later prime minister in Fianna Fáil governments, came to an early realisation after the war that more effective measures were needed to set the economy on the path of competitive efficiency and growth. Although his 1947 Industrial Efficiency and Prices Bill was never enacted, it was clear evidence of his concern; and it can be seen as a precursor of the more comprehensive measures of industrial survey, tripartite consultative and advisory machinery, grants for modernisation and adaptation and even unilateral reduction of protection which he put into effect in the early 1960s after the state had first applied for membership of the EEC.

Not only Lemass, but his counterpart in the Coalition government of 1954-57, William Norton, promised comprehensive tariff reviews but, as Professor Meenan notes, no observable consequences followed and protection was, indeed, intensified, though not deliberately, in the period 1956-58 by special charges intended to discourage imports and rectify a serious imbalance in external payments. During most of the 1950s, in fact, the risk of heavy balance-of-payments deficits was a serious constraint on development policies. Recurrent sterling crises also brought pressure on sterling area countries to curb imports and internal demand in order to avert a devaluation. Agricultural exports were still the predominant source of foreign earnings and they were subject to many vicissitudes, including unfavourable British pricing policies. It was not, indeed, until 1969 that industrial exports exceeded agricultural exports for the first time. The external deficits seemed at times quite menacing – the 1951 deficit was almost 15 per cent of GNP – and their absolute amounts could quickly exhaust the external reserves then directly held by the Central Bank, as distinct from the commercial banks. It was not until the 1960s, and the appearance on the world scene of the Eurodollar – a product of US trade deficits – that foreign borrowing on any significant scale became possible.

In any case, the instrument by which expansion would have been sought in the early and mid-1950s – the Public Capital Programme – was itself rather ineffective; the dominance of infrastructural and social (as distinct from more immediately productive) elements in the Programme gave a low output return for the capital investment. New policy orientations were needed which would bring private enterprise and initiative into play on a bigger scale.

Despite the difficulties, the despondency and the poor economic performance (less than 2 per cent annually by way of growth rate) of those years, the foundations of new policies for economic growth were being laid and the appropriate institutions established. In the early 1950s the Industrial Development Authority, Bord Fáilte, and Córas Tráchtála, had been set up. The industrial grants system, introduced in 1952, was extended in 1956. Tax reliefs for exports were introduced in that year by the Minister for Finance, Gerard Sweetman, who emphasised the need for 'a substantial increase in volume and efficiency of national production'.

## Phase 3 – Planned Development oriented to Free Trade – 1958-73

Nevertheless, as I have written elsewhere, the years 1955-56 had plumbed the depths of hopelessness. One of the recurring series of balance-of-payments crises was overcome but only at the cost of stagnation, high unemployment and emigration. The mood of despondency was palpable. Something had to be done or the achievement of national independence would prove to have been a futility. Various attempts were made to shine a beam forward in this dark night of the soul; they at least agreed on the need to devote more resources on an orderly basis to productive investment. Finally, over the winter and spring of 1957-58, a comprehensive survey of the economy, extending to its potentialities as well as its deficiencies, was prepared in the Department of Finance. This was presented to the government in May 1958 and published under the title *Economic Development* in November of that year, simultaneously with the *First Programme for Economic Expansion* which was acknowledged to be based largely upon it. This Programme changed the direction of policy, co-ordinated the development process and gave a fillip to confidence which, supported by buoyant world conditions, generated an outstanding economic performance in the 1960s. The GNP per capita, which in 1951 in Ireland was only 55 per cent of that in the UK, had by 1970 been lifted to 72 per cent.

The change of emphasis in traditional policy was remarkable. The aim of self-sufficiency, involving, for instance, protected or subsidised home production of wheat and sugar beet, had been pursued in agriculture as well as in industry; now the importance of the 85 per cent of Ireland's agricultural land which was under grass was expressly recognised. Not only, to oversimplify a little, did the new Programme put grass before grain but, on the industrial side, it put export-oriented expansion, even if under foreign ownership, before dependence on

protected and inadequate domestic enterprise. Successive programmes maintained this policy emphasis. The Programme's
abandonment of the old-fashioned protectionism was explicit:

> It would be unrealistic, in the light of the probable emerg-
> ence of a Free Trade Area, to rely on a policy of protection
> similar to that applied over the past 25 years or so . . . .
> Bearing in mind that the only scope for substantial expan-
> sion lies in the production of goods for sale on export
> markets, it is clear that there can be no place for weak or
> inefficient industries . . . . it will be the policy in future in
> the case of new industries to confine the grant of tariff
> protection to cases in which it is clear that the industry will,
> after a short initial period, be able to survive without pro-
> tection . . . .

To complete the obituary of industrial protection as an instrument of development policy, I may be permitted to look ahead
to the conclusion of a Free Trade Area Agreement with Britain
in 1965, following the failure of the original applications of
both countries to join the EEC, and the eventual absorption of
this bilateral pact in the transitional arrangements for their
joint entry into the EEC on 1 January 1973.

The place of protection in development policy was taken by
a more coherent and conscious expansionism, backed by rising
government capital expenditure and a strong private capital
inflow. The balance within public capital expenditure was
shifted towards productive investment. There was a steady net
capital inflow, much of it in the form of direct investment in
new industry. The change of outlook towards foreign participation in domestic development was symbolised by the transformation of the 'Control of Manufactures' into the 'Encouragement of External Investment' Act. At last it seemed more
sensible to attract the foreign industry here rather than watch
tens of thousands of young Irish workers leave to serve the
multinationals overseas. Tourism also prospered. The growth
of gross national product exceeded 4 per cent per annum on
average. For most of the decade this unprecedented performance was achieved without any major balance-of-payments

trouble and with only a moderate rise in prices. The Republic was enjoying a 'virtuous circle of growth'.[6]

A thorough review of industrial efficiency was undertaken in the early 1960s. Special grants, loans and tax incentives were provided to encourage firms to modernise and adapt to more competitive trading conditions. Tariffs were even lowered unilaterally. Foreign firms were offered generous grants to set up in Ireland and export their output. The heavy emigration of the 1950s had reduced the population to its lowest-ever level of 2.8 million in 1961. But the tide was already turning. By 1966 a rise of 66,000 was recorded and emigration has never since absorbed more than part of the natural increase. The population has by now climbed above its 1922 level. Professor Brendan Walsh has said:

> The reversal of the traditional pattern of heavy net emigration is probably the single most eloquent index of the improvement in economic and social conditions in the Republic over the recent past.

There was one period – 1965-66 – when a spurt in consumption caused imports to increase at a time when exports were curtailed by restrictive measures in the UK and the capital inflow fell away. Action was taken to damp down consumer spending but investment was sustained and above-average growth rates restored the decadal rate to 4 per cent p.a. within a few years. Towards the end of the 1960s the annual rise in prices took a steep upward turn, averaging over 8 per cent for the year to 1972. This was an experience by no means confined to Ireland and inflation was to be accentuated after the quadrupling of oil prices in late 1973. The withering of the bloom from the end of the decade onwards has enhanced rather than dimmed the bright memory of the 1960s. They have, in retrospect, taken on the aspect of a Paradise Lost.

## Phase 4 – 1973 to date

Joining the European Economic Community on 1 January 1973, cannot, however, be headlined as Paradise Regained, though Ireland's development has undoubtedly been helped by membership. Failure to realise the potential benefits to the full must be ascribed largely to indifferent management of our own affairs. This is evident particularly in Ireland's relatively high inflation rate and in excessive deficits, both budgetary and external, requiring undue recourse to foreign borrowing for unproductive purposes. The overwhelmingly affirmative vote in favour of joining the EEC reflected not only the strong desire of farmers for more assured and higher living standards but also a general wish to reduce the state's dependence on the British economy. Both these motivations have, at least in part, been vindicated despite the distortions and frustrations resulting from inflation, budgetary indiscipline and world recession. Farm income, having first received a major boost, was cut in recent years by the scissors effect of high labour and input cost increases in domestic currency operating on lower external price improvements. Substantial ground will be regained this year (1982) and farmers are undoubtedly better off and more secure in the EEC than they would be outside it. Reduced dependence on the UK is indicated by the fact that the UK is now the destination for under 40 per cent of our exports, as against 55 per cent in 1973, whereas the Continental EEC takes 30 per cent as against 21 per cent.

The annual 8 per cent average inflation of the early 1970s gave way, under the impact of the oil crisis, to 11 per cent for 1973, 17 per cent for 1974 and 21 per cent for 1975. An immediate effect of entry to the EEC was to add the impetus of food price increases to the already rampant inflation. Fortunately, there was a turn back in 1976 to an inflation rate of 18 per cent, followed by 14 per cent for 1977 and 8 per cent for 1978 – the world was recovering from the initial energy shock and the terms of trade against oil were improving. In 1979, however, under the pressure of new oil price increases, the inflation rate in Ireland swung upwards again with added impetus from high wage and salary increases and the reduced sterling value of the Irish pound subsequent to our abandonment of the old fixed parity on joining the European Monetary System in March of that year. The 1980 rate of inflation was over 18 per cent and the annual price rise has been close to 20 per cent ever since, almost twice the Community average. This disparity has impaired competitiveness. The threat to devel-

opment prospects is all the more serious, given the unprecedented level of unemployment (156,000) and the large number
of new jobs, up to 30,000 a year, needed to absorb the expanding young labour force associated with a rising population.
With unemployment high and jobs scarce everywhere, emigration is no longer an available escape hatch.

A general slowdown in world trade and abrupt changes in
competitive positions and external accounts were amongst the
effects of the sudden and steep increases in oil prices in 1973/4
and 1979/80. In Ireland, there was a fall in industrial employment between 1974 and 1977 but this fall had been more than
made good by 1979 when the second upsurge in energy costs
crippled the major industrial nations and created a deep and
still prevalent depression. Employment in Irish industry this
year is probably only at the same level as it was in 1974. Job
losses have been high. Some long-established businesses – in
textiles, clothing, footwear and metal fabrication – have had
to close down or contract. On the other hand, some of the
newer plants, induced to set up export operations in Ireland
by liberal grants and tax incentives, have found that high
technology and skills and significant added value provide the
key to success in a more fiercely competitive environment.

Two tragic policy errors have enormously aggravated
Ireland's development problem: the decision in principle in
1972 to resort to borrowing for current budgetary purposes
and the irrational optimism which underlay the resumption of
economic planning in 1977.

The philosophy before 1972 had been that, when the
economy needed an expansionary thrust, this could most effectively and safely be given by way of increased public capital
expenditure; foreign borrowing on a reasonable scale was
justifiable if it was being used to create additional productive
assets likely to generate resources at least sufficient to service
the debt. In 1972, with no valid justification in theory and, as
it proved, little practical necessity, this principle was deliberately abandoned leaving the door open, when the oil crisis
supervened, to resort on an extravagant scale to deficits in the
current budget and to virtual disregard of the need to adjust
to the pronounced change in economic circumstances. Over
the years 1974-76, £550 million was borrowed merely to meet

everyday expenses. In 1977 a brake was imposed and it seemed that a return to external and budgetary balance on current account, as well as to sound economic growth, might be in prospect, given the signs of recovery in the world economy and the evident abatement of inflation. The new government, however, opened up the throttle, incurring much increased current deficits in every year since. The state debt which was £1,200 million in 1972 is now, a mere ten years later, approaching £11,000 million. The most regrettable aspect of this accumulation of debt is how little it has contributed to national development: much of it has been used to finance current needs and little of it has generated increased output at competitive costs. In a country still sorely in need of infrastructural and other development, and short of jobs, it is inexcusable to waste borrowing potential – particularly foreign borrowing potential, which is necessarily limited – on unproductive and ephemeral uses.

Conscious planning of development was a casualty of the first oil crisis and when it did reappear in 1977, top-of-the-scale targets were set which could be realised if at all only in ideal conditions. Public expectations, never easy to contain, were thus inflamed, with effects on the rate of pay increase and the scale of expansion of public services which have rendered almost insoluble the problem of budgetary imbalance. Demand management sank in a sea of current deficits. Protectionism, abandoned in its explicit form, persists in covert ways and in an attitude of mind, e.g., in the readiness to 'inject' equity capital into inefficient, loss-making state enterprises on social grounds, despite the piled-up evidence that subsidised employment is not only poor and precarious in itself but impairs competitiveness generally and handicaps the healthy growth of the economy.

This year has brought indications both of a will to tackle the budgetary problem and, regrettably, of the aggravated tensions to which belated remedies, whether in the form of extra taxation or expenditure cuts, give rise. One good omen is the apparent readiness of the trade union movement to accept the general economic need for the rate of pay increase to be lower than the current rate of inflation. Industrialisation policy is currently being reviewed in the light of the 'Telesis' and

National Economic and Social Council's reports and a general economic and social programme for the next three years is to be issued this Autumn.

Clearly, there are four adverse factors on the employment scene which the strategists must seek to offset: 1. the world recession – transitory, one hopes, and amenable to co-ordinated action by the major industrial countries; 2. Ireland's high inflation rate – capable of being reduced by a combination of income restraint, productivity improvement and fiscal prudence; 3. growing competition from the newly developing countries of the Third World and 4. the uncertain implications of technological change. In relation to the last two factors, it would seem that we must keep moving up the scale in technology, quality, design and amount of value added in the production process if we are even to maintain saleable output and jobs, not to mention achieving the doubling of the 1973-80 rate of increase in manufacturing output which would be needed to provide full employment. One must agree with the recent remark of Dr D. J. Cogan of UCD that 'too much of Irish industry, both domestic and foreign-owned, is in competition with low-wage countries rather than with the high-income industrial nations.'[7]

## Conclusion

After sixty years of native government, the Irish workforce remains virtually at its original level. Only recently has the population risen above the $3\frac{1}{4}$ million of 1922. The intervening years have witnessed what is hoped to have been the final phase of the Irish diaspora; the loss of population through emigration has ceased and in today's depressed world is unlikely to revive. It might seem that there is not much to show so far for Ireland's development efforts over their whole range as outlined in this paper. The provision of adequate employment at acceptable remuneration for all who wish to work in Ireland is still an unrealised and tantalising objective; it came closest to attainment during the 1960s.

These broad and rather bleak observations must not be allowed to obscure the real gains which have been made under difficult conditions. The static workforce figure conceals an enormous change for the better in its composition and productivity.[8] The movement of labour from agriculture to industry has still a good way to go before the more stable patterns of France or Denmark are established. Industrialisation will have to be the main job provider for many years yet before Ireland can consider itself a 'post-industrial' society and rely mostly on service activities for gainful occupation of additions to its workforce.

One measure of the material progress made since independence is the fact that the typical Irish family is now at least three times as well off as its forerunner of the 1920s. Another is the ranking of Ireland amongst the 25 richest countries in the world. There have been significant improvements in health, education and social welfare but poverty, relative and absolute, still affects a disappointingly large minority and unemployment is inordinately high and still rising.

Material progress in the world at large seems fated to be slower for quite some time ahead. In Ireland itself the first one per cent or so of each year's economic growth will be needed simply to maintain individual living standards as the population continues to rise. Much of any further growth will have to be devoted to making good living standards which rest precariously on foreign borrowing. The unearned consumer resources supplied by balance-of-payments deficits, largely generated by current budget deficits, are of the order of six to seven per cent of Gross National Product. Eliminating this overstretch will take resolute action over a period of years and meanwhile will preclude any effective improvement in individual or social standards. Making the best of this situation, and turning to good account in competitive new activities the potential of a growing young workforce, better educated and trained than ever before, will be a major challenge to political, social and economic leadership.

When material wants, often stimulated by expensive publicity, can no longer be met on a rising scale, one hopes that there will be a renewal and spread of interest in satisfactions of a different order, such as those deriving from cultivation of the mind, enjoyment of a clean environment and healthy activities, the care of others and service to the community.

What I have said about Ireland's experience will make clear that the problem of development and its implications for peace and social stability is by no means confined to the countries of the Third World.

## Notes to Chapter 1

[1]L. M. Cullen: The Foundation of the Irish Economy (ed.)

[2]J. F. Meenan: 'The Irish Economy Since 1922', Liverpool University Press, 1970, p. 142.

[3]W. J. L. Ryan: 'Measurement of Tariff Levels in Ireland', *Journal of the Statistical and Social Inquiry Society of Ireland*, 1948-49, p. 109.

[4]First Finlay Lecture by J. M. Keynes, published in *Studies* of June, 1983.

[5]T. K. Whitaker: 'From Protection to Free Trade – The Irish Experience' (see chapter 3).

[6]K. A. Kennedy and B.R. Dowling, 'Economic Growth in Ireland: The Experience Since 1947', Dublin 1975.

[7]*Sunday Independent*, 25 July 1982.

[8]The number engaged in agriculture has fallen below 200,000 and is now balanced by the number employed in transportable goods industries; other forms of industrial employment bring the total number of jobs in industry to 330,000, with services employing 600,000 and some 200,000 out of work.

*T. K. Whitaker at time of appointment as Secretary, Department of Finance, May 1956.*

# 2 Capital Formation, Saving and Economic Progress

In this paper I assemble some facts and considerations regarding the relation of capital formation and saving to the raising of real incomes in Ireland. In other words, my concern is with national development and with some of the means necessary to attain it in our particular circumstances. The views expressed are purely personal.

## Comparative advances in real incomes

Concern has been expressed about the comparatively slow rise in real income per head in Ireland over the past thirty years. The varying degree to which economies were damaged during the war makes it difficult to interpret comparisons which stretch back to pre-war times. It will suffice to take 1949 as a starting point for three reasons. First, it is accepted that by then the countries with which we have most contact and in which developments have most influence on our economic and social conceptions had recovered from the effects of the war. Second, it was about that time that we began particularly to look to a greatly enlarged state capital programme as a means of economic progress. Third, it is recent experience and trends which are of most relevance to an examination of current problems.

In attempting to compare economic progress here and in other countries since 1949, one must rely on statistics which, though not satisfactory, are the best available, namely, indexes of gross national product. The term 'gross national product' expresses the value of the nation's output of goods and services, before any deduction is made for depreciation of capital assets. Just as personal income can be either consumed or saved so

19

gross national product can be applied either to consumption (private or public) or to 'gross capital formation'. If the 'gross' element could be eliminated, that is, if proper allowance could be made for maintaining existing capital, it would be possible to estimate net national product accurately; and on the basis of figures of net national product, converted into stable money terms, one could assess the real advance from year to year in a community's income and wealth. As things are, one must rely for comparative purposes on *gross* statistics, remembering, however, that 'gross national product' and 'gross capital formation' figures exaggerate, to an indefinable but substantial degree, the true position as regards real additions to income and capital.

## Table 1: Index of Gross National Product at constant prices, 1949-54

| Year | Ireland | Britain | All OEEC Countries |
|------|---------|---------|--------------------|
| 1949 | 100     | 100     | 100                |
| 1950 | 100.3   | 103.8   | 108.0              |
| 1951 | 101.4   | 106.4   | 114.6              |
| 1952 | 104.6   | 105.3   | 116.9              |
| 1953 | 107.2   | 109.6   | 122.8              |
| 1954 | 107.6   | 114.6   | 129.3              |

The gross national product indexes show clearly that the recent upward trend in output and real income is weaker here than in Britain and other OEEC countries. Taking 1949 as starting point, our gross national product had risen 7.6 per cent by 1954, as compared with 14.6 per cent for Britain and 29.3 per cent for OEEC countries generally (Table 1). On a *per capita* basis the differences are narrowed – for Ireland the increase being 7.7 per cent while the British and OEEC figures are reduced to 13.0 per cent and 24.3 per cent respectively. Our showing is thus improved by emigration, which has kept the population almost stable in contrast with the increases recorded in Britain and Europe generally. The slow rate of increase in real income here as compared with Britain is the more disappointing because of the statistical assessment that our average real income is only one-half that of Britain and, incidentally, about one-fifth that of the United States.

## Effects of emigration

While emigration may be viewed as a means by which both those who emigrate and those who remain at home can obtain a greater improvement in living standards per head than the increase in our national product warrants, it must be recognised, on the other hand, that a static or declining population has itself a restrictive effect on the growth of the national product. It makes development more difficult, giving an inflexible organisation and leading to reluctance to invest. With a stable population it is not usual to find a dynamic and expanding business activity. New investments are more risky and less profitable than in an economy that is growing quickly.

## Effects and risks of slow rate of advance

The failure of production here to rise as fast as in other countries is an unsettling economic and social influence, the more disturbing because, at least since the war, there is here, as elsewhere, a general expectation of year by year improvement of living standards irrespective of the trend in production. In our case, it is Britain more than any other country which sets the standard of our expectations in such matters as wage and salary levels and the pattern both of private consumption and of collective services (health, housing, education and social services generally). Moreover, the level of prosperity there not only affects our export trade and, therefore, our agricultural and industrial incomes, but also largely determines the rate of emigration because of its effect on the availability of employment in Britain on attractive terms.

The unsettling effect of a relatively faster advance in output elsewhere has been aggravated by the extent and frequency with which money (as distinct from real) incomes have been raised everywhere in post-war years. This feature of inflation obscures the necessary dependence of increases in *real* incomes on increases in productivity and encourages the belief that living standards can be improved more than the basic increase in output warrants. This belief is further encouraged by the possibility – limited and temporary though it is – of maintaining an inflated standard of living by incurring balance of payments deficits, that is, by making good the deficiency in output through imports paid for by selling external assets or incurring foreign debt. In this respect, the illusion is not that living standards can be raised more than productivity warrants but rather that this can go on for long. In the ordinary course, increases in money incomes which are not linked to increased output, become neutralised, in whole or in part, by higher prices and higher taxation. This shearing-off of nominal purchasing power is part of the inevitable process of reducing monetary demand to equality with the current physical output of goods and services.

If under the influence of external developments or of the natural desire for better conditions, a movement develops towards higher standards, for example of income, private consumption or social services and amenities, there is always the risk that it may outrun the rate of increase in national production. If this occurs, the first and most obvious effect will be a widening of the trade deficit, which means the consumption of foreign reserves and investments built up out of past savings. There will also be a tendency for prices to rise. It is, of course, part of the necessary stimulus to enterprise, investment and increased production that the home demand for consumer goods and services should be buoyant; but there is a point of excess at which the consequences, psychologically and in the credit field, of heavy and persistent balance of payments deficits are seriously prejudicial to economic progress.

Failure to keep pace with our neighbours in the rate of increase in real output of goods and services besides putting a strain on the economy in the way just described has also the effect of stimulating emigration, one of the potent causes of which is the attraction of living standards elsewhere. The industrial progress made over the past twenty years or so and the enlargement in recent years of the state capital programme have been substantial but in terms of employment they have not quite balanced the release of labour from agriculture; they have not resulted in a net increase in overall employment. In other words, the natural increase in the population, resulting from the excess of births over deaths, is still being siphoned off by emigration. There must, in these circumstances, be very

great doubt whether any immediate and practicable intensifi-
cation of industrialisation or capital development generally
can do more than absorb a fraction of the natural increase in
the population, which is of the order of 25,000 per annum. But
even if additional jobs could be created year by year at this
rate it would not necessarily mean an end to emigration, even
to such emigration as is due solely to economic causes. There
would be only a limited curb on emigration unless the jobs
created – and all other jobs, too – were such as to yield as good
a life as could be obtained by emigrating. A high rate of
economic development and competitive efficiency in production are indispensable conditions of even a partial solution of
the emigration problem.

## Acceptability of the standard of living

The standard of living regarded as acceptable is, indeed, of
critical importance – a point to be borne in mind when considering proposals for the creation of employment and the stemming of emigration through an increase in public and private
investment in Ireland. It has been pointed out that, if everyone
were content to accept, say, 1926 standards of living, we could
support at present a population some forty per cent greater
than our actual population; but neither the community as a
whole nor its individual members, including many of the
emigrants themselves, would accept this depression of current
living standards as a condition of full employment at home.
Another way of putting this is that, if emigration ceased
altogether our population would rise at the rate of $1\frac{1}{2}$ per cent
per annum, assuming fertility remained unchanged. The rate
of increase in real output here over the years 1949-54 was not
quite $1\frac{1}{2}$ per cent per annum. So there would never be any
improvement in the present standard of living, if emigration
ceased and our recent rate of increase in output were not
raised. In the United States, on the other hand, real output
has been increasing so much faster than population that over
forty years the standard of living has doubled. In Britain, if
the population does not rise much, the recent rate of increase
in real output may double the standard of living in 25 years.
These comparisons point to the likelihood of emigration con-

tinuing on a large scale unless our rate of increase in output can be greatly accelerated. It would, indeed, need to be almost trebled if we were to keep all our people at home and double our present living standards in 25 years. If we do not keep pace with other countries in material progress, who can confidently predict that emigration will not continue virtually unabated?

## Increased output – the primary need

The mere giving of employment, to the neglect of the productive element in it, can obviously afford no lasting easement of the emigration problem. On the contrary, insufficiently productive employment necessitates a redistribution of real income in favour of those who are not adequately supporting themselves by output for which there is an economic demand. This redistribution may take place in ways not immediately recognisable, e.g. through higher taxation to finance the net debt charges on public works or through higher prices or inferior quality of protected products. Whatever form it takes, it represents a lowering of real incomes for many in the community and so tends to aggravate the unsettling influence and unfavourable comparisons with conditions elsewhere.

It is much wiser to concentrate on measures to increase production rather than on direct or immediate means of giving employment. Employment is desired as a means of securing an acceptable livelihood but it will not sustain itself unless it is adequately productive. In an expanding economy, however, where real incomes are rising and the demand for goods and services is growing, opportunities for useful and continuing employment will arise automatically. There is no conflict between what are termed 'socially desirable' and 'economic' objectives. 'Socially desirable' objectives will not be permanently realised merely by increasing 'social' investment. The erection of houses, schools and hospitals – socially desirable in themselves – will, of course, provide employment but the employment ceases once the period of construction is over and the unemployed man is left with facilities which, if he remains unemployed, will contribute but little to his standard of living. Socially desirable objectives are not attainable on a permanent basis except through the appropriate means, namely, increased production which itself must be of goods and services satisfying, either directly or by exchange for imports, the needs of consumers.

## Increased capitalisation not the only means

If we want a rising standard of living we must do what is necessary to achieve a rising volume of output; and if we are not content with the present rate of increase in output we must do what is necessary and possible to accelerate it. It would, however, be a mistake to think that a faster rate of increase in output is a matter merely of stepping up the volume of home investment ('domestic capital formation').

It is true that there is a close relationship between output per head and the amount of capital per head but there are other conditions of economic progress no less important than increased capitalisation. The first of these is the development of a better appreciation of the dependence of material progress on individual output. Others are a raising of the general level of education, health and skill, the loosening of restrictive practices, whether of employers or employees, the practical encouragement of initiative and enterprise, the adoption of improved methods, techniques and principles of organisation and management both in agriculture and industry, and a greater readiness to apply scientific advances. Attention to matters such as these may yield even greater increases in production than direct capitalisation in the form of new plant and machinery though this does not, of course, imply that increased capitalisation may not in due course be required. It is essential for sustained and balanced progress that an increase in productive capital should be supported not only by advances in education and technical training but also by the provision of basic utilities and amenities, including power supplies, good housing and transport services. Harmonious development calls also for suitable fiscal and monetary policies designed to increase the supply of savings and the incentive to invest in productive enterprises. As between countries, differences in climate, political institutions, educational and technical facilities, individual attitude to work, trade union outlook and

B

policy can be as important as differences in natural resources or in the volume of investment in causing divergent rates of development. Economic growth is, in fact, a complex process depending on social, psychological and political as well as economic and technical factors.

Although there are differences in natural resources as well as in other factors as between Ireland, Britain and other European countries, it is not inappropriate to seek an explanation of different degrees of economic progress partly in differences in the rate of capital formation. If we find relatively low capital formation without any obvious superiority in organisation, methods, technical skill, etc., it is safe to conclude that an increased rate of capital formation is one of the essentials if we are not to fall further behind in material progress. In reading the statistics one must bear in mind that 'gross capital formation', apart from containing an indefinite element of maintenance and replacement of existing capital, covers every form of capital from an electric generating station to a cinema, as well as stocks of raw materials and finished consumer goods. If, however, we look first at the figures of gross capital formation, without regard to the constituents, we find that the proportion of gross national product devoted to gross capital formation in 1938 was low in Ireland – a mere 10 per cent – by comparison with the average for OEEC countries in that year, which was 15 per cent. The corollary to this low level of gross capital formation was that the proportion of income consumed rather than saved was higher than in most other European countries. For the years since 1949 the position is shown in Table 2 from which it will be seen that the Irish proportion is

## Table 2: Gross Domestic Capital Formation as a percentage of Gross National Product at constant prices, 1949-54

| Year | Ireland % | Britain % | All OEEC Countries % |
|------|-----------|-----------|----------------------|
| 1949 | 14.7 | 13.0 | 17.7 |
| 1950 | 15.3 | 11.3 | 17.6 |
| 1951 | 16.3 | 16.2 | 19.2 |
| 1952 | 12.4 | 12.8 | 17.3 |
| 1953 | 16.2 | 14.3 | 17.6 |
| 1954 | 12.9 | 14.9 | 18.4 |

still below the European average. For 1954 the Irish percentage of 12.9 is, in fact, lower than the percentage for Britain, Belgium, the Netherlands, Italy, Germany, France, Denmark, Norway and Sweden and compares with an average of 18.4 per cent for Western Europe generally.

An allocation of 12.9 per cent of national production to *gross* capital formation is altogether insufficient if we desire to provide a rising standard of living for a growing population. The experience of other countries suggests that an increase in real national income by a certain amount requires an increase in the volume of *net* capital formation by about three times that amount. If the natural growth in our population were retained within the country and we wished to double our living standards in 25 years, we would need to allocate to *net* rather than *gross* capital formation 13 per cent or more of the national product. This would require not only a marked increase in savings but also a greater concentration of capital formation on directly productive purposes.

Indexes of *gross* capital formation, including and excluding stocks, for Ireland, Britain and OEEC countries generally since 1949 are given in Tables 3 and 4. Table 3 shows more clearly than percentages the deficiency in our allocation of resources to domestic capital formation because it allows for the relatively slow growth in our national product. We make a better showing in Table 4, which refers to *fixed* capital only, and, therefore, excludes stocks. It should be emphasised that the 'gross capital formation' covered by the tables relates only to the domestic scene; no allowance is made for changes in external capital. Many countries have little or no net external capital and when measuring additions to national capital may safely confine their attention to domestic capital formation. In our case, however, changes in the external capital position must be taken into account as well as estimates of domestic capital formation if a true picture is to be obtained of the trend in *national* capital. This point, which is further developed later, is quite independent of the merits of repatriating external capital. It is a truism that if domestic capital formation is accompanied by an equivalent reduction in external capital there is no net addition to national capital. The tables must, therefore, be read in the knowledge that in every year covered there was a deficit in the Irish balance of payments and a corresponding net reduction in external capital resources.

### Table 3: Index of Gross Domestic Capital Formation at constant prices, 1949-54

| Year | Ireland | Britain | All OEEC Countries |
|------|---------|---------|--------------------|
| 1949 | 100 | 100 | 100 |
| 1950 | 111.5 | 90.0 | 107.2 |
| 1951 | 119.8 | 132.9 | 123.9 |
| 1952 | 94.2 | 103.6 | 114.3 |
| 1953 | 125.5 | 120.3 | 122.3 |
| 1954 | 100.3 | 131.4 | 134.3 |

### Table 4: Index of Gross Domestic Fixed Capital Formation at constant prices, 1949-54

| Year | Ireland | Britain | All OEEC Countries |
|------|---------|---------|--------------------|
| 1949 | 100 | 100 | 100 |
| 1950 | 114.5 | 103.7 | 110.0 |
| 1951 | 117.0 | 101.5 | 114.8 |
| 1952 | 121.0 | 101.5 | 116.1 |
| 1953 | 129.0 | 114.0 | 126.2 |
| 1954 | 130.0 | 119.7 | 137.9 |

Note: Tables 1, 2, 3, 4 and Table 6 have been compiled on the basis of OEEC definitions and are, therefore, presumed to be comparable. The main difference between the official Irish estimates and those based on OEEC definitions is that the latter take account of the value of changes in the number of livestock on farms.
Methods of measuring depreciation vary widely as between the different countries. In Ireland, the wear and tear allowances of the Revenue Commissioners for income tax purposes are taken as depreciation of existing industrial capital; in agriculture, the cost of machinery purchased is taken as depreciation; no allowance is made for depreciation of land or buildings.

Sources: *OEEC Statistical Bulletin,* January, 1956 and *Seventh Annual Report of OEEC.*

The fact just mentioned reinforces the conclusion that the proportion of gross national product devoted to capital formation in Ireland is low. An alternative expression of this conclusion is that the proportion of income *saved* is low by comparison with Britain and most other European countries. Saving is the means by which resources are made available for capital development. Everyone who is earning an income has the choice, after the essentials of life are met, of consuming or saving. Saving entails sacrifice of immediate consumption possibilities and can make sense only on the basis of an expectation that the application of the incomes saved will increase the ability to consume at some future time. This expectation can itself be realised only if the income saved is used for productive investment in the sense of building up capital assets which will enlarge the flow of income in the future. The dilemma of poorer countries is that there is less income left over for saving and capital formation after the essentials of life are met. They are also exposed to the attraction of the higher consumption standards of richer neighbours. The normal means of escape from this dilemma – or 'take off' mechanism as it has been called – is the raising of agricultural productivity through education and research, improved methods, drainage, fertilisation and mechanisation. In close association with the generation of additional productive power and savings in this way, manufacturing industry can be developed and public utilities and services expanded.

It is not within the scope of this paper to discuss in any detail how production might be raised in agriculture, industry or other spheres. Some reference to recent trends and future potentialities is, however, necessary if our position is to be understood.

## Agriculture

Comparisons with other countries in regard to agricultural development must be subject to many qualifications because of differences in soil, climate, market and other conditions but the progress here in recent years, though relatively slow, at least establishes the possibility of further and, perhaps, more rapid advance. Excluding turf, the gross volume of agricultural output rose by 11.3 per cent over the period 1949-54, i.e. at an average rate of 2 per cent per annum. The corresponding average rate for OEEC countries generally was 5 per cent per annum. The relatively low net output per acre here as compared with countries in which agriculture is highly developed is also a pointer to the scope for further improvement. An improvement would yield increased incomes and enlarge both the fund of savings for capital development and the consumer demand to stimulate such development.

Substantial assistance is being granted to agriculture, both directly and indirectly, from public funds. Actual monetary assistance is of the order of £11 million per annum, including provision for the relief of rates, for educational and advisory services, for improvement of farm buildings, development of better seeds and breeding strains, land rehabilitation, fertilising, grain storage, eradication and control of disease. Besides these direct aids, guaranteed prices and markets are provided for various products, protection is afforded by import prohibitions and controls, and direct taxation of farming incomes is on a favourable basis. It seems desirable, as a general principle, that the assistance afforded to agriculture should be directly linked to the objective of increased production rather than be given as a general subvention. It is also desirable that, as the standard of living expected by farmers rises, the urge to have more to spend on new wants should be satisfied by greater output rather than by redistributive devices such as higher subsidies or guaranteed prices. The importance of agriculture as a source of exports and, therefore, as a means of defraying the cost of imports of necessary commodities, underlines the need for a competitive level of price and quality of agricultural products.

Subject to these qualifications, the means which are already being adopted or in contemplation may reasonably be expected to result in a faster rate of increase in agricultural output in the future. Doubtless other means could also be employed; and there may be a case for testing, on co-operative principles, some at least of the methods of capitalisation, organisation and management which prevail in industry.

## Industry

The second main source of increase in real national product is industry. In our base year 1949 the level of industrial output was low here even by comparison with countries which suffered war damage. The increase in net industrial output over the five years 1949 to 1954 was 28% as compared with 40% for OEEC countries generally. Our increase is based in part on State-financed building activity and the consequential stimulation of production of building materials, furniture, etc., to meet arrears of demand; this type of production may not be as firmly based as the production of goods for which there is likely to be a continuing and growing demand in the home and export markets. It has also to be remembered that the recent increase in output in some industries is based on the import of materials (for conversion into consumer goods) for which we have to pay by drawing down external capital; here again there must be some doubt whether the increase is firmly based. Output per head in a number of Irish industries is below British standards. Distinctiveness has, in some cases, proved capable of overcoming cost disadvantages in the export market but it would obviously be safer to rely on competitiveness. Prolonged protection, sheltering high domestic costs or inferior quality, blocks both the incentive and the capacity to expand production for export markets. Modification of protection, improvements in industrial organisation, and a closer gearing of pay to productivity are necessary supplements to the positive efforts which are being made – not without success – to improve the range, quality and design of Irish products and promote exports.

While the opportunity for industrial expansion afforded even by our limited home market has not yet been fully availed of, it would be unduly restrictive to concentrate attention on the home market alone. It is much more important that industrialists, whether native or foreign, should be induced to establish industries here capable of competing in export markets. Most of the more obvious opportunities in the home market, especially in the food and clothing lines, have probably already been exploited. The new industries of the future call for more capital, more technical skill and greater operating efficiency so that the world, and not a mere 3,000,000 people, will be their potential market. If this view is correct, tariff protection may have to give way to other stimuli, such as grants towards the initial capital cost of factories or towards technical training. The importance of the larger industries from the employment angle is not widely appreciated. In fact, the total output of firms employing less than 100 workers each – which constitute the majority of our industrial units – amounts to little more than one-third of the output of manufacturing industries as a whole. In other words, the larger firms supply two-thirds of the output of manufacturing industry and provide also two-thirds of the employment.

An industrial expansion based mainly on agricultural raw materials has to many seemed the most sensible form of development in our circumstances, as being more natural, more secure and of greater assistance to our balance of payments. There has, in fact, been considerable development of this kind in recent years, particularly in the processing and canning of beef, ham and vegetables. It is to be hoped that it will be maintained. In general, however, progress in building secondary industries on an agricultural foundation depends on competitive efficiency in the production of the basic agricultural materials.

Rigid control of industrial profits, except where high protection made it a necessary safeguard, would be inconsistent with the desire for maximum industrial development. Even where protection is necessary to reserve a market (because of traditional consumer preferences or large-scale advertising of foreign products) but the industry is otherwise competitive, it would be unwise to control profits to such a degree as to discourage expansion of output or improvements in technique. It is well to remember that in many countries undistributed profits are now the greatest source of savings, personal savings having dwindled under the impact of inflation and other influences to a small proportion of total savings.

## Other forms of production

Apart from the raising of production in agriculture and industry, some scope may exist for further development of certain services such as tourism. In transport we are not obviously backward and, indeed, as regards services generally, including administration and distribution, we appear to have reached an adequate stage of development. It is, at any rate, the basically productive activities which stand in greatest need of expansion.


## Dilemma of poorer countries

Less developed countries, being at the disadvantage of starting from a lower standard of living, find it much more difficult to set aside even the same fraction of income for capital building as the more highly developed countries. Yet, unless they make more rapid strides in other means of raising output, it is precisely these countries which must set aside a relatively greater fraction if they are ever to catch up in living standards. We find countries like Federal Germany and the Netherlands in recent years devoting much higher proportion of their national product to capital formation than, say, the United States or Britain and their people stinting themselves and living uncomfortably for a time in order to build up productive capacity. A poorer country which continues to save and allocate to productive capital purposes a smaller proportion of income than relatively rich countries like the United States or Britain must fall progressively further back in the race for material betterment.


## Constituents of capital formation

Further light is thrown on the comparatively slow advance of Ireland in real income per head by a study of the constituents of gross domestic capital formation. It is only by analysis of the total that a distinction can be made between capital formation yielding a flow of goods and capital formation providing the services and amenities associated with an already high level of production and consumption. 'Social' capital formation can contribute indirectly to increased production by improving the health, education and efficiency of workers and their families but even this indirect contribution will not be secure unless it is founded on an adequate amount of 'economic' investment. While it is, of course, necessary that there should be a building up of capital in the form of houses, hospitals, schools and roads in association with the accumulation of capital in agriculture, industry and commerce, it is just as necessary to ensure that there is a proper balance between the two types of investment. The balance will naturally vary as between richer and poorer countries. It is to be expected that poorer communities wishing to make rapid material progress would apply their limited savings predominantly to raising output in agriculture and industry, thus laying the foundations for a lasting increase in employment and the standard of living.

## Preponderance of housing

In most European countries these basic productive activities have been receiving a higher proportion of the available capital than in Ireland. Here for many years dwellings have been the greatest single claimant on capital resources. Table 5 shows that over the six years 1949-54 dwellings alone formed as high a proportion of gross domestic capital formation as agriculture, mining, manufacturing and other construction combined. In Britain, Germany and Belgium housing had to take a lower place in the early post-war years than the rehabilitation of

## Table 5: Ireland: Constituents of Gross Domestic Fixed Capital Formation, 1949-54 (£ million)

|  | 1949 | 1950 | 1951 | 1952 | 1953 | 1954 | Total |
|---|---|---|---|---|---|---|---|
| Agriculture, etc. | 3.1 | 3.3 | 5.2 | 5.2 | 6.7 | 7 | 30.5 |
| Mining, etc. | 1.1 | 1.0 | 1.2 | 0.8 | 1.0 | 1 | 6.1 |
| Manufacturing and Construction | 5.6 | 7.4 | 8.2 | 9.0 | 10.0 | 10 | 50.2 |
| Electricity, gas and waterworks | 5.2 | 6.2 | 7.4 | 7.6 | 7.8 | 9 | 43.2 |
| Transport and communications | 7.2 | 7.5 | 7.9 | 9.8 | 12.4 | 12 | 56.8 |
| Dwellings | 12.0 | 13.9 | 15.5 | 15.8 | 14.3 | 14 | 85.5 |
| Public administration | 1.1 | 1.3 | 2.3 | 3.1 | 2.2 | 2 | 12.0 |
| Other services | 11.3 | 12.7 | 13.0 | 17.8 | 19.9 | 19 | 93.7 |
| Total | 46.6 | 53.3 | 60.7 | 69.1 | 74.3 | 74 | 378.0 |

Source: *Returns furnished to OEEC for Seventh Annual Report.*

industry and trade and it is only in the past few years that special efforts have been made to overtake arrears. Within the past year decisions have again been taken in Britain to slow down new building. The proportion of gross fixed capital formation represented by dwellings (24 per cent on average for 1949-53, 19 per cent for 1954) is, in fact, higher in this country than in countries which, like Ireland, suffered virtually no war-time destruction, e.g., Denmark with 17.9 per cent and Norway with 17.1 per cent for 1954 (Table 6). In connection with these differences in policy it has to be recognised that it is less difficult to make provision for housing out of a vastly expanded national product and, on the other hand, that it is easier to rebuild industrial capacity than to create it. If, however, more savings were made and were devoted to raising basic production, housing and other services could be paid for by a higher proportion of the population out of their improved real incomes and would, therefore, entail less call on the existing real incomes of the community at large.

### Table 6: Percentage Distribution of Gross Domestic Fixed Capital Formation in various countries in 1954

|  | Ireland | Britain | Denmark | Norway | Sweden | Germany (Federal Republic) | Italy |
|---|---|---|---|---|---|---|---|
|  |  |  |  | Percentage |  |  |  |
| Agriculture, etc. | 9.5 | 3.8 | 8.7 | 9.7 | 5.7 | 8.2 | 14.0 |
| Mining, etc. | 1.4 | 3.5 | — |  |  | 5.7 | 2.1 |
| Manufacturing and Construction | 13.5 | 25.9 | N.A. | 18.5 | 20.8 | 23.8 | 22.9 |
| Electricity, Gas and Water Works | 12.2 | 12.5 | 4.8 | 6.0 | 9.7 | 9.1 | 6.2 |
| Transport and Communications | 16.2 | 11.4 | 21.9 | 31.6 | 24.8 | 10.8 | 16.0 |
| Dwellings | 18.9 | 26.5 | 17.9 | 17.1 | 23.9 | 28.5 | 23.3 |
| Other | 28.3 | 16.4 | 46.7* | 17.1 | 15.1 | 13.9 | 15.5 |
| Total | 100 | 100 | 100 | 100 | 100 | 100 | 100 |

*Includes manufacturing and construction.

Note: The above table should be read in association with particulars of the percentage of gross national product at factor cost derived from agriculture and industry in the various countries in 1954 in Table 7.

## Table 7: Percentage of Gross National Product at factor cost in 1954

|  | Agriculture, etc. % | Manufacturing Industries % |
|---|---|---|
| Ireland | 30.7 | 25.8* |
| Britain | 4.8 | 37.6 |
| Denmark | 19.3 | 18.9 |
| Norway | 13.9 | 29.9 |
| Sweden | N.A. | N.A. |
| Germany   (Federal   Republic) | 10.9 | 48.3* |
| Italy | 24.6 | 29.9 |

*Includes mining and electricity, gas and water works. See Note to Tables 1 to 4.

Source: *Returns furnished to OEEC by member countries for seventh annual report.*

## Real increase in capital-building is small

Passing now to the detail of recent Irish experience, we find (Table 8) that gross domestic capital formation, which was £17 million in 1938, has averaged roughly £70 million in recent years; this is true whether changes in stocks are taken into account or not. This fourfold increase in monetary terms greatly exaggerates the *real* increase in gross *domestic* capital formation which is of the order of only 50 per cent because of the fall in value of money since 1938. Further allowance must be made for proper maintenance and replacement of existing capital and for depletion of external capital in assessing the true accumulation of real *national* capital. Even from the figures given in Table 8, where the Central Statistics Office deprecia-tion allowance is treated as adequate, it will be clear that the net annual addition in recent years to real national capital is very much less than 50 per cent above the 1938 level. A level of 10 per cent to 15 per cent above 1938 might be closer to the truth.

## Table 8*: Ireland: domestic capital formation, 1938 and 1949-54

| Year | Gross | | | Net Domestic Fixed Capital Formation | Index of Volume of Gross Fixed Capital Formation |
| | Including Changes in Stocks | Fixed Capital Only | Depreciation | | |
| | £ million | | | | 1938 = 100 |
| 1938 | 17.1 | 17.1 | 4.2 | 12.9 | 100 |
| 1949 | 45.1 | 46.6 | 9.0 | 37.6 | 117 |
| 1950 | 56.8 | 53.3 | 11.2 | 42.1 | 134 |
| 1951 | 73.6 | 60.7 | 12.2 | 48.5 | 137 |
| 1952 | 58.7 | 69.1 | 13.0 | 56.1 | 142 |
| 1953 | 77.9 | 74.3 | 14.0 | 60.3 | 151 |
| 1954 | 69.0 | 74 | 15 | 59 | 152 |

*Note: The figures in the above and following table are official Irish estimates; they do not include the value of changes in the number of livestock on farms. See note to Tables 1 to 4 for method of measuring depreciation.

Source: *Irish Statistical Survey*, 1954.

## Table 9: Ireland: Changes in net national capital formation and current savings, 1938 and 1949-54 (£ million)

| Year | Net Domestic Capital Formation | Change in External Capital | Net Increase in National Capital | Current Savings |
| 1938 | 12.9 | +2.0 | 14.9 | 14.9 |
| 1949 | 36.1 | —9.7 | 26.4 | 26.4 |
| 1950 | 45.6 | —30.2 | 15.4 | 15.4 |
| 1951 | 61.4 | —61.6 | —0.2 | —0.2 |
| 1952 | 45.7 | —8.9 | 36.8 | 36.8 |
| 1953 | 63.9 | —7.0 | 56.9 | 56.9 |
| 1954 | 54.0 | —5.5 | 48.5 | 48.5 |

See Note to Table 7.

Source: *Irish Statistical Survey*, 1954.

## High proportion of state-financed capital expenditure

Another point worthy of note is that state-financed capital expenditure is now a much greater proportion of the total than in 1938. It was only about one-seventh of the 1938 figure whereas in recent years it has been one-half or more of the total. The growth in the relative importance of state-financed capital outlay obviously necessitates careful consideration of the character of that outlay and the form it gives to domestic capital formation as a whole. Tables 9 and 10 make it clear

## Table 10: Ireland: Constituents of State Capital Programme 1947/48-1954/55 (£ million)

| | 1947/8 | 1948/9 | 1949/50 | 1950/51 | 1951/2 | 1952/3 | 1953/4 | 1954/5 | Total |
|---|---|---|---|---|---|---|---|---|---|
| Housing | 0.91 | 3.20 | 8.98 | 11.06 | 12.67 | 11.91 | 9.85 | 10.49 | 69.07 |
| Sanitary Services | 0.19 | 0.44 | 0.72 | 0.69 | 0.63 | 0.88 | 1.31 | 1.12 | 5.98 |
| Hospitals | 0.12 | 0.08 | 0.05 | 0.09 | 0.14 | 0.40 | 3.27 | 2.38 | 6.53 |
| Electricity Development | 3.00 | 4.00 | 4.00 | 4.60 | 8.80 | 8.60 | 7.10 | 5.60 | 45.70 |
| Turf Development | 0.88 | 0.80 | 1.08 | 1.04 | 1.27 | 1.19 | 0.70 | 1.44 | 8.40 |
| Agricultural Development | 0.08 | 0.41 | 2.21 | 3.13 | 3.91 | 4.13 | 3.87 | 4.25 | 21.99 |
| Afforestation | 0.20 | 0.21 | 0.25 | 0.43 | 0.76 | 0.58 | 0.65 | 0.70 | 3.78 |
| Fisheries | 0.03 | 0.03 | 0.09 | 0.08 | 0.10 | 0.16 | 0.11 | 0.09 | 0.69 |
| Schools and Other State Buildings | 0.28 | 0.43 | 0.60 | 0.71 | 0.95 | 0.98 | 1.23 | 2.02 | 7.20 |
| Telephones | 0.34 | 1.23 | 1.25 | 1.80 | 2.60 | 1.95 | 1.05 | 1.40 | 11.62 |
| Transport | 1.66 | 1.61 | 5.07 | 0.77 | 0.89 | 0.97 | 3.77 | 1.38 | 16.12 |
| Industrial Credit | — | — | — | 0.19 | — | 0.50 | 0.25 | — | 0.94 |
| Mianraí Teo | 0.03 | 0.02 | 0.04 | 0.02 | 0.01 | 0.02 | — | — | 0.14 |
| Tourism | 0.10 | 0.01 | — | — | — | — | — | — | 0.11 |
| Insurance | 0.11 | — | — | — | — | — | — | — | 0.11 |
| University Buildings | — | — | — | — | — | — | 0.20 | — | 0.20 |
| Wireless Broadcasting | — | — | — | — | — | — | 0.05 | — | 0.05 |
| Min-Fhéir Teo. | — | — | — | — | — | — | 0.01 | 0.02 | 0.03 |
| Ceimicí Teo. | — | — | — | — | — | — | — | 0.10 | 0.10 |
| Alginate Industries | — | — | — | — | — | — | — | 0.01 | 0.01 |
| National Development Fund (Expenditure) | — | — | — | — | — | — | 1.17 | 1.86 | 3.03 |
| Total | 7.93 | 12.47 | 24.34 | 24.61 | 32.73 | 32.27 | 34.59 | 32.86 | 201.80 |

that the present pattern of our domestic capital activity is shaped by the state capital programme.

Over the eight years 1947/48 to 1954/55, state-financed capital outlay amounted to £202 million, of which £82 million represented expenditure on housing and hospitals. If capital works financed by the Hospitals Trust Board from its investments and by local authorities from non-state borrowings were included, the preponderance of housing and hospitals would be even greater. Moreover, the rapid growth of state-financed investment in post-war years – from £8 million in 1947/8 to an average of £33 million over the three years 1952/3 to 1954/5 – has been marked by a great expansion in works of mainly social benefit rather than of a directly productive nature. Much of the benefit of power development is absorbed directly in the domestic use of electricity and turf, rather than used to expand industrial and agricultural production, and thus the basic

## Table 11: Ireland: Summary of constituents of State Capital Programme, 1947/48-1954/55 (£ million)

| | 1947/8 | 1948/9 | 1949/50 | 1950/1 | 1951/2 | 1952/3 | 1953/4 | 1954/5 | Total |
|---|---|---|---|---|---|---|---|---|---|
| Housing and Sanitary Services | 1.10 | 3.64 | 9.70 | 11.75 | 13.30 | 12.79 | 11.16 | 11.61 | 75.05 |
| Hospitals | 0.12 | 0.08 | 0.05 | 0.09 | 0.14 | 0.40 | 3.27 | 2.38 | 6.53 |
| Power Development | 3.88 | 4.80 | 5.08 | 5.64 | 10.07 | 9.79 | 7.80 | 7.04 | 54.10 |
| Agricultural, Fishery and Forestry Development | 0.31 | 0.65 | 2.55 | 3.64 | 4.77 | 4.87 | 4.63 | 5.04 | 26.46 |
| Industrial and Mining Development | 0.03 | 0.02 | 0.04 | 0.21 | 0.01 | 0.52 | 0.26 | 0.13 | 1.22 |
| Schools and other Construction | 0.28 | 0.43 | 0.60 | 0.71 | 0.95 | 0.98 | 1.43 | 2.02 | 7.40 |
| Communications | 2.00 | 2.84 | 6.32 | 2.57 | 3.49 | 2.92 | 6.04 | 4.18 | 30.36 |
| Other | 0.21 | 0.01 | — | — | — | — | — | 0.46 | 0.68 |
| Total | 7.93 | 12.47 | 24.34 | 24.61 | 32.73 | 32.27 | 34.59 | 32.86 | 201.80 |

capacity of the community to afford amenities. It is also true that some of the state investment under other 'economic' as distinct from 'social' headings is not immediately or adequately productive of increases in real incomes and, further, that the totals include an element of replacement of existing capital as distinct from new capital formation proper. When so much of our limited national savings is being channelled into housing and other building, it is a disappointment to find that the value obtained for it is impaired by a fall in labour productivity in building as compared with pre-war.

## Financing of state capital needs

Considering that state-financed capital is so large a proportion of total capital formation and that most of the savings of public and private companies are needed sooner or later for renewal and extension of industrial and commercial capital, it is not surprising that, taking one year with another, all the available personal savings are needed to support the State Capital Programme. For this they are absorbed both directly and indirectly, mainly through the collection of small savings by the Savings Banks and the sale of Saving Certificates and through public and bank subscriptions to National Loans. When to the requirements of the State Capital Programme (which up to 1954-55 inclusive covered the Electricity Supply Board), there is added the capital needed by Dublin and Cork Corporations and by Córas Iompair Éireann, a total is reached which is higher than even aggregate personal savings will cover. The position in recent years may be summarised in Table 12.

It is to be noted that total personal savings averaged about £30 million for the four years 1952-55. In effect, since the exhaustion of Marshall Aid Counterpart, the excess of public capital requirements over available savings has had to be met by realisations of sterling securities both by the commercial banking system and by the state itself. The potentialities of this method of finance have been much reduced and a marked upsurge in personal saving is needed if public capital outlay is to continue at the desired rate.

## Table 12: Excess of Public Borrowing over Public Subscriptions

| | 1952-53 to 1954-55 (annual average) | 1955-56 |
|---|---|---|
| | £ million | £ million |
| 1. Net borrowing by the state (including Electricity Supply Board) Dublin and Cork Corporations and Córas Iompair Éireann | 36 | 41 |
| 2. Amount obtained from public (including externs) | 26 | 27 |
| 3. Excess of 1. over 2. | 10 | 14 |

## Productivity of public capital outlay

Comment must be made not only on the relation of public capital requirements to the supply of savings available but also on the productivity of public capital outlay. It is clear that the state capital programme at present contains a large proportion of works which do not yield an adequate direct return. The effect of the growth in non-productive and inadequately productive assets appears in a comparison between the interest and sinking fund charges on the state debt and the receipts from state assets. The net annual increase in the charge against taxation because of the state capital programme is roughly £2 million at the present level of interest rates. Any buoyancy which the revenue displays – for whatever reason – is preempted to this extent.

## The need for savings

At several points already in this paper I have stressed what is axiomatic but nevertheless often forgotten, namely, that the rate of national development is ultimately determined by the capacity and willingness of the community to save. It would be pointless to complain of the low level of national capital formation unless it led to a recognition of the need for greater savings to support more development expenditure. Recognition by itself is not enough. The community must actually forego to a greater extent than heretofore the opportunity of consuming if it wishes to make more resources available for capital formation. Present sacrifice is unavoidable. I am leaving out of account deliberately the possibility of external borrowing 1. because it is limited, 2. because the terms might be onerous, and 3. because, in any event, such borrowing would have to be repaid either from future savings or by realisation of external assets. Reference will be made later to the extent to which our accessible sterling assets have already been used or committed in support of domestic capital formation. The future potentialities in this direction are limited in relation to the scale of our capital requirements. In any case, realisation of external capital does not of itself add to national capital. It entails merely a geographical redistribution of existing national capital and the guiding principle should be to achieve this redistribution in such a way as to maintain or improve the total product, not to use up past accumulations to sustain a present standard of consumption exceeding our real production.

## The question of forced savings

Our external resources were acquired under the compulsion of war-time shortage of imports and we neither hope nor wish for a recurrence of that form of forced saving. Saving enforced by taxation yielding a budget surplus is a recognised means of curbing inflation but if it is too severe or too prolonged it may defeat its own purpose by leading to dissaving in other ways and to inadequate provision for private capital replacements and extensions. A deliberate policy of inflation, which is another way of securing forced savings, would require a virtually closed economy to be fully effective and would, of course, be socially inequitable. In our circumstances, any substantial addition to the volume of money, not matched by increased production, must result initially in a heavier draw on external capital as well as in higher domestic prices, the second effect becoming the more serious according as the first required to be controlled to protect the exchange value of the currency.

## The Keynesian 'multiplier'

Leaving forced savings aside, there are some who discern in Keynesian doctrine the possibility of achieving higher levels of employment and income without any prior sacrifice of consumption standards. It is argued that an expansion in capital expenditure, financed otherwise than from current savings, would lift the levels of income and employment and thus generate the savings necessary to support the higher capital outlay. To discuss this idea fully would involve too great a digression but some consideration must be given to its applicability to our circumstances before we go on to the prospects of an increase in voluntary savings as ordinarily understood.

Keynesian doctrine differs from the classical theory in drawing a sharp distinction between conditions in which a country's resources of men, land, materials and capital are fully employed and these in which they are not. The essence of the theory is this: that income and employment depend on effective demand and that effective demand is determined by the propensity to consume and the volume of investment. Keynes believed that consumption normally increases by a lesser amount than income when income is rising and he assumed that the propensity to consume (which, of course, is the inverse of the propensity to save) was relatively fixed in a given community over a short period of time. Accordingly, his theory was that, in the short run, income and employment are, in effect, determined by the level of investment, by which he meant capital formation at home. Indeed, given the proportions of new income which are consumed and saved, it is possible, according to Keynesian theory, to tell how much income and employment will increase as a result of any given increase in investment. Assuming that resources are not fully employed at the start, an increase in investment will cause a multiple increase in income and employment, the 'multiplier' being related to the marginal propensity to consume. What this means is that if, in a closed system, four-fifths (say) of any increase in income is consumed (and one-fifth saved), the effect of a sustained increase in investment will be to generate consumption-spending within the country which will ultimately raise the national income by five times the primary increase in investment. At the heart of the theory is the recognition that saving and investment are done by different people and at any moment may not necessarily be equal. Inequality between them, however, produces changes in incomes and employment which tend to bring them back into equilibrium. If savings exceed investment this equilibrium is attained at the expense of incomes and employment; hence the efficacy in such circumstances of an increase in investment in raising incomes and employment to a higher level.

There are, however, important qualifications to this theory and to the principle of the 'multiplier':

1. It has been well said that 'the multiplier is not a quasi-magical device for expanding employment through the economic counterpart of internal combustion. It gives a laborious increase in income, won only after many successive injections. The successive injections necessarily amount to many times the so-called multiplier effect, and they must be kept up indefinitely (from some source) if the increase in income is to become permanent'.

2. The 'multiplier' might work in a country completely closed to the outside world in which at the start there were idle resources. Then an increase in investment would generate a series of new incomes and the voluntary savings made out of the increase in incomes would tend, eventually, to cover the investment outlay and make it self-perpetuating. In the real world, however, there are few, if any, completely isolated economies and the effects of the creation of new incomes are, therefore, not wholly retained within the system. Much of the new incomes would be spent on imports – initially perhaps the greater part – and the process of generating incomes might cause

such a serious upset in the balance of external payments – with loss of external resources or reduction of the exchange value of the currency – as to impair public confidence and negative the initial boost given by the increase in income investment.

3. The theory does not promise full employment at any level of incomes, a point of particular relevance to a country in which the availability of higher real incomes elsewhere operates, through emigration, to eliminate 'idle resources' at home. Rates of pay which are out of line with the international value of the products of home labour at the existing rate of exchange may be a serious obstacle to the attainment of full employment. This is only a specific way of saying that the new investment must at least be productive at the existing levels of prices and costs if it is to be relied upon for a sustained increase in real incomes and employment. Otherwise the initial increase in activity will become bogged down in rising costs and taxation at home and in external payments difficulties; and emigration will remain the principal means of access to employment yielding the desired level of real income.

4. In any case, the facts of recent Irish experience are not in accord with the basic assumption on which the theory rests, viz., that consumption increases by a lesser amount than income when income is rising. In three out of the seven years 1948-54 (and doubtless also in 1951) the increase in national consumption exceeded the increase in national income. This erratic experience is associated with the prevalence of inflationary conditions since the war, conditions the opposite of those in which Keynesian theory was first formulated.

5. It is also well to stress that full employment cannot be made to order. Experience suggests that it is a matter even in highly developed countries of good luck as well as good management. For a country like ours it depends

at least as much on how things are going in the outside world – and more especially on the level of prosperity in Britain – as on the efforts we ourselves may make to increase our prosperity. This is not to say, of course, that we cannot take effective measures to raise real incomes and employment or that wrong policies here could not be positively harmful.

It is also relevant to note that, although some countries have operated policies based to some extent on Keynesian theory, the full implications of the theory still remain to be tested in practice. In essence the idea we have been discussing, in so far as it envisages capital outlay – private and public – in excess of current savings, represents merely a continuance or extension of what is already taking place here with the discouraging outcome commented upon earlier. It is in effect a plea for even heavier state capital outlay (probably involving enlargement of an already high proportion of social investment) at greater cost in terms of external capital resources, but without any certainty of a net improvement in real national income. It offers no escape from the fact that the building up of national capital, real income and self-sustaining employment depends on the utmost expansion of output in ways which are sparing of capital, on a greater volume of current savings, and on the use of savings to the greatest possible degree for productive purposes.

## Irregularity and insufficiency of current savings

It is apparent that current savings are not sufficient even to support the present relatively low rate of net domestic capital formation. The deficiency over the six years 1949-54 amounted to £123 million, which had to be supplied by drawing on external capital resources, with a corresponding reduction in net savings and in net *national* capital formation:

## Table 13: Savings deficiency

| | £ million | | | | | | |
|---|---|---|---|---|---|---|---|
| | 1949 | 1950 | 1951 | 1952 | 1953 | 1954 | Total |
| 1. Net domestic capital formation (i.e., the gross figure less the CSO deduction for depreciation) | 36.1 | 45.6 | 61.4 | 45.7 | 63.9 | 54 | 306.7 |
| 2. Current Savings | 26.4 | 15.4 | —0.2 | 36.8 | 56.9 | 48 | 183.3 |
| 3. Savings Deficiency | 9.7 | 30.2 | 61.6 | 8.9 | 7.0 | 6 | 123.4 |
| 4. Draw on External Capital | 9.7 | 30.2 | 61.6 | 8.9 | 7.0 | 6 | 123.4 |
| 5. Net National Capital Formation | 26.4 | 15.4 | —0.2 | 36.8 | 56.9 | 48 | 183.3 |

The figures of 'draw on external capital' express the net effect of outward and inward movements of capital and therefore allow both for Irish investment in, e.g. British securities, and for British investment in, e.g. our National Loans. Contrary to the belief held in some quarters, there has been no net reduction in the availability of capital for Irish enterprises as a result of private investment in extern stocks and shares because the sales of such stocks and shares have exceeded the purchases; thus, over the period 1949-54 the net realisation of extern stocks and shares was £17.2 million, as shown in the Balance of Payments Statements.

## Savings position

The figures of current savings show considerable variations from year to year and as current savings are the sole basis of additions to *national* capital it is important 1. to assess the validity of the figures and 2. to inquire into the possibility of securing a sustained increase in the volume of savings. Separate estimates are available of (a) savings by public and private companies (i.e., undistributed profits, tax reserves, etc.), (b) savings – more usually dissaving through budgetary deficits – by public authorities and (c) personal savings. The third category, personal savings, is still in this country the largest element in total savings but, unlike the other figures, it is not directly ascertained. The figures in Tables 14 and 15 for 1952, 1953 and 1954 give an idea of the sources of savings.

## Table 14: Gross and net savings

|  | £ million | | |
| --- | --- | --- | --- |
|  | 1952 | 1953 | 1954 |
| Savings by public and private companies | 12.0 | 14.4 | 16 |
| Savings by public authorities | 1.6 | —3.8 | —5 |
| Personal savings | 25.0 | 43.2 | 37 |
| Gross Current Savings | 38.6 | 53.8 | 48 |
| Corrected for stock appreciation | 36.8 | 56.9 | 48 |
| Deduct External Dissaving | 8.9 | 7.0 | 5.5 |
| Net Savings | 27.9 | 49.9 | 42.5 |

Although the estimates of personal savings are residuals, the estimates of net savings as a whole tally reasonably well with rough approximations arrived at directly, e.g.:

## Table 15: Forms of personal saving

|  | £ million | | |
| --- | --- | --- | --- |
|  | 1952 | 1953 | 1954 |
| Net increase in Savings Bank deposits and Saving Certificates | 6 | 6 | 6 |
| Subscriptions by Irish public to issues of public authorities | 17 | 20 | 13 |
| Increase in Irish deposits of the commercial banks | 6 | 17 | 20 |
| Increase in deposits with building societies and net saving through insurance companies | 3 | 6 | 5 |
| Total | 32 | 49 | 43 |

The categories of positive savings included above do not purport to be exhaustive or completely exclusive and the attributed figures are subject to some reservations.

## Conditions of increase in saving

The need for an increase in net savings is obvious in view of the inconsiderable advance so far made in the rate of accumulation of real national capital as compared even with 1938, when the level was low in relation to OEEC countries generally. Having regard to the moderate level of income per head, the absence of any large body of wealthy citizens, and the attraction of the consumption standards of richer neighbours, it is difficult to do much by exhortations or inducements to increase the flow of savings. Former incentives to individual saving have been somewhat weakened by collective provision for personal contingencies such as unemployment, ill-health, widowhood and old age. Any significant and sustained increase in national savings can flow only from a prior increase in real national income providing the community generally with more to spend at once in improving their living standards as well as with more to save for future betterment. In turn, an increase in real national income depends on the utmost expansion of productivity in agriculture and industry by means which are sparing of capital and the productive investment of present savings, i.e., their application to purposes which will generate a lasting and progressive increase in real income. The non-productive use of savings entails not only present loss but also forfeiture of the future returns which sound investment would yield. Genuinely productive enterprises can afford to offer attractive yields to investors and thus stimulate savings.

Next to productive use of savings as a condition of national progress, is real stability in money values. Nothing can be more destructive of savings and consequently of the will to save than monetary depreciation. Indeed, in Britain, where there is an extensively organised and publicised national savings movement, rising prices and the resulting fall in the value of money negatived for some years all efforts to secure additional small savings. It is, therefore, a necessary condition of a substantial increase in savings not only that real incomes (including profits) will have increased but also that confidence in the value of money will not be seriously upset. It is possible that a slight upward tendency in the price level over a long period would not be harmful but certainly a marked annual increase in prices, besides causing social injustice in many ways, must in time undermine the propensity to save. While monetary depreciation is a deterrent to saving, it should at the same time be remembered that the greatest corrective of monetary depreciation is the addition to the supply of goods and services which productive investment of savings will ensure.

## Mode of application of savings

Because current savings are insufficient to maintain even a low rate of capital formation and therefore of economic growth, it is all the more desirable that they should be applied in ways which will give the maximum immediate increase in real incomes, thus enlarging the community's capacity to save more and enjoy concurrently a higher living standard. It can scarcely be claimed that this test is met by the manner in which we have used our limited supply of savings; the proportion devoted to increasing basic production in agriculture and industry has obviously been too small. There can be no question of the need for considerable investment in housing, hospitals, schools, transport and other utilities intended to raise the general well-being of the community, even though this is not reflected in a lasting and real increase in spendable incomes; and it is natural that investment of this kind should have to be publicly financed in large measure. But, when state-financed investment is so large a proportion of total domestic investment and the raising of freely disposable incomes in real terms is so important, there can equally be no gainsaying the need for a large directly productive element in the state capital programme, whether in the form of state enterprise or assistance to private producers. It would be much easier to reconcile these needs in an economy in which real incomes and savings were expanding but the possibility of expansion itself depends on a more directly productive use of existing savings and that in turn depends largely on the character of state capital expenditure.

## Capital for industry and commerce

The requirements of public authorities being in excess of the *total* personal savings available, internal financing (from undistributed profits and reserves) is the only source of capital on which industry and commerce can safely rely. This emphasises the desirability of curbing the growth of taxation and of a more liberal attitude towards profit-making; in this way, the conditions for economic development of national resources by private enterprise would be made less difficult. Few will invest their money in schemes which may or may not succeed if they get only 7 per cent or so in the event of success and nothing in the case of failure, while at the same time they can get a safe 5 per cent on government or government-guaranteed stock. The need for a change is all the more apparent when one considers the inadequacy of the present rate of investment in manufacturing industry. Table 5 (on p.34) shows that this investment amounts to only £10 million a year, *gross*. Deducting from this figure an appropriate allowance for depreciation and for replacement of existing capital, it is certain that the new capital going into manufacturing industry is not more than £7 million to £8 million a year and may be even less. The disappointing rate of industrial development is also revealed by the fact (recorded by the Central Bank in its 1955 Report) that, of the total new capital raised over the calendar years 1950-54 by issues of marketable securities, industry and commerce accounted for only £8.9 million out of £112.9 million. It may not be possible to point to particular developments which did not come to fruition because of the restrictive effects of public capital outlay on its present scale but it cannot be doubted that these effects will become the more significant the longer public authorities continue to absorb all the available personal savings and force up the level of taxation. It is hard to counter the argument that at least some personal savings should be left for private enterprise to work on.

### Inevitability of present sacrifice

There must be some sacrifice of *current* welfare and consumption if there is to be any economic development at all in the future. Presumably some small gains will continue to be made in real national income even if conditions stay as they are but they will be inadequate to meet the expectations of even a stable population. It may be too much to expect a substantial reduction in current consumption and the only realistic hope may be that more of the increment in real national income will go into savings and productive investment rather than into immediate consumption. Even this involves a sacrifice, a sacrifice which everyone would need to understand and accept as an inevitable condition of a higher rate of permanent improvement in living standards. It has also to be realised that economic development here is made all the more difficult by the population situation and calls for greater sacrifices than in a country with an increasing population, apart altogether from the special difficulties in regard to standards and expectations occasioned by our close contact with Britain. The Emigration Commission put the point well when they said 'the mind and spirit of the people must change so that they possess the necessary degree of resolution not only to develop the economy fully but also to accept readily the sacrifices and hard work which this would involve' (para. 480 of Majority Report).

## Conclusions

The principal conclusions of this paper are:

1. To avoid losing ground in the improvement of real incomes by comparison with other countries, particularly Britain, and, indeed, to maintain present consumption standards without drawing on capital, our national product needs to be enlarged and a greater proportion of it devoted to capital formation. Failure to keep pace with advances in Britain is a stimulus to emigration.

2. The raising of output in agriculture and industry should have a higher priority in the allocation of savings. The utmost use should be made of means of raising output which are sparing of capital so as to make savings go as far as possible and thus relieve the immediate sacrifice in consumption.

3. The building up of national capital and consequently the improvement of national living standards depend (a) on the most productive use of savings and (b) on an increase

in current savings. To the extent that our limited supply of savings is applied to objects other than a permanent increase in production, a drag is imposed on material progress and the opportunities for self-sustaining employment are restricted.

4. Saving and production should be encouraged and excessive consumption discouraged. As saving is largely a function of income this means primarily that capital development of a *productive* character should be stimulated. There should be a liberal attitude towards profits to encourage their expansion and use for productive purposes. Assistance to agriculture and industry should be directed specifically towards the development of productive capacity.

*Harold Wilson, Prime Minister of Britain, with Jack Lynch, Minister for Finance and Seán Lemass, Taoiseach in 1965.*

# 3 From Protection to Free Trade – The Irish Experience

May I begin by congratulating the University of Exeter, and, in particular, its Professor of Social Administration, Dr Robert Leaper, as well as the Irish universities and Institute of Public Administration for arranging to honour an outstanding Irish statesman of our time by establishing a commemorative series of lectures to be given alternately in Exeter and in Dublin. To be asked to give the first Seán Lemass Memorial Lecture is a special privilege which I gratefully acknowledge. I regard it as a great honour. It is also a personal pleasure to be for the first time in Exeter.

The influence which Seán Lemass exerted on Ireland's economic and social development and political evolution extended over many years and bore fruit in different ways. Its effects can be traced not only domestically, in such domains as industry, energy, transport, social and administrative organisation but also in the Republic of Ireland's political and economic relations with Northern Ireland, Great Britain, the European Economic Community and the world at large. The monuments to his achievements include national air and shipping fleets as well as a large number of manufacturing and service industries and promotional bodies. Out of this richness of record I will take only one theme: to trace the movement of a man's thought and action across a policy spectrum, from high protectionism to free trade. I was fortunate, as Secretary of the Department of Finance from 1956 to 1969, to have been close to Seán Lemass during his final period as Minister for Industry and Commerce (1957 to 1959) and his tenure of office as Taoiseach (1959 to 1966). I can, therefore, draw on my own experience in dealing with the latter part of the transition towards free trade in contemplation of EEC membership.[1]

55

How Seán Lemass applied his talents as a member for thirty-three years of an Irish government can be fully understood only by reference to his family background and the motivation and experience of his youth. He was born in Dublin in 1899 and went to O'Connell School (Christian Brothers) where he was an exhibition winner. He grew up during a period of intense nationalist activity. His grandfather had been a Parnellite member of Dublin Corporation. He himself took an early interest in politics and joined the Volunteers at fifteen. He took part in the 1916 Rising and the subsequent War of Independence before being interned in 1920. Like many another active person condemned to physical inactivity, he gave his mind as free a range as possible. As an ardent nationalist, he read Arthur Griffith's writings and came under the influence of his economic views. Arthur Griffith was himself a disciple of the German apostle of protection, Friedrich List, and adopted his National System of Political Economy as a headline for much of his own propaganda. Indeed, he wished to see List's book in the hands of every Irishman. Griffith's teachings are summed up in *The Resurrection of Hungary* in which he reproduced the arguments (with acknowledgements to List) which he had advanced in 1905 in favour of a Sinn Féin policy of developing Ireland's 'manufacturing arm' with the aid of tariff protection, particularly for infant industries. Griffith emphasised the interdependence of agriculture and industry and the concern of Sinn Féin 'to give Ireland back her manufacturing arm, not to make fortunes for dishonest manufacturers' who had no need of protection. Griffith's views had a profound influence on Lemass; they can indeed be said to have laid the basis of his life's work.

When the Irish Free State was founded in 1922, Lemass was still in jail. Shortly after his release in 1923 he was elected to the Dáil but did not take his seat. He subsequently helped form a new political party, Fianna Fáil. As one of the secretaries of the party, he spent the next few years moving around the country organising branches and preparing for the next election. In this capacity his administrative abilities first became apparent.

Offering a policy which included the imposition of a wide range of protective tariffs, the new party gained a strong minority position in the general election of 1927. They took their seats and Lemass gradually assumed the role of opposition spokesman on economic affairs. In this capacity he pressed for increased tariffs on imports. It may seem strange that he should have to castigate the tardiness of the then government in following the Sinn Féin principles of Arthur Griffith. But one of the leading spokesmen of that government, Kevin O'Higgins, Minister for Home Affairs, had earlier moved to a critical stance:

> The propagandist writings of any one man cannot be accepted simply as revealed truth, requiring no further investigation, something that must be accepted for ever as beyond question, beyond doubt, beyond the need of examination.[2]

It is true that a few moderate tariffs were introduced during the twenties but they were certainly not designed in scope or degree to promote the ideal of self-sufficiency.[3] Perhaps this reluctance to embrace an outright protectionist policy can be explained by the first Irish government's desire to establish the standing of the state in the eyes of the world by observing a rather strict orthodoxy in this as well as in other economic and financial matters. Free trade was the accepted commercial philosophy of the day. Moreover, agriculture was by far the stronger arm of the economy and the government leant towards this side of the Sinn Féin policy balance. It was hoped that the benefits of agricultural prosperity would percolate to other sectors of the economy, leading in time to an expansion of home industries. A Tariff Commission was set up to consider tariffs on certain imports but it moved slowly and cautiously.

In 1928 Lemass made a speech in the Dáil which clearly defined his views on the policy which should be pursued:

> We believe that Ireland can be made a self-contained unit, providing all the necessities of living in adequate quantities for the people residing in the island at the moment and probably for a much larger number. . . . Until we get a definite national policy decided on in favour of industrial

and agricultural protection and an executive in office prepared to enforce that policy, it is useless to hope for results.[4]

In 1932 Fianna Fáil were voted into power and Seán Lemass
became Minister for Industry and Commerce. Thus the stage
was set for a vigorous policy of protection and industrialisation.
The drive towards protection was reinforced by a dispute with
Great Britain – the so-called 'Economic War' – which stimulated recourse to tariffs and quotas as retaliatory devices.
Internationally, also, the trend of events was running against
free trade and in favour of resort to national protectionism.

The 'Economic War' centred on the refusal of the new
government to pay certain land purchase annuities to the
British government: the details need not concern us here. What
is relevant is that the British government decided to recoup its
losses by imposing duties of 20 per cent *ad valorem* on Irish
cattle and on the other main Irish agricultural exports to the
United Kingdom. These duties were later increased in severity.
These were not the only restrictions placed on Irish exports.
It was decided to exclude Ireland from the preferential tariff
agreements which were negotiated amongst members of the
Commonwealth at the Ottawa Conference in 1932. It was
hardly surprising, therefore, that the new government should
have pursued its policy of self-sufficiency with more political
zest than economic calculation. In 1936 the so-called 'Coal –
Cattle Pact' marked the first step towards resolving the difficulties between the two countries, and in 1938 an agreement
was signed which in effect brought the 'Economic War' to an
end. This agreement, although partly revised in 1948, formed
the basis of trade between the two countries until the Anglo-
Irish Free Trade Area Agreement in 1965. It provided for
review by the Irish Prices Commission of existing protective
duties and other import restrictions, for the holding of this
review *first* 'upon the classes of goods for which the Government
of the United Kingdom request early consideration' and for
full right of audience before the Commission for UK producers
and manufacturers. The advent of World War II, however,
effectively prevented any reduction in tariffs; in fact, it heightened the degree of Ireland's isolation and self-reliance.

The protectionist policy of the nineteen thirties received valuable support from a famous economist – John Maynard Keynes. Keynes, while mentioning the dangers of economic nationalism, spoke out in favour of a move towards greater self-sufficiency, declaring to his audience at the first Finlay Lecture in University College, Dublin, on 19 April 1933:

> I sympathise, therefore, with those who would minimise rather than with those who would maximise, economic entanglement between nations. Ideas, knowledge, science, hospitality, travel – these are the things which should of their nature be international. But let goods be homespun whenever it is reasonable and conveniently possible and, above all, let finance be primarily national.[5]

and again

> . . . . if I were an Irishman I should find much to attract me in the economic outlook of your present government towards self-sufficiency.

Neither Friedrich List nor Arthur Griffith could have put it more forcefully. Unlike them, Keynes spoke when all was in place – the time, the opportunity, the mood and the man. It is understandable that less attention was paid to the 'fundamental question' which Keynes also posed in his lecture, whether 'Ireland is a large enough unit geographically, with sufficiently diversified natural resources, for more than a very modest measure of national self-sufficiency to be feasible without a disastrous reduction in a standard of life which is already none too high'. The answer Keynes himself suggested to this question is interesting, in view of Seán Lemass's signature much later (1965) of the Anglo-Irish Free Trade Area Agreement:

> I believe, I should answer that it would be an act of high wisdom on the part of the Irish to enter into an economic arrangement with England which would, within appropriate limits, retain for Ireland her traditional British markets against mutual advantages for British producers within the wide field which for long to come will not interfere with

Ireland's own developments. I should see nothing in this the slightest degree derogatory to her political and cultural autonomy. I should look on it merely as an act of common-sense for the preservation of the standard of life of the Irish, at a level which would alone make possible the country's new political and cultural life.

In those early years of the 1930s the world at large was in the grip of the Great Depression; the prices of primary products had plummeted, the demand for goods had fallen catastroph-ically, unemployment was severe and widespread. In 1931 the new government in England announced its intention of impos-ing a tariff – the first general British tariff since the eighteen fifties – and of protecting British agriculture. The practical and theoretical considerations supporting free trade were thus undermined and no inhibition lay in the way of a policy of protection aimed at securing self-sufficiency. On the contrary, the sharpness of the British reaction to the withholding of the land annuities caused protection proper to be enveloped in a heated atmosphere of retaliation which was hostile to any careful adjustment of aid to need. On several occasions in the 1932-38 period the desirability of a more scientific basis for the tariffs was suggested to Lemass by the Secretary of his Depart-ment, only to receive an Augustinian reply: the advice was appropriate but premature. Lemass did not, however, object to the provisions in the 1938 Anglo-Irish Trade Agreement for tariff reviews.

One of the first acts of the new government in 1932 was to introduce the Control of Manufactures Act which was aimed at restricting, to a minority position, foreign ownership and board membership of Irish manufacturing companies. The intention was to lay the foundation of a domestic industrial base:

> We are endeavouring to undertake and promote rapid indus-trial development in this country. We are in the process of imposing a system of protective tariffs designed to ensure the production in this country in much greater volume of goods which were produced here heretofore and some classes

of goods which were not produced in this country before this.[6]

With the same purpose in mind, the government, realising the undeveloped state of the industrial capital market and the absence of financial facilities for new industries, set up the Industrial Credit Company in 1933 to remedy these deficiencies.

The Control of Manufactures Bill was vehemently attacked by the opposition in one of the longest debates of the new Dáil. A wide variety of arguments, legal, political, administrative and economic, were adduced against it. One deputy, J. J. Byrne, in the course of a speech, put some rhetorical questions which may be read as indicating the general state of mind as well as the position of industry at that time:

Will capital be attracted or repelled if this Bill passes? Is there any attraction for the investment of Irish capital if the Bill becomes law? Do not men who possess capital realise the shortcomings from which Irish industrialists suffer? Do they not realise that they have not the experience of their competitors either in technical processes of manufacture or in large scale production? Do they not realise that when people invest capital they do not ask 'is this an Irish or a foreign firm' but rather 'what are they going to receive on any money they invest'?[7]

The truth lay between this pessimism and the optimism reflected in the expectation of a 'rapid industrial development' which would be foreign-dominated unless legislative provision were made otherwise.

A few figures will give an idea of the zeal with which what Professor Meenan has called 'the last surviving example of a predominantly free-trading state' was transformed into one of the most highly protected in the world. At the end of 1931, the list of tariffs covered 68 articles including 9 revenue tariffs. In the Finance Act of May 1932, the new Fianna Fáil government imposed *ad valorem* duties ranging from 15 per cent to 75 per cent on 38 classes of goods with specific duties on 6 other classes. Following the Emergency Imposition of Duties Act, which provided for the imposition of retaliatory duties, the next major round of tariffs was introduced in October 1932 with *ad valorem* duties ranging from 15 per cent to 75 per cent on a further 29 classes of goods (including component parts for motor vehicles, ropes and yarns, and coffin plates) and specific duties on 7 commodities (including food items and machinery). In 1933 *ad valorem* duties ranging from 22½ per cent to 75 per cent were imposed on 22 classes of goods (including heavy electrical equipment, mattresses, leather goods and candles, to name but a few) and specific duties on 15 classes. In 1934, 45 further commodities were made subject to import duties; in 1935 *ad valorem* duties ranging from 20 per cent to 100 per cent were imposed on 29 classes and specific duties on 17 goods; in 1936, 44 new duties were imposed; in 1937, 31 new duties were imposed and in 1938 14 new duties were added.[8] Tariffs on intermediate products piled up to create a pyramid of protection for some final products. There was not much time for tea-breaks in the Department of Industry and Commerce in those years!

Estimates of the tariff levels obtaining in 1931, 1936 and 1938 have been made by Professor Louden Ryan of Trinity College, Dublin, and they show how the intensity of protection mounted.[9] The calculations are based on a representative list of commodities bearing either a specific duty or an *ad valorem* duty, and altogether some 161 commodities subject to tariff protection, but not to revenue duties, were considered. The resulting tariff level indexes by comparison with a *nil* rate for 1924, were as follows: 1931 9 per cent; 1936 45 per cent; 1938 35 per cent. The year 1931 was chosen to measure the level of protection reached under the selective policy of the previous government. The year 1936 marked the high-water mark of tariff protection by the Fianna Fáil government, Séan Lemass being Minister for Industry and Commerce. The year 1938 saw the signing of the Anglo-Irish Trade Agreement, completing the settlement of the Anglo-Irish dispute initiated by the Coal–Cattle Pact of 1936; some tariffs had been reduced or abolished in the intervening period. The calculations are based on figures which represent the 'potential' height of the tariff wall and do not allow for abatement of the tariffs in special circumstances. On the other hand, the protective effect of quota restrictions is not measured by the index. Professor Ryan estimated that the prevailing UK tariff level in 1937 was about 65 per cent of the corresponding Irish tariff level. The table in which this estimate appears also contains estimates of the relative tariff levels of other countries at that time; with figures of 152 for Germany (relative to Ireland's 100), 70 for Switzerland, 55 for the United States and 53 for Japan, the table is striking evidence of the international incidence of protection before World War II.

The percentage duty applicable to particular categories of imports into Ireland was high and where the basic value was low had often to be underpinned by a minimum specific duty. As a category, fuels were subject to an *ad valorem* rate of approximately 250 per cent, foods to 72½-82 per cent, textile products to 35½-37½ per cent, but such was the prevalence of protection in those pre-war years that even these rates had, individually, near counterparts in some European countries or in North America. *The Economist* calculated in 1938 that 1,947 articles were subject to restriction or control in the Irish state. These restrictions were administered with thoroughness and few exemptions were granted. Licences to import goods duty-free were given only if the prospective importer could show that no reasonable substitute was available from home producers. On the other hand, it is only fair to the recipients of such unscientifically generous protection to say that most of them did not take full advantage of the high tariffs in fixing their domestic prices; many regarded the full tariff as a safeguard against dumping and relied in practice on a lower degree of price differential, more closely related to productivity and cost differences.

Reviewing the progress made towards self-sufficiency in the cramped circumstances of those pre-war years, one cannot record spectacular success but nevertheless there was progress, and this was seen to be worthwhile in the scarcity conditions of war and post-war years. Rather indiscriminate particulars of 'the number of new industries and extensions of existing industries' were published periodically, but the best indication of the extent to which industrialisation had proceeded before World War Two is afforded by the following summary:

|                                                    | 1926     | 1931     | 1938     |
|----------------------------------------------------|----------|----------|----------|
| Value of *total* net industrial output             | £23m.    | £26m.    | £35m.    |
| Index of volume of total industrial production, 1929=100 | 92  | 102      | 149      |
| Numbers employed in industry                       | 102,515  | 110,589  | 166,513  |

Sources: *Irish Statistical Bulletin*, March 1973; *Statistical Abstract* 1955.

It was many years later – after the scarcities had disappeared and the supporting structure of education, power, communications and finance had been strengthened – that significant progress was realised. When Lemass retired to the backbenches towards the end of 1966, the volume of industrial production (1929=100) had reached 452 – though figures such as these are best interpreted as rough indications only – the numbers employed in industry were over 260,000 and industrial exports amounted to £128 million, as against a mere £5 million in 1938. Indeed a few years later, in 1969, industrial exports exceeded agricultural exports for the first time. This growth in output was accompanied by another encouraging development – an increase in the size of firms, a trend likely to continue during the coming years.

But this is to take a glimpse forward from those pre-war days when industry – much of it small in scale – was almost entirely confined by cost considerations to a protected and stagnant home market, the agricultural arm having been weakened by the prolonged dispute with Britain. It has been estimated that, whereas in 1931 the average income per head in Ireland was 61 per cent of that in Britain, by 1939 the corresponding figure was 49 per cent.

> While protection had created a whole complex of vested interests not necessarily compatible with present efficiency or future prosperity, emigration, by removing some of the pressures for change, contributed its share to what seemed the immutable inertia of Irish economic life.[10]

When the war came, Lemass was given charge of the newly created Department of Supplies where his dynamic energy, his decisiveness (and eagerness to decide) and his organisational capacity received full scope.[11] The scarcity of essential supplies made protection irrelevant and protective duties were suspended for all practical purposes in 1942. Only as supplies became fully available in the post-war years were they gradually put into effect again.

With the insight into the industrial situation afforded by his experience as Minister for Supplies, it was natural that Seán Lemass, on his return to Industry and Commerce, should reassess the merits of the policy of hurried and indiscriminate protection pursued in the pre-war years. He was too intelligent a man not to learn from experience and too patriotic to neglect any lessons relevant to the long-term development of the Irish economy. This pragmatic nationalism was his outstanding characteristic and it showed up constantly in his approach to economic as well as to political problems.

One sign of it was the increasing concern he displayed about the cost and price effects of high protection and the complacency and inefficiency it induced. The Prices Acts of 1932 and 1937 had not been very effective: the legislation was directed against profiteering rather than high costs of production and the possibility of restraining prices by reducing tariffs and allowing more foreign competition was not, in effect, entertained. Speaking on the second stage of the Control of Prices Bill, 1937, Lemass had said:

> In relation to most industries I have tried to promote a reasonable amount of competition, but I think it is wrong to assume that competition is always an unmixed blessing.... Competition may be all right on paper and in textbooks but in actual practice it is often the cause of many social evils.[12]

But the obvious deficiencies of enterprise, management and technique in many protected industries, and the deeper realisation of the enormity of the task of industrialisation gained by his wartime experience, convinced Lemass that more effective measures were needed to set the economy on the path of competitive efficiency and growth. So in 1947 he introduced an Industrial Efficiency and Prices Bill. This was a watershed in his thinking. He proposed to establish a Commission which should exercise

> a continued supervision over the efficiency of industries engaged in the production of protected commodities and shall endeavour to improve the efficiency of such undertakings by giving expert advice and assistance and by consultation with the representatives of the industries concerned. (Industrial Efficiency and Prices Bill, 1947—Explanatory Memorandum)

The chairman of the Commission, acting with the Minister's consent, could undertake a special enquiry into the efficiency of an industry. If the Commission decided that this was below a reasonable standard, measuring efficiency by reference to such matters as the quality and cost of the products by comparison with similar products in other countries, the arrangements for purchasing of materials and the economic use of capital and labour, the Minister was to have the power to give a direction to the manufacturers to make such changes as were necessary to promote greater efficiency in the industry.

Furthermore, the government was empowered to set the maximum profit which a firm could make and if the firm made any excess profit then the Minister could claim that excess.

The Bill was not solely concerned with punitive measures; there were also provisions for helping industries to develop. One such provision was the establishment of development councils for industries, which would be mainly concerned with

> promoting by voluntary efforts the efficiency of industries which the council represents. The functions of a development council were to include the promotion of scientific research and of enquiries into the methods of production and the management and use of labour. A development council was also to be concerned with the extension of facilities for technical training of workers and the promotion of improved standards and design and standardisation of products and of market research. (Explanatory Memorandum).

A development council to encourage cooperation between firms in the supply of materials and equipment and the coordination of production, marketing and distribution was also envisaged. The Bill also proposed to re-establish the Prices Commission and to extend its investigatory scope to include services as well as commodities.

This mixture of carrot and stick, for those infant industries loth to grow up, never got a chance to prove itself. The coalition government which took office in 1948 did not proceed with the legislation and it is now chiefly of interest as an indication of Lemass's concern at the time – a concern which extended also to the fragmented state of trade union organisation – and as a precursor of the more comprehensive measures of industrial survey, tripartite consultative and advisory machinery, grants for modernisation and adaptation, and even unilateral reduction of protection which he put into effect in the early 1960s after applying for membership for Ireland in the EEC.

The Fianna Fáil government were out of office from 1948 to 1951 and again from 1954 to 1957. The final phase of transition from protection to free trade coincided with Lemass's own final period in government from 1957 to 1966 for the seven last years of which he was Taoiseach (Prime Minister). This period was preceded by a dark night of the soul, shared by the principal politicians both in and out of office and by concerned citizens and public servants. For the first half of the nineteen fifties economic progress had been brought almost to a standstill by balance of payments and other difficulties. The years 1955 and 1956 had plumbed the depths of hopelessness. One of the recurring series of balance of payments crises had been overcome – indeed, the basis laid for a surplus on current account in 1957 – but at the cost of high unemployment and emigration. The mood of despondency was palpable. My own impression of the state of the nation at that time is set out in the following passage:

> A sense of anxiety is, indeed, justified. But it can too easily degenerate into feelings of frustration and despair. After 35 years of native government people are asking whether we can achieve an acceptable degree of economic progress. The common talk amongst parents in the towns, as in rural

Ireland, is of their children having to emigrate as soon as their education is completed in order to be sure of a reasonable livelihood. To the children themselves and to many already in employment the jobs available at home look unattractive by comparison with those obtainable in such variety and so readily elsewhere. All this seems to be setting up a vicious circle – of increasing emigration, resulting in a smaller domestic market depleted of initiative and skill, and a reduced incentive, whether for Irishmen or foreigners, to undertake and organise the productive enterprises which alone can provide increased employment opportunities and higher living standards. There is, therefore, a real need at present to buttress confidence in the country's future and to stimulate the interest and enthusiasm of the young in particular. A general resurgence of will may be helped by setting up targets of national endeavour which appear to be reasonably attainable and mutually consistent.[13]

Lemass himself had reacted to Ireland's evident failure in the post-war world of reconstruction and development by presenting, when in opposition, a simple 'Keynesian' prescription of increased public investment to generate 100,000 new jobs and provide full employment in five years. His ideas were expounded in a supplement to *The Irish Press* and subsequently to party members in Clery's Ballroom in early 1956. Other studies of the deficiencies of the Irish economy were also undertaken around this time. These included a paper on capital formation, saving and economic progress, which I read to the Statistical and Social Inquiry Society of Ireland in May 1956 [see Chapter 2] and reports of the Capital Investment Advisory Committee, which had been established in 1955. These various products of the dark night of soul-searching at least agreed on the need to devote more resources on an orderly basis to productive investment. Finally, over the winter and spring of 1957-8, a comprehensive survey of the economy, extending to its potentialities as well as its deficiencies, and containing a systematic set of proposals for action, was prepared in the Department of Finance. This was presented to the government in May 1958 and was published under the title *Economic Development* in November of that year, simultaneously with the *First Programme* for *Economic Expansion* which was acknowledged to be based largely upon it.

Lemass, as Tánaiste (Deputy Prime Minister) and Minister for Industry and Commerce, chaired the cabinet committee which put this First Programme into final shape. Here again his pragmatic nationalism was in evidence, for the Programme indicated a distinct and courageous change of emphasis in the traditional policy of his party. The aim of self-sufficiency, involving, for instance, protected or subsidised home production of wheat and sugar beet, had been pursued in agriculture as well as in industry; now the importance of the 85 per cent of Ireland's agricultural land which was under grass was expressly recognised.

> Grass is the raw material of our principal export trade, beef and cattle, of milk production and of sheep and lamb production. While the outlook for milk products in export markets is uncertain, there is fortunately little doubt that there will be a continuing demand for meat. We are singularly well situated to take advantage of this prospect....[14]

Not only, to oversimplify a little, did the new Programme put grass before grain but on the industrial side it put export-oriented expansion – even if foreign-owned – before dependence on protected domestic enterprise. The new policy was stated straightforwardly as follows:[15]

> It would be unrealistic, in the light of the probable emergence of a Free Trade Area to rely on a policy of protection similar to that applied over the past 25 years or so. Assuming that a Free Trade Area is set up in Western Europe and that Ireland joins the Area, the Government will, of course, still be prepared, in suitable cases, to grant protection to worth-while new industries up to the limits permissible under the rules of the Free Trade Area, but it must be expected that in future the criterion to be applied in determining what is 'worth-while' will be very much stricter than hitherto. Bearing in mind that the only scope for substantial expansion lies in the production of goods for sale on export markets, it is clear that there can be no place for weak or inefficient industries. Even where only the home market is

involved, it must be accepted that such industries place a burden on the economy generally and render other industries less able to meet foreign competition. Hence it must now be recognised that protection can no longer be relied upon as an automatic weapon of defence and it will be the policy in future in the case of new industries to confine the grant of tariff protection to cases in which it is clear that the industry will, after a short initial period, be able to survive without protection. The rules of the Free Trade Area will require a gradual and systematic reduction in existing tariffs.

The industrial Free Trade Area then envisaged never came into being. It was viewed as an alternative to a wider Common Market, and Britain would have preferred it because it had no agricultural implications. It was, however, effectively killed by French opposition. The Six held fast to their Common Market and the outer Seven (Britain, the Scandinavian countries, Austria, and Portugal) formed the European Free Trade Association. Ireland had been pressing hard in the original Free Trade Area negotiations for a transitional period of some twenty-five years for the gradual elimination of industrial protection, in this respect claiming the same derogations as Greece and Turkey. When the break-down occurred and Europe split into sixes and sevens, Ireland was isolated. Much thought was devoted during the period, 1959 to 1961, at Lemass's insistence as Taoiseach, to ways of overcoming this isolation. In particular, the possibility of special bilateral trade arrangements with Britain and the question of joining EFTA were studied. The Secretaries of the four main economic Departments – Finance, Industry and Commerce, Agriculture, and External Affairs – met frequently as a committee reporting on these matters to a cabinet committee chaired by Mr Lemass. The correspondence which passed between the four Secretaries – particularly Finance and Industry and Commerce – was intended also for the eyes of the Taoiseach and other Ministers on the cabinet committee and may be presumed to have had some influence on policy.

This was, in fact, a 'crunch' period in the move to free trade. Despite recognition of its probable inevitability, free trade, naturally enough, was not universally welcome and the original impetus towards it ran the risk of running into the sands of frustrated isolation. The Department of Industry and Commerce was concerned about the sensitivity of Irish industry to external competition, to shifts in demand, and, worse still, to dumping. There was apprehension about the risks of industrial setback and unemployment inherent in even a gradual commitment to dispense with protection. In the Department's view, even if protection was intended only for infant industries, most Irish industries, if one excluded the war years and their aftermath, were still in their 'teens'. While the risks involved in premature withdrawal of protection were acknowledged, the following were the chief points on the other side of the argument:

1. Protected manufacture for a home market of present population and purchasing power and already well exploited offered little prospect of *increased* employment.

2. In an increasingly competitive world, in which real wages would be rising, continued high protection could not guarantee the maintenance of existing employment in Ireland at *acceptable* real wages.

3. If employment opportunities were to be created for the fresh thousands seeking work every year – indeed even if existing employment were to be safeguarded – industry must quickly become more efficient so that its products could be sold on an increasing scale in export markets.

4. The rapid and general increase in industrial efficiency required by national progress could most effectively and advantageously be secured by accepting an external commitment to reduce tariffs, accompanied by appropriate internal incentives and aids towards industrial adaptation and modernisation.

Lemass had been convinced since 1958 of the inevitability of free trade and his frequent contacts with European economic ministers at the OEEC had helped towards his gradual Europeanisation. His mind is revealed in a statement made by him when concluding the adjournment debate on government policy on 11 December 1959:

> The world trend, however, is towards freer trade and we must not blink our eyes to it. The Common Market is already making gestures towards a world agreement. Whatever may be the outcome of negotiations with Britain or the EFTA or anyone else, we must face up to the fact of our having to reduce our protective measures at some time and not too far ahead at that. Indeed there is a case for doing it in our own interests apart from external arrangements. Everybody concerned, whether in management or as workers in industry, must face up to the prospect and prepare for it.[16]

A pamphlet published about that time by the Federation of Irish Industries recognised the imminent necessity for progressive reduction of protection leading eventually to free trade, and claimed that Irish industry was sufficiently strong and adaptable to meet the situation successfully.

This more open view of Ireland's future trading relations was reflected in the decision in 1960 to join GATT and was confirmed beyond all doubt in the decision to apply for membership of the European Economic Community in 1961. This application had to be put aside in 1963 when de Gaulle exercised his veto on British membership. Ireland saw more problems than advantages in trying to pursue the goal of independent membership which was probably unrealisable in any event. So again there was a setback and the search had to be renewed for an alternative interim trading framework offering some benefits in return for the only thing Ireland had to offer – a progressive lowering of tariffs. In the end, after two brave unilateral and across-the-board 10 per cent tariff cuts in 1963 and 1964, intended not only as notices of serious intent to Britain and the EEC but also as spurs to internal reorganisation and adaptation, the interim framework was found. In the new world of free trade areas and common markets, it naturally conformed to accepted patterns; it took the form of a free trade area with Britain with some element on the agricultural side of a common market character. The Free

Trade Area Agreement, signed by Lemass in December 1965, provided for the immediate removal of the remaining British tariffs on Irish manufactures (mainly on synthetic textiles) together with concessions and assurances for the Irish meat trade in return for the progressive removal over ten years of all Irish protection against British manufactures. This Agreement held the field until it was subsumed into the transitional arrangements for the entry of both countries into the European Economic Community on 1 January 1973.

I have run ahead to complete the obituary of protection, or at least to register its fatal decline, and have given less than proper attention to important complementary policies which eased it out of the Irish economic system without as much upset or redundancy as some originally feared. In a recent publication[17], it has been estimated that the number of potential (not actual) jobs lost as a result of the expansion of imports attributable to AIFTA and other competitive factors was no more than 2,000 in 1969-70. Moreover, economic progress has continued, though somewhat erratically: over the period 1966 to 1973 the real increase in GNP has been over 35 per cent.

One of the first moves towards achieving a more efficient, outward-looking industrial sector was the Industrial Development (Encouragement of External Investment) Act passed in 1958. This removed the restrictions on foreign ownership of capital in Ireland embodied in the Control of Manufactures Act and reinforced the steps already taken by the previous government, through the Industrial Development Authority, to attract foreign industry from a wider range of countries.

The title is eloquent testimony to the change in policy engendered by the frustrating experience of continued emigration and lukewarm external interest in exploitation of Irish resources. During the debate on the Bill, Mr Lemass said:

> I believe this Bill will be effective in what it sets out to achieve. What does it hope to achieve? Its object is to attract external capital into new industries and into industries with export possibilities and in that way to put more people into employment. It is not to put existing factories out of business but to ensure that the capital which can be attracted will be channelled into the activities which we want to promote.[18]

In industry, the main objective of the First Programme was to encourage private enterprise – 'the private sector will be the principal source of new productive projects' – while at the same time switching public capital resources to productive purposes. Foreign capital was to be actively attracted by means of more liberal capital grants, export tax concessions and other incentives. The Finance Acts of 1959 and 1960 extended the tax concessions of profits and investment originally introduced in 1956. The Industrial Credit Company was given greater resources for making loans to industry. By making existing as well as new industry eligible for the benefits of the Industrial Grants Acts, it was hoped to develop the entire industrial sector.

It would be unfair to give the impression that Lemass was the only politician who had reconsidered traditional policies in the light of experience. The export tax incentives introduced by the coalition government in 1956 were available for all, whether native or foreign, and Mr Gerard Sweetman, Minister for Finance in that government, declared:

> The real need at the present time is for a substantial increase in the volume and efficiency of our national production.[19]

Speaking in 1957, Deputy Norton (leader of the Labour Party) declared:

> It is not very important what the Minister does at the moment with regard to the Control of Manufactures Act. Speaking for my own part I should like to say that we recognise it is out of date, that it has lost its early significance, that there is a change in the whole industrial and economic situation and that in contemplation of these circumstances the Act should be modified, if not in fact abolished altogether. Except for the purpose of the directional powers it gives the Minister it has little or no value in the present circumstances.[20]

Much of the basic organisation for the industrial expansion of the 1960s was laid during the 1950s – including the establishment of the Industrial Development Authority (1950), Córas

Tráchtála (the export promotion body) in 1952, and Foras Tionscail (the grant-giving authority), also in 1952. The first export tax reliefs followed in 1956.

Shortly before Lemass succeeded de Valera as Taoiseach in 1959, he asserted that 'the historic task of this generation is to ensure the economic foundation of independence'. If there was failure to achieve economic goals, this would set the political gains to nought. Furthermore, the growth in the economy was to be achieved by means of an outward-looking, competitive approach. There was to be no more hiding behind stultifying trade barriers: the industrial forest must be cleared of dead-wood and new growth created.

Expert foresters were sent in to survey and report. A Committee on Industrial Organisation was established, the members being drawn from trade union and employers' organisations as well as the public service, and teams with economic and technical backgrounds conducted surveys for this Committee of the main industries as a basis for recommendations on the measures to be adopted to prepare them for intensive competition. The Department of Agriculture similarly reviewed the agricultural processing industries and the Industrial Reorganisation Branch of the Department of Industry and Commerce a further twenty-four industries. The general finding, as one might expect, was that most firms needed to invest in new machinery and to rationalise the whole productive process, from raw material buying to marketing. Measures of cooperation and integration were needed. Special Adaptation Councils were recommended for most industries. The government decided to make available, for a finite period, special grants, loans and tax incentives to encourage firms to modernise and adapt to more competitive trading conditions.

Undoubtedly, the confidence and responsiveness of industry during all this adjustment phase were greatly increased by the success – far beyond the initial modest expectations – of the First Programme for Economic Expansion. To find the economy growing year by year at a rate of 4 per cent with no trouble on the balance of payments front and prices rising only moderately was a psychological tonic for the whole community. Even later, under the more specifically ambitious Second Programme, when expectations ran ahead of resources, the balance of payments deficit never quite regained its former frightening and inhibiting power, partly because the financing of the deficit by capital inflows, autonomous or arranged, became easier; indeed, these inflows tended to raise the external reserves and not just offset their depletion.

Relations between the state and both sides of industry, indeed between the 'social partners' themselves, were also improved by the active interest in industrial welfare manifested by all the surveys, the financial aids offered, the tax reliefs granted, the concern to safeguard and promote employment and improve training facilities and the participation in the shaping of policy through the National Industrial Economic Council. This Council was set up in 1963 to advise the government on the principles which should guide the development of the economy; its membership included representatives of industry and the trade union movement, university professors of economics and other distinguished persons outside the public sector as well as a few public servants. As its chairman, my judgment on the Council cannot claim objectivity. It seems to me that its chief value lay in its being a forum for continual analysis of economic and social problems and for enlightening discussions. *Ex parte* and committed views were softened under exposure to fact and argument. The best work of the Council was done in studying the conditions on which full employment might in time be attained – 'the arithmetic of a full employment policy' as it was called – and in outlining the principles of a prices and incomes policy. The Council's examination of the Second Programme and, annually, of the economic prospect also helped towards more widespread understanding of critical issues.

I have no doubt that this intermeshing of cooperative study and action played a significant part in preparing Ireland, psychologically and technically, for the approach of free trade. The disposition to face it – indeed, the general recognition that only if Irish manufactures could attract an increasing *export* demand was there any hope of escape from unemployment, under-employment and emigration – was not impaired by the failure to get into the EEC at this time nor by the 15 per cent levy on manufactured imports which Britain imposed in 1964, nor by the re-emergence of domestic inflationary problems in

1965. The impetus carried through to the signing of the Anglo-Irish Free Trade Area Agreement at the end of that year.

In retrospect, one can scarcely doubt the economic advantage to Ireland of the time gained through the reluctance of France (at least) to see Great Britain in the EEC, of the surveys and adaptation measures taken in the 1960s and of the experience provided by the tariff reductions of 1963 and 1964 and under the AIFTA.

Seán Lemass did not live to see Ireland formally enter the European Economic Community; he died in 1971, having retired altogether from politics the year before. One can, however, safely assert that this pragmatic nationalist, who had erected the high tariff wall in the 1930s to shelter Ireland's infant industry, would have been happy to see it razed to the ground in return for the benefits to Ireland of membership of the Community. He would have been gratified that many of the 'infants' were strong enough to make their way against Continental as well as British competition. No doubt he would still have misgivings. But I suspect these would relate more to Ireland's relatively high current rate of price and cost inflation rather than to the dismantling of protection. He had always, like many others, been apprehensive about the effects of removal of the lowest 10 per cent or so of the protective shield. I remember assuring him that the pound sterling was almost certain to be devalued again in advance of Britain's entry to the EEC and that this, whatever its disadvantages, would at least afford both countries some 'residual' protection against the stronger Continental members. On top of the formal devaluation of 1967, the floating of sterling since mid-1972 has had this effect. Ireland's main problem is to hold its competitive position in relation to Britain. It has been estimated that, as late as 1966, the tariffs and export incentives were the equivalent of a 19 per cent devaluation of the Irish currency in relation to sterling; that is, their removal on a unilateral basis without reciprocal concessions by Ireland's trading partners would require a devaluation of this magnitude to restore equilibrium in the balance of payments.[21] Given that the tariff instrument has been set aside, that export aids may not endure for ever, and that the EEC is committed to move towards a monetary union in which exchange parities will be irrevocable, Seán Lemass would undoubtedly endorse all the emphasis which Ireland has placed on the need for effective Community policies financed by adequate regional, social and investment funds to mitigate the economic imbalance between the member countries. These matters are now the concern of other statesmen. We can salute Seán Lemass for having so effectively pursued policies which have taken Ireland from the embattled and impoverished protectionism of the 1930s into the more exposed but also better-off 1970s.

## Notes to Chapter 3

[1] Text of Seán Lemass Memorial Lecture delivered at the University of Exeter, 17 January 1974. I am indebted to Adrian Masterson, M.Sc. (Econ), an economist on the staff of the Central Bank, for substantial help in preparing this lecture.

[2] *Parliamentary Debates*, Dáil Éireann. Vol. 16, Col. 1884, 30 June 1926.

[3] For a summary of pre-1932 protective attitudes and actions, see Professor James Meenan's *The Irish Economy Since 1922*, pp. 137-141.

[4] *Parliamentary Debates*, Dáil Éireann, Vol. 22, Cols. 213/4, 22 February 1928.

[5] Reproduced in *Studies* of June 1933 under the title 'National Self-Sufficiency'.

[6] *Parliamentary Debates*, Dáil Éireann, Vol. 42, Cols. 1234/5, 14 June 1932.

[7] *Parliamentary Debates*, Dáil Éireann, Vol. 42, Col. 1270, 14 June 1932.

[8] Figures derived from various Finance Acts. See also Professor James Meenan *The Irish Economy Since 1922*, pp. 142-3.

[9] Paper read on 3 December 1948 to the Statistical and Social Inquiry Society of Ireland entitled 'Measurement of Tariff Levels for Ireland, For 1931, 1936, 1938'.

[10] This is the rather harsh judgment of Professor F. S. L. Lyons in *Ireland Since the Famine*, pp. 611-612.

[11] For most of his time in ministerial office, in Industry and Commerce and Supplies, Seán Lemass had the good fortune to be assisted, and at times creatively inspired, by a Permanent Secretary of outstanding quality, John Leydon.

[12] *Parliamentary Debates*, Dáil Éireann, Vol. 69, Col. 264, 7 October 1937.

[13] *Economic Development*, 1958, page 5.

[14] *Programme for Economic Expansion*, November 1958, (Pr. 4796), p. 12.

[15] ibid. pp. 37-8.

[16] *Parliamentary Debates*, Dáil Éireann, Vol. 178, No. 9, Col. 1574, 11 December 1959.

[17]McAleese and Martin, 'Irish Manufactured Imports from the UK in the 'Sixties: The Effects of AIFTA', Economic and Social Research Institute, Paper No. 70, May 1973.

[18]*Parliamentary Debates*, Dáil Éireann, Vol. 166, No. 9, Col. 1131, 27 March 1958.

[19]*Parliamentary Debates*, Dáil Éireann, Vol. 159, Col. 1603, 25 July 1956.

[20]*Parliamentary Debates*, Dáil Éireann, Vol. 163, Cols. 481/2, 2 July 1957.

[21]Dermot McAleese, 'Effective Tariffs and the Structure of Industrial Protection in Ireland', Economic and Social Research Institute, Paper No. 62, Dublin, June 1971.

*Jack Lynch, Taoiseach, T. K. Whitaker, J. C. Nagle and Donal O'Sullivan en route to London for the trade negotiations.*

# 4 Financial Turning-Points

## The Early Years

The first twenty-five years (1922-47) of budget-making in this state were marked by scrupulous respect for the principles of Adam Smith and Gladstone. There was a strong faith in the desirability of keeping government to a minimum and allowing money to fructify in the pockets of farmers, businessmen and individuals; and a matching disbelief in the virtue of public spending as a remedy for economic or social ills. Keynes paid a fleeting visit to Dublin in 1933 when he spoke in support of the new protectionist policy but his views on demand management, no less than the implications of the spreading political commitment to full employment, began to make their impact only in the immediate post-war years.

The principal aim of financial policy in the 1920s and 1930s was to confirm and strengthen the stability and repute of the new state. The means to this end were the choice of an absolute parity with sterling for the new Irish currency and the exercise of a budgetary discipline which strictly limited the growth of public expenditure and debt. So effectively was this policy applied, despite the high cost of suppressing a civil war and of restoring basic services afterwards, that Exchequer outlay, current and capital, which started off at £30 million in 1922-3 had been cut to under £27 million by 1930-31, or by at least as much as the general fall in the price level over that period. Even fighting the so-called Economic War in the depressed 1930s did not cause a notable rise in public expenditure: it was still under £36 million in 1939-40 though by then the price level was rising again. Typical of the outlook and doctrine of

81

the pre-Keynesian thirties are the following quotations from Department of Finance files of 1932:

> the balancing of the budget is not an object of purely academic importance that can be deferred till times are better: it becomes more necessary than ever when times are bad that the state can be shown to be living within its income

and

> the time has come not to extend the system of public works for the relief of unemployment but to reduce it drastically.

On 31 March 1939 the public debt was £45 million and it is almost incredible that it rose by as little as £20 million over the seven years to 31 March 1946. Ireland came through the Second World War with an aggregate of £16 million in current budget deficits, a sum which would last barely a week at our recent rate of deficit financing!

## Turning Point No 1 – 1950

It was to be expected that the first turning point would occur in the early post-war years, given the combined influence of the new significance and responsibility attached to public expenditure and borrowing in economic policy, the pent-up demand for consumer and capital goods, and the financial means provided both by the wartime accumulation of sterling assets and the availability of Marshall Aid loans and grants.

Dr Ronan Fanning in *The Irish Department of Finance, 1922-58*, from which I have taken the pre-Keynesian dicta cited above, traces the development of a new approach, starting with the participation of two junior officers of the Department (Patrick Lynch and myself) in a debate on full employment at the Statistical and Social Inquiry Society of Ireland on 27 April 1945. It was evident that Keynes, Beveridge and the British *White Paper on Employment Policy* had made their mark: there was explicit recognition that demand was an inherently unstable quantity and that positive action by governments through budgetary policy was necessary to maintain and stabilise it. Though the years 1947 to 1950 were plagued by continuing commodity scarcities, dollar shortage, sterling devaluation and the inflationary effects of the Korean War, the yeast of new thinking was at work, stimulated by Mr Frank Aiken's interest as Minister for Finance (1945-48) in cheap credit, Mr Sean McBride's advocacy as Minister for External Affairs (1948-51) of 'repatriation' of sterling assets to finance an enlarged public capital programme, the need to construct a plausible case for Marshall Aid, and argumentation as to the right use of the Marshall Aid 'counterpart funds'. Only a couple of months after the shock of the sterling devaluation of September 1949, the then Taoiseach, Mr John A. Costello, delivered a speech to the Institute of Bankers in Ireland, drafted by his economic adviser, Patrick Lynch, which installed at the centre of economic policy the principle of sustaining an adequate level of demand by way of public investment. This principle was reaffirmed in Mr McGilligan's budget speech of 1950, one of a long series of which I was the principal draughtsman. Thus the 1945 debate was carried into explicit policy formulation.

The first overt sign of a new approach to financial policy was not in itself of great absolute magnitude nor, indeed, could it be said to be of Keynesian inspiration. The introduction of a capital budget in 1950 was an innovation prompted by Patrick Lynch but recognised as an appropriate move by his Finance contemporaries. For many years it had been customary to make a deduction from current expenditure at budget time for 'items of a capital or abnormal nature'. Typically, however, the amount of the deduction before 1939 was only a few hundred thousand pounds. With the outbreak of war, the deduction rose at first to over £2 million, airport construction and afforestation joining defence equipment and public works as borrowing charges, but fell back to an average of just over £1 million a year for the remainder of the war period. It was Mr Aiken's budget of 1946 which, by introducing a Transition Development Fund of £5 million as a voted service financed from borrowings, made the first major break with tradition. This Fund was 'to operate during the next two financial years, and from it contributions would be made 'towards the extra capital expenses of state organisations and local authorities which are attributable to post-war transitional difficulties such as high prices of materials and shortage of equipment'. The year 1946/7 also saw the first post-war expansion of non-voted capital expenditure – the provision for Exchequer issues for electricity and turf development, telephones, local loans and tourism went up to £3½ million, as compared with an expenditure of less than £¼ million in 1945/6. The stage was therefore set for a more extensive and formal classification of voted services as being of a capital nature and, on that account, 'proper to be met from borrowing'. This concordance, however, had its roots in traditional accountancy rather than in new economic theory which would relate the manner in which public capital expenditure should be financed (whether by new credit creation or by a budget surplus) to the state of the economy. Accounting convention, political advantage and practical economic justification joined hands, however, in 1950. This particular year may therefore be considered to be a distinct turning-point in financial policy.

For the first time the Estimates for 1950-51 showed a division of Supply (or Voted) Services into Capital Services and Other Services. The total of Capital Services was £12,113,680 – roughly one-seventh of voted expenditure and a much larger amount than had ever previously been designated as a borrowing charge. Indeed, Mr McGilligan's 1949 budget had merely deducted £600,000 from the Supply Services for 'items of a capital or abnormal nature' and he said in his 1950 speech that the comparable figure for 1949-50 according to the new 'Capital Services' classification would have been some £4½ million. There was, therefore, a material increase in the deduction and it was doubtless to allay alarm that provision was made for an annuity to be charged against revenue to redeem the relevant borrowing over 30 years.

The 1950 budget speech contained a series of expository paragraphs on the economic obligations of the state, the need for increased investment, the question of repatriation of sterling assets and other matters of topical interest. Already, in his 1949 speech, the Minister for Finance had outlined the main considerations applicable to the spending of the Irish currency proceeds of Marshall Aid borrowings and had expressed approval of developmental expenditure which added to employment, improved amenities and increased security, even though it did not yield a direct money dividend sufficient to offset the corresponding debt charges. This, in the light of later developments, was an ominously liberal concession.

The Note Regarding Capital Services which prefaced the Estimates Volume for 1950-51 described them as:

> services which, although provided for by Votes, are regarded as proper to be met from borrowing because of their capital nature. The existence of capital items in the Supply Services has been recognised in the past in the framing of the annual Budget, when a deduction for capital items has usually been made from the total for Supply Services before arriving at the amount of expenditure chargeable against current revenue. In view of the considerable expansion in expenditure of a capital nature provided for out of voted moneys it has been decided to draw special attention to capital items by means of a note appended to Part II of each Estimate in which they occur . . . . For a full account of capital outlay financed by borrowing regard must, of course, be had not only to the Capital Services included in this volume but also to the direct issues from the Central Fund to the Electricity Supply Board, the Local Loans Fund, etc., estimates of which appear in the White Paper of Receipts and Expenditure published prior to the annual Budget.

A note in heavy type appeared as a footnote to individual Estimates:

> Included in the above Estimate of £      are the following items which are regarded as Capital Services and, therefore, proper to be met from borrowing:—
> Subhead . . . . . . . .

The 1951-52 Estimates Volume was drawn up on the same basis, the prefatory note including a reference to the provision made in the Central Fund Services for the redemption over a thirty-year period of the borrowings incurred for voted Capital Services.

I shall continue to note the changes in presentation which

took place in the years following 1951-2 because they reflect not only the altered economic and political background but also the rejection in favour of a more Keynesian approach of the simple accounting axiom that capital expenditure was, ipso facto, proper to be met from borrowing.

In an article in *Administration* (29/2) Dr Frank Gould has drawn attention to the expansionary thrust of public expenditure during the period of the first Inter-Party government (1948-51). The ratio of public expenditure to GNP rose sharply; indeed, public expenditure grew more than $2\frac{1}{2}$ times as fast as GNP, the highest rate for any period of government. As he says, this is attributable not only to post-war catching-up with maintenance and development arrears and satisfying of pent-up demand but also to ideological influences on government. It was clearly facilitated by the transfer to borrowing of services previously chargeable against current revenue, as well as by the availability of Marshall Aid counterpart funds.

## Intermission 1952-8

In 1951, however, there was not only a change of government but a deterioration in the economic scene. The rapid domestic expansion and the 1949 devaluation of sterling, which raised import prices but not agricultural export prices, caused balance of payments problems which were reinforced in 1950 by the effect on raw material prices of the Korean War. The result was a deficit in the 1950 balance of payments of £30 million which soared to £62 million in 1951, almost 15 per cent of GNP. The new Fianna Fáil government took severely corrective budgetary action in 1952. Mr MacEntee, as Minister for Finance, had strong reservations about voted Capital Services because of their political background and the doubtful quality, in his view, of some of the components. Within the Department unease had grown on economic grounds about the automatic equation of 'Capital Service' and 'proper to be met from borrowing'. The result of all this was that the Estimates Volume for 1952-53 dropped the classification altogether.

The 1952-53 note regarding 'Capital Services' reads:

Attention is drawn to the fact that the procedure of designating particular items in the Supply Services as 'capital services and, therefore, proper to be met from borrowing', which was inaugurated in 1950-51, has not been followed in this Volume. The reasons are (1) that it is necessary to reconsider the validity of the description 'capital service' in particular cases: (2) that it is only in the context of the Budget that a full estimate of Exchequer outlay on capital and current account will be available; and (3) that the extent to which capital expenditure may be met from borrowing can be assessed only in relation to the general economic and financial position, including the outlook in regard to national savings, which will be reviewed in connection with the Budget.

The 1952 Budget, however, was severe enough – it was described by the principal Opposition spokesman as 'cruel, unjust and unnecessary' – without adding back the former 'capital services' as items to be met from current revenue rather than borrowing. The Minister for Finance excused himself in the following terms:

> The deficit we face on current and capital account combined, however, is so great and the problem of dealing with it so serious that it seems unwise to deflect attention from it by a controversy as to whether some millions more or less in the voted services may be legitimately charged to 'capital'. In this Budget, therefore, I propose to present the figures on current and capital account on the same lines as were adopted by the previous Government, leaving over to a later stage in the rehabilitation of our finances the determination of the extent to which it is strictly justifiable to treat items of recurring voted expenditure as proper, even in principle, to be financed by borrowing.

This Augustinian procrastination extended throughout the life of the new government. Indeed, not only was the practice of borrowing for voted 'capital services' continued but new items were added. At the same time, however, the overriding budgetary principle of meeting current expenses out of current revenue and applying borrowing capacity to national development purposes was constantly reiterated. In his 1953 Budget Mr MacEntee answered those who advocated a less conservative policy, involving flexible recourse to current budget deficits, as follows:

> Advocates of this policy do not realise that the contribution of the state towards the stimulation of economic activity is determined, not by deficits on the current budget but by the overall effect of state expenditure, capital as well as current. They overlook the extent to which in recent years total state outlay has exceeded the resources drawn from the public in the form of current revenue and savings and has been financed by putting new money in circulation one way or another.

It is a pity that these words were not re-read before a more easy-going doctrine, devoid of Keynesian or other orthodoxy, was adopted in 1972 with significant consequences in later years.

Financial policy in the MacEntee period (1952-4), and indeed in the Sweetman period (1954-7) which followed it, was sensitive to the risk of external payments disequilibrium and to recurrent sterling crises. In the first period, total public expenditure grew at less than half the rate of GNP and, in the second, at just over half. There was only a slight growth in real terms in annual public capital expenditure over the period 1952-1958. In 1955, a combination of pay increases and easy credit conditions caused a large external deficit to recur at a time when Britain was in recession and imposing import surcharges. The government acted to curb consumer demand and social capital expenditure. Special import levies were imposed which were paid into a Capital Fund rather than used as current revenue. The balance of payments was turned around quite quickly but GNP fell a little in 1956 and was barely positive in 1957.

Kennedy and Dowling 'do not claim that the slow growth rate of the 1950s was solely due to the absence of a sufficiently expansionary fiscal policy, or that it would necessarily have been feasible then to maintain a rate of growth of demand sufficient to secure as good a growth rate of output as in the 1960s' but they do maintain that 'a reasonable rate of growth of demand led by an expansionary fiscal policy could have been safely sustained had there been a less restrictive view of the balance of payments constraint and less concern about increasing the national debt'.[2] Subsequent commentators have tended to follow this line which focusses on only some effects of fiscal expansion and shows insufficient appreciation of the practical constraints which precluded expansionary policies for most of the 1950s. At this period, our predominantly agricultural exports depended precariously on conditions in the British market; external deficits of menacing size could, and did, arise with little warning; the external reserves under direct Central Bank control were low; and foreign borrowing possibilities were virtually non-existent. I have unpleasant recollections of the difficulty of raising even a few million pounds on a short-term basis in London in 1956. It was not until the 1960s, when U.S. payments deficits created the Euro-dollar market, that foreign borrowing on any significant scale became possible and it was only in 1969 that the sterling holdings of the commercial banks were finally centralised in the Central Bank.

Voted 'capital services' have retained their status to this day, new items being added from time to time. With the return of an Inter-Party Government, the 1955 Estimates for Supply Services again had a prefatory note followed by a summary of these services by vote and subhead; and the Estimates of Receipts and Expenditure for the first time showed a division into Capital Services and Other Services, replacing the asterisk and footnote which had until then drawn attention to the capital component. It is significant that the prefatory Note Regarding Capital Services for 1955-6 and subsequent years contained no reference to 'proper to be met from borrowing'. The Finance Accounts were the last official publication to take any cognisance of voted 'capital services'. It was not until 1967-8 that Account No 1 drew attention to this element in the 'above the line' expenditure set against current revenue receipts.

## Turning Point No 2 – 1958

Even in the darker years of the 1950s sight was not lost of the need for radical change if economic growth – and indeed the viability of the economy – were to be assured. New institutions were established with this end in view – the Industrial Development Authority, An Foras Tionscal, Bord Fáilte, Córas Tráchtála and the Irish Management Institute. The system of grants for new industries was introduced in 1952 and extended in 1956. The tax reliefs initiated in that year were a powerful incentive to expansion of industrial exports. The mood of the time, however, was one of depression. Emigration was exceptionally heavy and a declining population presaged continuing contraction of the home market and of housing and other social needs.

In a paper to the Statistical and Social Inquiry Society of Ireland in May 1956, (see Chapter 2) before my appointment as Secretary of the Department of Finance, I drew attention to the slow growth of GNP in Ireland since 1949 as compared with Britain and other EEC countries, the relatively low ratios of capital formation and savings to GNP in Ireland and the rather high proportion of capital formation of a social as distinct from an economic character. The paper suggested that savings needed to be increased and used more productively so that capital investment could be raised and the national product enlarged as a basis for improved individual and social standards. At the same time as a Capital Investment Advisory Committee was sitting, a comprehensive review of development opportunities and policies was being undertaken in the Department of Finance. This was completed by May 1958 and published in November of that year under the title *Economic Development* shortly after the appearance of the *First Programme for Economic Expansion,* which itself owed its inspiration and nearly all its content to *Economic Development.* The result was a substantial change in the direction of policy, a purposeful co-ordination of development effort and, most importantly, a transformation of disillusionment and despondency into hope and confidence. It was recognised that reliance on a shrinking home market offered no prospect of satisfying Ireland's employment aspirations and that protectionism, both in agriculture and industry, would have to give way to active and competitive participation in a free-trading world. In agriculture, the development of grasslands and their products was to take precedence over the objective of self-sufficiency in cereals and, in industry, export-oriented expansion, even if under foreign ownership, was to be preferred to dependence on protected but inadequate domestic enterprise. Successive economic programmes maintained this policy emphasis.

An essential element in the new approach to economic management was a redressing of the balance between economic and social investment in the public capital programme. This programme would gain support from a rising level of domestic savings, based on steady growth in real national income, and domestic savings could be supplemented by reasonable recourse to foreign borrowing to promote productive home investment. *Economic Development* had set down both the advantages and disadvantages of such borrowing (Chapter 4, paras. 35-39). The balance was considered to be in favour of accelerating Ireland's economic progress through 'an inflow of external capital directed to types of development which would increase the country's productive capacity and which would bring with it new techniques and methods.' Explicit warning was given, however, that external payments difficulties would tend to curtail internal credit and, therefore, 'borrowing from abroad except for adequately productive projects, apart from being objectionable in itself, might result in less money being available for capital purposes from home sources.'

Policy became, in fact, more expansionary than was at first envisaged but this was an appropriate Keynesian response at a time when Irish costs were competitive and world trade was buoyant.

In the 1960 budget, attention was being drawn to 'the manner in which we are already turning to good account the opportunity . . . to apply more of our resources to productive purposes.' The provision for all forms of building was down but this was much more than offset by a 'remarkable shift' of public investment towards industry, agriculture and air transport. By 1962 it was being claimed that for the third year in succession the momentum of economic advance had been maintained, with the cumulative increase in GNP being almost 15 per cent. In 1963, for the first time, a separate paper on the

Capital Budget was published to encourage greater interest in and closer examination of 'the contribution which the large and growing volume of public capital expenditure makes to national development'. The point was made that 'the community is not yet saving adequately for development needs', with the result that, of the total prospective public capital expenditure of over £79 million, £12 million might have to be found from banks and similar sources.

In 1964, it was being stressed, in relation to the Current Budget, that 'a budget deficit which would add to spending and widen the balance of payments gap would be indefensible' while, in relation to the Capital Budget, various warning signs were being flashed – about the high rate of increase in public capital expenditure and the relevant debt service charges, the need for critical review to make sure that the components were genuinely of a capital nature and the old reservation as to the propriety of financing capital expenditure from borrowing in all circumstances. On this last point the relevant remarks, which no Keynesian could fault, were:

It was pointed out as long ago as 1952 that the method of financing public capital expenditure needs also to be considered from time to time. Regard must be had to the manner in which the Current Budget is being financed and to the prevailing economic conditions. When the Current Budget is in surplus, purchasing power is, in effect, being withdrawn from the public by taxation and made available to finance capital expenditure. In inflationary conditions this is desirable, provided the taxation is not itself so high as to cause a countervailing drop in private savings. On the other hand, a deficit in the Current Budget involves borrowing and it is necessary to take care that total borrowing, on both capital and current account, is not excessive in relation to the state of the economy.

The correct classification of items as capital and current is under review having regard to the nature of the items and the rules of classification now generally applied in national accounting systems. The appropriate method of financing the total of public expenditure, current and capital, cannot, however, be settled once and for all but must be considered from time to time in relation to economic conditions. It is rather a question of what change should be made between one year and another so as to moderate tendencies towards inflation or deflation. At the same time, it is considered desirable that items which may now be incorrectly classified as capital should be identified so that, as and when appropriate for economic reasons, their cost might be transferred, in whole or in part, to current account.

In the early 1960s not only the capital but the current element in public expenditure grew strongly with the result that Dr Gould's ratio of total public expenditure to GNP is 1.31 for the years 1962 to 1965. The sustained and rapid advance of the economy was a new experience, supported by favourable trends in world production and trade. The population ceased to be depleted by emigration. Industrial exports climbed above the level of agricultural exports for the first time. Prices rose only moderately and the balance of payments deficits, though on the upturn, gave cause for no great anxiety – they were more than balanced by private capital inflow and the external reserves were increasing. It is scarcely to be wondered at that all this unusual economic buoyancy incited expectations of substantial improvements in public services as well as personal income; expectations even in bleaker times tend to outrun resources. In 1964 the minority government of Seán Lemass, facing two critical by-elections, approved a national pay settlement well in excess of productivity trends. During 1965, the spurt in expenditure generated by large money income increases and liberal bank credit caused an upsurge of imports at a time when exports were handicapped by British import restrictions. The private capital inflow which had supported investment for years fell away sharply and the old bogey of an excessive external deficit loomed up again. Fiscal and monetary action was, however, taken to moderate the growth in consumption, means were found to circumvent the British import restrictions and public capital outlay was critically re-appraised and revised in a White Paper published in October 1965.

In the White Paper it was noted that public capital expenditure had much more than doubled over the six years 1959/60 to 1964/5. The resources provided by increased domestic output and the capital inflow had been sufficient, until recently, to meet the demands of rising expenditure both on consumption and capital formation. But the situation had changed on the resources side and it had become an urgent problem of economic management to equate total demand with total supply. The balance of payments expressed the relationship between domestic demand and resources; the rising scale of deficits indicated undue pressure on the demand side which must be abated since 'a large-scale drain on external reserves or expansion of external debt could neither be justified nor sustained.' The abatement necessitated a slowing down of the upward trend in incomes, a revival of savings, a curbing of credit expansion, a reduction of £30 million in public capital expenditure and some curtailment of current expenditure. On the resources side, the government obtained an exceptional supplement of £20 million by borrowing from the Central Bank and announced its intention of seeking a further temporary supplement through foreign borrowing. The express proviso was made that 'external borrowing by the Government will not be resorted to other than temporarily and the Government will be concerned to ensure that the proceeds are applied to productive investment, and not consumption, in order to create the future current earnings needed to discharge the indebtedness and maintain permanently a higher balance between demand and resources.' The Paper acknowledged that deferment of expenditure by postponing or slowing down projects was unwelcome but claimed that the corrective action being taken was inevitable and 'far from drastic.'

The Minister for Finance (Mr Jack Lynch) had, indeed, to reinforce the corrective measures within a few months. In an exceptionally early budget for 1966/7, he announced a stabilisation of public capital expenditure – it was to be even somewhat below the £101 million expected for 1965/6 – until the resources for it grew sufficiently to enable expansion to be resumed. Public capital outlay had been outrunning the non-inflationary means available to finance it; and there was no stomach for raising taxes to finance it even in part from a current budget surplus. In 1964/5 total budgetary financing had required £13½ million from the banks and £5½ million from external borrowing; these figures had risen to £31½ million and £15 million respectively in 1965/6. A Eurodollar borrowing had not been proceeded with in December 1965, but, in addition to the £20 million from the Central Bank, the equivalent of £8 million had been borrowed from the International Monetary Fund and £7 million through a Sterling/ Deutschemark loan.

The 1966 budget speech is notable for what was said on two matters later to assume critical importance – borrowing to meet current budget deficits and foreign borrowing. On the first, Mr Lynch declared:

> A deliberately arranged deficit in the current budget can in times of serious economic depression be justified as a means of reactivating the economy. No such justification for what is called 'deficit financing' exists in this country today . . . we are suffering from such pressure of spending by Government and people that we have outrun our resources and are incurring too big a deficit in our balance of payments . . . Spending which exceeds the resources drawn from current domestic incomes, whether as taxation or savings, and has to be met by drawing down reserves or increasing external debt, is a cause of inflationary pressure and both higher prices and a balance of payments deficit are the outcome . . . We are now in a position that continuance of the public capital programme, even at its stabilised level, is impossible without the support of external capital . . . If we run a deficit on current account, the borrowing incurred to finance it will subtract from our capacity to finance capital expenditure . . .

On the second topic, Mr Lynch had this to say:

> On the principle of foreign borrowing, I might add a few words. There can be no reasonable objection to supplementing, within moderation, our current domestic savings in order to finance a well-balanced domestic capital programme. The qualifications are, however, important and

must be kept in mind. A 'well-balanced domestic capital programme' is one in which directly productive expenditure bulks large. 'Moderation' must be measured in relation both to the extent of the deficit already existing in the balance of payments and to the prospect of being able to continue to borrow these supplementary needs on acceptable terms. Ireland already benefits from a large inflow of investment capital and the Government's short-term aim is to reduce the deficit in our external payments to a level corresponding to that inflow. We must ensure, therefore, that the way in which the public capital programme is financed contributes to the achievement of this aim and to the eventual replenishment of our external reserves. To keep direct foreign borrowing over the next few years within a moderate annual limit is desirable both for this reason and because such borrowing owing to the world shortage of capital is both difficult and dear.

The stabilisation of public capital expenditure aimed at in the 1965-7 period, though politically difficult, was not on its face a contradiction of government policy which, as expressed in the *Second Programme for Economic Expansion*, envisaged just such a levelling off by 1965 'and thereafter a progressive increase in private investment in industry, agriculture and services according as GNP rose.' In the event, the steady growth of resources expected in the Programme was not realised, policies were not put in force to realise the assumption of private sector growth, and the stabilisation of public capital outlay, which proved to be strictly temporary, was accepted reluctantly as a necessity rather than welcomed as a virtuous stage in national development.

The 1966 budget did its work well. The deficit on current account, which had threatened to widen, was transformed into a surplus; public capital expenditure was held just below £100 million, which meant a contraction in real terms. The new Minister for Finance (Mr C. J. Haughey) considered it justifiable to raise the total to £108.6 million for 1967/8 as a stimulus to the economy which had grown only slightly in the previous two years. His budget speech contained an interesting echo of previous orthodoxy about the definition of capital items and the impropriety of always financing them from borrowing:

> Another matter which must be kept in mind is the desirability of reckoning as capital only such expenditure as genuinely merits this description. Expenditures which do not add to the national stock of capital, or must be repeated every year to maintain their effect, are suspect from this point of view. There is, of course, a distinction between the accounting principles involved here and the economic principles which must determine, from year to year, how much of total Government expenditure should be financed from taxation and how much from borrowing. Last year, a significant change occurred through the conversion of a deficit of £8 million on current account into a surplus. This year, a reflationary rather than a deflationary budget is called for and it would not be appropriate to increase taxation in order to cover any of the items now classified as capital. The question must, however, remain open for consideration in relation to the circumstances of future years.

Years later the question still remains open – indeed, the prospect is now exceedingly dim that it will ever be a practical issue in budgetary policy.

During Mr Haughey's tenure of Finance (1967-70) and under his successor Mr Colley the secular rise in public expenditure, capital and current, was resumed. Dr Gould's ratio of the growth of public expenditure, as compared with GNP, in the period 1966-9 is 1.38 and it remained well above unity in the early 1970s. This faster growth of public expenditure than of national output was occurring during a period of greatly accelerated inflation; the typical 3 per cent to 5 per cent p.a. price rise of the early and mid 1960s had given way towards the end of the decade to inflation rates of $7\frac{1}{2}$ per cent to 9 per cent p.a. This was a universal trend accelerated in our case by the eventual impact of the sterling devaluation of 1967. External payments, brought into balance over the years 1966-8, had again developed a marked list and deficits of the £70 million-a-year order were being incurred at the turn of the decade. Total public expenditure, which had been 25 per cent of GNP in 1956, had reached 40 per cent by 1972 and the Exchequer borrowing requirement had risen from 4 per cent to 7 per cent of GNP. Moreover, the rate of increase was accelerating. Buoyancy of revenue in inflationary conditions, with output and incomes rising, eased the pressure to control expenditure which is normally exerted by the political unpopularity of having to impose additional taxation. One bulwark had, however, held – no one had yet undermined the disciplinary safeguard of not deliberately incurring deficits in the current budget. The abandonment of this safeguard marks a new and adverse turning-point in financial policy.

## Turning-Point No 3 – 1972

The domestic economic problems of 1972 were not such as could be solved by adopting a more expansionary fiscal policy. Both the Central Bank[3] and the Economic and Social Research Institute were emphasising that the chief enemy was cost inflation: the rate at which pay had been increasing was inconsistent with the retention of a competitive position and injurious to national growth prospects. The terms of trade were already worsening as a result of the international rise in commodity prices. The government was being advised not to accentuate Ireland's relatively high inflation rate by raising domestic costs through indirect taxation. The economic portents, with the referendum on EEC entry imminent, were darkened by the serious implications for Anglo-Irish relations tourism and trade of 'Bloody Sunday' (30 January 1972) in Derry and the burning of the British Embassy in Dublin a few days later. Yet 1972 was the year when the shades of Keynes were impiously invoked to justify the expansion of internal demand by deliberate resort to credit creation and borrowing in order to finance budgetary deficits on current account.

In the months before the budget, the Central Bank had been urging that any expansionary move intended to offset low growth and rising unemployment should be undertaken only in return for a firm commitment by the trade unions to moderation in the forthcoming negotiations for a National Pay Agreement. It was emphasised also that any expansion of public expenditure should be confined to productive outlay, especially where overtaking of arrears or acceleration of progress was desirable in the light of EEC membership and where the tempo of activity could later be relaxed: instances given were telephone development, the main roads and housing. However, when it became clear that, besides adding to public capital expenditure, it was proposed to depart openly for the first time from the tradition of attempting to balance the current budget, I argued strongly as Governor of the Central Bank against this 'dangerous innovation' which was unnecessary as an economic stimulus, would remove one of the few remaining disciplines and would disturb confidence. As I reminded the same Minister (George Colley) in Seanad Éireann years later (25 January 1978), I insisted that it was not the current account deficit that mattered in Keynesian theory but the deficit in the budget as a whole, capital as well as current. It was proper to rely on the capital budget to provide the expansionary stimulus. In this way, I contended, more direct value would be obtained in terms of jobs and lasting assets, while, in practice, capital expenditure was more flexible than current expenditure, which consisted so largely of irreducible items like pay, pensions, and social welfare. Once a large current deficit had been allowed to appear, the government would find it extremely hard on political grounds ever to close the gap again, even when this course was dictated by sound economic principles.

These arguments proved unavailing. The 1972 Budget provided for a current account deficit of £28 million and the taking into the Exchequer from the Central Bank for current purposes of £7 million of accumulated surplus income – additional spending power which, with the increase of £30 million in the public capital programme, was expected to raise the national growth rate by about $1\frac{3}{4}$ per cent. The Minister's presentation was as follows:

> When introducing the supplementary budget in October, 1970, I indicated that, while over most of the 1960s, a deliberate policy of deficit budgeting would have been contrary to the requirements of our general economic situation, the Government would in future aim at a deficit when economic activity was depressed and at a surplus in condi-

tions of inflation. I have to consider whether on this test I should seek to balance the budget this year or should aim at either a surplus or a deficit. Present and prospective economic circumstances provide no clear-cut, unambiguous answer to this question. The rate of price increase is still high and the balance of payments position is weak. Nowhere is inflation more marked than in labour costs. In 1971, the rate of increase in unit labour costs in this country was second highest amongst European countries, and there is little indication that we are losing this unenviable place in the league tables. Whatever our hopes, there is no certainty that the new National Pay Agreement will diminish the pace of cost inflation. These factors would suggest that the budget should be directed at containing inflationary pressures or, at least, not adding to them.

On the other hand, the economy is, for the third year in succession, running at well below capacity. Unemployment is high. We lack the economic buoyancy required to tackle quickly and effectively the adaptation which membership of the EEC will demand. If priority were given to these factors, budgetary policy should be primarily directed at improving the growth performance of the economy.

Faced with these competing requirements, the Government have opted for growth rather than stability. The level of Government expenditure this year will, therefore, be determined by reference to our economic requirements and will not be cut back to the estimated yield of revenue. There will not be any increases in taxation, and the resultant deficit in the current budget will be financed mainly by borrowing.

The Minister's statement implies that demand expansion was the correct response to a problem concerned primarily with output costs. It shows no recognition of the point so forcefully made by the Central Bank that it was the total budgetary deficit (capital and current combined) that was, in any case, relevant to Keynesian expansionary theory. It is scarcely credible that his failure to appreciate this could have been due to ambiguity in the advice he received from his Department. Nor is there any admission in the Minister's speech that, in a country still lacking many infrastructural facilities, it would have made much more sense to borrow only for additional capital expenditure, particularly where foreign borrowing was involved. His attempt to found his decision on remarks made when introducing a supplementary budget in October 1970 is weak: the focus of those remarks was on the desirability of planning for a current surplus in times of inflation and the Minister was excusing his practical inability to follow that course. Perhaps the advice tendered by the Department was not sufficiently clear and authoritative or perhaps the Minister himself preferred, on short-term grounds, to adopt an expedient which enabled him to be generous with income tax reliefs and social welfare benefits in the lead-up to national pay negotiations and the EEC referendum. That the Minister was far from certain of the correctness of his policy is evident from the vivid acknowledgment in his budget speech: 'I may be fuelling the fire of inflation rather than the engine of growth'.

Whatever the explanation (which historians will no doubt unearth) the consequences were most unfortunate, not indeed immediately in practical terms because the current deficit in 1972-3 turned out to be a mere £5 million, followed by a deficit of only £10 million in 1973-4, but rather in the misguided dismantling of a disciplinary safeguard and in the creation of a spurious respectability for fiscal decisions of a nature and on a scale which in their cumulative effect have misused and almost exhausted our foreign borrowing potential and have deprived fiscal policy of its capacity to serve as an instrument of economic management.

The pause on the brink of the slippery slope was deceptive. By 1974 heavy deficits and foreign indebtedness were being incurred for current purposes in disregard of the desirability of using foreign borrowings only for purposes which would raise national productivity or at least leave behind useful additions to national capital in the form of a better communications system, new educational buildings, houses or other social assets.

The other regrettable legacy of 1972 was the failure to clinch, as a pre-condition of an expansionary budget involving no tax increases and liberal social welfare improvements, the *quid pro quo* of a commitment by unions and employers to moderate rates of pay increase. This was the most essential policy goal if cost inflation were to be contained and the highest value in employment terms obtained from expansion of public outlay and borrowing. Wages and salaries had for some years been rising much faster in relation to output and prices than in Britain and other competitor countries. A highly inflationary national pay agreement was, however, arrived at in mid-1972 with scant recognition of the budgetary concessions. This agreement, as Professor Charles McCarthy has shown, gave, over a period of seventeen or eighteen months, a 21 per cent increase (following the 1970 Agreement's 17.9 per cent) to a typical male worker.[4] The same man was to get an increase of 29.4 per cent in 1974 and 16.6 per cent in 1975. The remissness of 1972 was the first of a series of failures to make sure in advance that budgetary risk would be at least partly recompensed by incomes restraint.

Much of the Central Bank's criticism of financial policy after 1972 was directed *against* the impropriety of borrowing abroad to finance current expenses and *towards* convincing the government that, with more incomes restraint, more jobs could be sustained and created with less aggregate borrowing, whether on current or even on capital account.

The general election of March 1973 took place before a budget had been introduced. This responsibility fell to the incoming Coalition government, succeeding to power only a few months after Ireland's entry to the EEC and weighed down with expensive pre-election commitments. The agricultural price increases resulting from Ireland's participation in the Common Agricultural Policy were beginning to boost an inflation rate which had been constant at 9 per cent per annum since the start of the decade but which was to rise to over 11 per cent for 1973 and, yielding to the added pressure of oil price increases, to 17 per cent for 1974 and 21 per cent for 1975.

It was my hope that the new government would resist the temptation to load its pre-election commitments on to its borrowing requirement. The growth rate of GNP was rising, unemployment falling, consumer spending, investment and exports increasing. The public capital programme was being

increased and it would be quite unnecessary and unjustifiable
to add the further stimulus of a large current deficit. If current
expenditure could not be reduced sufficiently by economies
and deferrals, and additional taxation were needed to reduce
the current deficit, this should preferably take the form of a
widening of the scope of income tax (bringing farmers into the
net) rather than an increase in indirect taxation.

The Central Bank also repeated its concern at the failure to
come to grips with another, and related, domestic source of
inflation – high labour cost increases. The Bank had been
urging strongly on the government the desirability of finding
a wider and better-informed context for pay settlements than
the periodic bargaining confrontations between employers and
trade unions leading to national pay agreements. Acquiescence
in the measures needed to contain inflation was, the Bank
argued, more likely to be obtained if a degree of consensus had
been reached amongst the main sectoral interests about the
potential for economic and social development for a period of
years ahead, the conditions for realising that potential and the
manner in which the gains might be shared. The Bank saw
this consultative and educative process as the principal argument for proceeding with a Fourth Programme in succession
to the Third, which had run out in 1972. The government,
however, became preoccupied with more immediate problems
and, in the aftermath of the oil crisis, pleaded uncertainty as
a reason for not going ahead, although arguably some light is
never more necessary than in a fog. It was not long, indeed,
before the government began to scoff at the very idea of a
Programme at such a time. The Minister for Finance was
particularly scornful in his 1975 budget speech (15 January
1975): 'of all the tasks which could engage my attention the
least realistic would be the publication of a medium or long-
term economic plan based upon irrelevancies in the past,
hunches as to the present and clairvoyance as to the future'.

Some respect for a plan as a comprehensive and coherent
set of economic and social policies and as an aid to democratic
consensus must however have survived or been revived by the
representations of the Central Bank and others. The Minister
for Finance's budget speech of 1976 not only voiced a firm
purpose of amendment about borrowing for current purposes

– the deficit was to be phased out over a three-year period – but devoted a long passage to outlining the purpose of a new medium-term economic and social programme the preparation of which was already under way. He announced that a Green Paper would be published to 'present frankly the options open to the country over the next five years' with a view to achieving 'national commitment to a plan for economic revival'. A Green Paper on Economic and Social Development, 1976-80 appeared in September 1976, but was still being analysed and discussed when the general election of mid-1977 swept Fianna Fáil into office with a programme embodying such irrational optimism as to undermine credibility and distort, by exaggerating the potential for progress and for individual and social gain, the framework in which the vital consensus of unions and management would be sought regarding the pre-conditions of orderly progress.

To return to 1973/4, expansionary fiscal policies which (besides higher social benefits and reduced local rates) included a 23 per cent increase in public capital expenditure, induced an abnormal rate of economic growth (of the 7 per cent order) in 1973 but at the cost of raising both the external deficit and internal prices. The momentum of growth was already falling in the fourth quarter of the year when the sudden quadrupling of the price of oil completely altered not only the Irish but the world economic scene.

As Governor of the Central Bank I was urging as early as December 1973, that since we faced a real emergency we should, for reasons of social equity no less than economic exigency, take the measures necessary to cope with it. It was unfortunate in this respect that public consciousness of the gravity of what impended was quite limited and doubly unfortunate that a headline for 1974/5 wage and salary increases might be set before there was a wide realisation of the irresponsibility of aggravating the coming production and employment crisis by rates of money income increase which could make even a reduced output unsaleable. The reduction in the community's real income occasioned by the rise in energy costs could not be offset by money income increases: these would be illusory and add to inflation. The government was therefore urged to intervene in the national pay agreement discussions, alert the parties to the grave deterioration in economic prospects and seek more moderate terms.

It was, I fear, not only public consciousness of the gravity of the new turn of events that was lacking: the government's reaction was also slow and inadequate. In part, this may be attributed to their preoccupation in the early days of December 1973, with the final phase of the Sunningdale negotiations on Northern Ireland. The government decided not to intervene and ministerial speeches, while they stressed the seriousness of the economic outlook, confined themselves to exhorting trade unionists to abide by the terms of the new pay agreement. No attempt was made to have these terms revised and an opportunity was let slip of trying to put the economy in a position to get through the critical years that followed with less unemployment and less foreign borrowing.

The budget of 1974 was to cover the nine months 1 April to 31 December, so as to align Ireland with the calendar year system applicable to the public finances of the original EEC countries. The budget-makers were confronted with a formidable current deficit and with the dilemma of cutting expenditures or raising taxes to narrow the current account gap. The dilemma was dodged by resort to borrowing. Two doctrinal influences favoured the choice of this soft option: the flabby perversion of Keynesian theory relating to deficit financing promulgated in the 1972 budget and the advice against allowing the oil crisis to exert an uncontrolled deflationary effect which various international bodies had issued in its immediate aftermath. Foreign borrowing on a less substantial scale would have been justifiable to ease the massive deflationary shock of the oil price increase but it ought not to have been predominantly for current purposes and should have been seen as allowing a temporary respite to make basic corrections in real incomes. It is regrettable that the euphemism of 'recycling' of oil revenues seemed to make foreign borrowing to finance a current deficit, and thus sustain internal demand, not only less questionable but positively meritorious.

The Central Bank felt constrained to argue against such a lenient interpretation of international advice in its 1974 Report:

There is in many countries a disposition, following the sharp raising of oil prices, to favour somewhat uncritically a counter-policy of expanding domestic demand and borrowing more abroad. This policy should be pursued cautiously as a means of gaining time for a smoother adjustment to this adverse turn in the terms of trade. It is not possible for life to go on just as before after such a major increase in energy costs. There cannot but be a real disimprovement, or at least a slower rate of improvement, in economic and social standards in oil-importing countries. More has to be produced for sale abroad to pay for the higher-priced fuel; correspondingly less is available to raise domestic living standards. . . . Prudence, apart from practical exigencies, would forbid prolonged reliance, year after year, on large-scale foreign borrowing as a means of financing external deficits. . . .

Although increased resort to current deficits over the years 1974 to 1976 was defended as a stimulus to economic growth – with annual rates of growth much below 4 per cent being considered unacceptable – it was never explained why such a stimulus could not more appropriately have taken the form of borrowing to accelerate the provision of capital assets and the remedying of infrastructural deficiencies. At least in part the explanation must be that tax reliefs and social welfare improvements have more immediate and widespread popularity. Anxiety was at times expressed about the dangers involved in continued heavy recourse to foreign borrowing for current purposes but it was not until 1976 that a brake was imposed and further current account deterioration halted.

| Year | Current Exchequer Deficit (£m) | Exchequer Borrowing Requirement (£m) | |
|---|---|---|---|
| | | Foreign | Total |
| 1973-4 | 10 | 44 | 206 |
| 1974 (9 mths) | 92 | 147 | 310 |
| 1975 | 259 | 164 | 601 |
| 1976 | 199 | 324 | 506 |
| 1977 | 187 | 71 | 545 |

Over the period of Coalition government, both current and capital expenditure rose rapidly, Dr Gould's ratio of growth of public expenditure to GNP being 1.37. The foundations of government revenue had not been enlarged or strengthened sufficiently to make good the erosions resulting from continual concessions. Indeed, much effort was vainly expended on the replacement of death duties by complicated forms of capital taxation much less productive of revenue.

In a supplementary budget in 1975, which had the unusual distinction of being based largely on the advice of the National Economic and Social Council, food, fuel and transport subsidies were introduced to slow down both price and income inflation. Under the 1975 national pay agreement, provision had been made for quarterly increases in pay by reference to the previous quarter's increase in the consumer price index. The budgetary measures secured a slight fall in the price index in the third relevant quarter, thus justifying no pay increase, and reduced the increase in the final quarter of the agreement to 2.8 per cent. The total pay increase for the second half-year of only 2.8 per cent contrasted with a minimum increase of 12 per cent in the first half-year of the agreement.

This more active concern by the government was maintained during 1976. As a fairly moderate seven-months pay agreement embodying a two-months' pause was drawing to a close in October of that year, talks were initiated with the employers and trade unions suggesting a standstill on wage increases in 1977 in return for tax concessions and investment in job creation. The 1977 budget was the first to make public policy commitments of this kind expressly contingent on prior agreement on pay moderation – it had been accepted that a standstill was not obtainable. A relatively moderate pay agreement was, in fact, ratified in return for the budgetary concessions. The 1977 budget was also notable for its note of hope: 1976 had been an encouraging year and 'things were looking up again'. Industrial production had grown by 10 per cent, national output by $3\frac{1}{2}$ per cent. Inflation had subsided and exports were expanding. The transition to economic recovery was marked by 'the sharp reduction in the current deficit and borrowing requirement'. Now that the economy was on the way to being restored to health the need to continue such a policy was clearly reduced. Against this more virtuous prospect, the sins of the past could be excused and even extolled. Unjustifiably it was claimed to be 'undeniable that the heavy borrowing *to finance growing current deficits* as well as capital spending was the correct response to the economic situation then facing us' (my italics).

## Turning Point No. 4 – 1977-78

On the whole, however, the new orientation of policy and the success of the 1977 budget in curbing the growth of pay, public expenditure and borrowing mark a turning-point in financial policy. It proved to be a short-lived manifestation of reform. A Fianna Fáil government with a different policy emphasis came to office after the mid-year general election, trailing an expansionary manifesto which, despite an effort to convert it into a formal plan (White Paper *National Development 1977-1980*) was the political basis for a pro-cyclical budget involving an unprecedented current deficit and Exchequer borrowing requirement in 1978.

Fianna Fáil's first budget after their return to power in 1977 was launched on 1 February 1978. The economic background, as described in the budget speech, was one of exceptional growth – 'twice the EEC average' – and a 'dramatic fall in inflation' (exaggerated by the effect of subsidies). 'Useful progress' in raising employment and tackling unemployment was also recorded – non-agricultural employment had risen by 12,000 during 1977, unemployment had fallen by 6,000 in the second half of that year. Tourism was 'buoyant', the external payments deficit 'reasonable'. World demand for Irish exports would continue to grow in 1978; competition would be tougher but 'if income increases are moderate and competitiveness is thereby increased', market share could be substantially enlarged. The income increase target, deriving from the Manifesto, was 'about 5 per cent'. The Minister took the view that 'to give priority, in the short-term, to achieving a further substantial reduction in borrowing would have involved a severely deflationary budgetary stance'. Not only, therefore, did the budget jettison the reform programme which had already reduced deficit financing and borrowing but, despite strong signs of economic recovery and no evident need for a budgetary boost, the throttle was deliberately opened again, by way of tax cuts and expenditure increases, and the current deficit was doubled in one year. The resultant jump in public borrowing to 13 per cent of GNP was said to be 'only a temporary feature' of the government's 'overall strategy to restore economic stability and confidence'. The prospective balance of payments deficit, while large, was nevertheless 'supportable'.

A 'purpose of amendment' was revealed in the undertaking that the current deficit and borrowing requirement were to be 'greatly reduced' in the following years. It will, however, scarcely be a surprise to find that this intention was not fulfilled. The record is as follows.

| Year | Current Deficit (£m) | Exchequer Borrowing Requirement (£m) | |
|------|----------------------|----------------|-------|
|      |                      | Foreign | Total |
| 1978 | 368 | 23 | 810 |
| 1979 | 509 | 509 | 1,009 |
| 1980 | 541 | 566 | 1,217 |
| 1981 | 802 | 1,285 | 1,722 |
| 1982 | 988 | 1,148 | 1,945 |

Although a Coalition government was in office from June 1981 to March 1982 and introduced corrective measures in July 1981, all the substantive budgets of this stretch of years were the responsibility of Fianna Fáil governments.

The national debt, which stood at £1,422 million in 1972, and £4,229 million in 1977, had risen to £10,195 million by the end of 1981 according to the 1981 Finance Accounts. By year end 1982 it reached the order of magnitude of £12,800 million. The foreign debt component climbed from £127 million in 1972 to £1,039 million in 1977, £3,794 million at the end of 1981 and to £5,200 million by the end of last year. The 1981 Finance Accounts also show that by December 1981 the government had guaranteed the principal of, and interest on, loans of which the principal outstanding was £2,198 million (including £1,144 million of external obligations). By year end 1982 government-guaranteed debt may be of the order of £2,800 million (compared with a level of guaranteed debt of £316 million in 1972).

Terms such as 'policy', 'strategy' or 'rationale' would clearly be unapplicable to such a destabilisation of the public finances. The overt explanations for this disastrous course of events are to be found in successive budget speeches and in the various Green (discussion) and White (decision) Papers published over the period.[5] The first of these, the White Paper published in January 1978, was a mirror-image of the pre-election manifesto. It described the 'significant increase in Government expenditure and substantial tax cuts' which were to be the chief features of the 1978 budget as an initial stage in implementing the manifesto; in subsequent stages 'stability would be restored to the Government's finances through revenue buoyancy, control of expenditure and an enhanced private sector contribution to the process of development'. In fact, however, the economic environment created for the private sector by fiscal policies made the realisation of this hope impossible.

What I have termed the 'irrational optimism' of this and subsequent plans was apparent in the main objectives stated: a regular 7 per cent per annum increase in national output for the years 1978 to 1980 and a 75,000 reduction over these three years in the numbers out of work. The prospect of a high rate of increase – 6 per cent per annum – in consumption standards was held out. There was, as I said in Seanad Éireann on 17 May 1978, no allowance for contingencies, inadequate discussion of the stringent conditions necessary to attain the objectives, no precaution against the disruption of confidence by failure to do so and undue reliance on global demand expansion rather than selective supply side measures. The White Paper was a 'short-cut to planning' and the educational process of involving the social partners in consideration of alternative growth ratios, of the conditions necessary to achieve them and of the proper allocation of the resources so made available had unfortunately been foregone.

The new (and, as I thought, unnecessary) Department of Economic Planning and Development did attach considerable importance to this consultative process as a framework for settlement of incomes and of economic and social advance. All the Papers issued, however, held to top-of-the-scale objectives which could be realised only in an ideal world. Indeed, the June 1978 Paper envisaged 100 per cent employment by 1983. The risk that the growing balance of payments deficit might prove to be a constraint was ignored. The official scenario being so rosy, it is scarcely surprising that the well-intentioned process which led to the National Understanding of 1979 did not, in fact, yield the degree of incomes moderation needed by an economy already beginning to be upset by the second series of oil price increases and the onset of world recession. In the buoyant days of 1977 to 1979, however, any criticisms of programmes as being over-ambitious or unduly vulnerable tended to be met by the rejoinder that, while they might prove to be so, in the interests of the young in particular nothing less could be attempted.

By 1980 a new mood had set in. Growth had slowed down, inflation had received a new impetus and the balance of payments position had worsened, causing a drop of some £300 million in official reserves despite heavy foreign borrowing. The Department of Economic Planning and Development had been wound up by the new Fianna Fáil Taoiseach, Mr C. J. Haughey, and both he and the new Minister for Finance, Mr Michael O'Kennedy, were voicing an earnest commitment to reducing the external deficit and the level of government borrowing. The budget speeches of 1980 and subsequent years, however, reveal a lack of complete conviction; they contain expressions of self-exculpation, indeed of self-praise, for not yielding fully to the dictates of orthodoxy. Successive Ministers for Finance have appeared more as pre-conversion than post-conversion Augustines.

In 1980, for instance, the Minister, acknowledging that it might be said that he ought to have done more to reduce borrowing, righteously claimed that the government 'were not prepared to allow the need for budget stringency to override the necessity to move towards tax equity and to protect and improve the circumstances of the less well-off, whether in employment or dependent on social welfare'. In 1981, the Minister, Mr Gene Fitzgerald, having attacked those who spoke of disorder in the national finances, admitted that 'it might be argued that, ideally, the reduction in the current deficit – and consequently in the borrowing requirement – should be greater.' 'However,' he declared, 'harsh measures could cause severe hardship.' And in 1982, even after the failure of years of attempted reform, the then Minister, Mr Ray MacSharry, displaying pride in a 24 per cent increase in current expenditure, could speak of having to find 'a balance between the need to keep borrowing as low as possible and the obligation to ensure that all opportunities for economic and social progress are fully exploited'. After such a declaration, and in the light of the conspicuous collapse of budgetary estimation, the words 'nevertheless' and 'gradually' in the following assertion should be seen as significant:

> The Government are, nevertheless, firmly committed to bringing the current deficit under control and gradually eliminating it.

In fact, one of the most disturbing features of the administration of the public finances in recent years is the chasm that has opened up between budgetary projections and actual results, as the following comparison indicates:

## Current Deficit (£ million)

| Year | Budget Projection | Actual | Excess of Actual over Projection |
|------|-------------------|--------|----------------------------------|
| 1979 | 289 | 522 | 233 (81%) |
| 1980 | 347 | 547 | 200 (58%) |
| 1981 | 495 | 802 | 307 (62%) |
| 1982 | 679 | 988 | 309 (46%) |

The underestimation of current deficits, and consequently of the Exchequer borrowing requirement, has been so seriously disproportionate as to invalidate the whole budgetary exercise. Over-runs of expenditure and, latterly, a short-fall of revenue have contributed.

This technical criticism reinforces the two main policy criticisms applicable to recent years: increased borrowing over a period (mid-1977 to mid-1979) when borrowing could and should have been reduced because the economic climate was improving and the need for expansionary action diminishing; and the incurring of foreign debt on much too large a scale by a developing country merely to meet everyday expenses.

For the period 1977-82 the ratio of growth of public expenditure to growth of GNP was 1.69, by far the highest for any Fianna Fáil term of office. The ratio reached a peak in 1981 and has since fallen.

The discipline of being a participant in the European Monetary System since March 1979 has not proved to be as contagious and automatic as was originally expected. Domestic policies have failed to establish a convergence between Ireland's income and cost trends and those of our EMS partners. We abandoned a fixed relationship with sterling in favour, in effect, of a rather less fixed relationship with the Deutschemark, although only a minority – some 30 per cent – of our economic transactions take place in EMS currencies. Some 70 per cent are still being conducted in currencies, notably sterling and the US dollar, which are outside the EMS and which, from our standpoint, have fluctuated, at times favourably but at times unfavourably, in relation to the EMS group. The appropriateness of our exchange rate policy has come increasingly into question.

While critical attention is usually concentrated on the waste involved in borrowing abroad to finance everyday expenses, it is even worse, of course, to use foreign borrowings to finance so-called 'capital' expenditure which not only yields no return but generates continuing loss which has to be borne by consumer or taxpayer. The public capital programme is riddled with economically unsound and dubious social elements. Much of the argument for massive state injections of 'equity capital' is suspect as a euphemism for permanent subsidisation by the taxpayer. Transfers of a marginal character continue to be made from time to time from current to 'capital' services in order to lighten the pressure on the current budget. Even meritorious capital outlay may be carried out by methods that fail to give value for money. The overall rate of return on public capital outlay, as Professor Kieran Kennedy has shown and ministers have acknowledged, has fallen to a very low level. Reform of the Irish public finances must, therefore, be concerned not only with the outsize current deficit but also with the large part of capital expenditure which burdens rather than enriches the community.

## Turning-Point No. 5?

It would be satisfactory if one could conclude this review by signalling with confidence the appearance of a new turning-point. What is required for any such definition is not simply good intentions: a commitment to reform has marked the declarations of Ministers for Finance for some years past and is undoubtedly present in the new Coalition government which assumed office on 14 December 1982. The 1983 budget introduced on 9 February shows signs of being such a turning point but a final judgment must await further experience of its economic and financial impact. While current public expenditure, despite cuts, claims a higher proportion of GNP in 1983 (43.3 per cent as against 41.6 per cent in 1982), public capital expenditure and total Exchequer borrowing have been reduced as a percentage of GNP, the latter to 13 per cent as against 16.5 per cent. Total public expenditure, for the first time in many years, is projected to rise more slowly than GNP.

It must, in fairness, be acknowledged that the Fianna Fáil government, by placing a brake on the rate of pay increase in the public sector and by specific cuts in services, made 1982 one of the rare years when current expenditure was held at its intended level. The Fianna Fáil plan, *The Way Forward*, published in October 1982, envisaged a continuation of this more careful policy. The incoming Coalition government has also imposed cuts and transferred charges for services from tax-payer to user in order to keep within the Estimates provision for voted services published by its predecessor. Experience of economy exercises suggests that, once a service has been introduced, its withdrawal or modification is painful and unpopular and that the most effective way to curb public expenditure is by not being liberal in introducing new, or improving old, services. Budgetary arithmetic dictates that only if the main components (pay and pensions, social welfare and debt interest) are controlled – and it is obvious how this must be approached – will any curbing take place.

I end with a table which highlights the state of Ireland's public finances at the various turning-points identified in this review.

## Government Expenditure and Borrowing

| Year | Current Expenditure | | Capital Expenditure | | Total Expenditure | | Borrowing | |
|---|---|---|---|---|---|---|---|---|
| | £m | % GNP | £m | % GNP | £m | % GNP | £m | % GNP |
| 1922 | 30 | 20 | 1 | — | 31 | 20 | 3 | 2 |
| 1950 | 77 | 19 | 25 | 6 | 102 | 26 | 23 | 6 |
| 1958 | 126 | 22 | 38 | 7 | 164 | 29 | 21 | 4 |
| 1972 | 665 | 29 | 251 | 11 | 916 | 40 | 151 | 7 |
| 1977 | 1,944 | 36 | 695 | 13 | 2,639 | 49 | 545 | 10 |
| 1982 | 5,897 | 50 | 2,000 | 17 | 7,897 | 67 | 1,945 | 16 |

The tendency for 'getting and spending' by government to bulk ever larger in national activity has been common to many Western countries over this sixty-year span but nowhere, I believe, to a more marked degree than in Ireland.

## Notes to Chapter 4

[1]Patrick Lynch was later appointed Professor of Political Economy (Applied Economics) at University College, Dublin.

[2]*Economic Growth in Ireland: The Experience Since 1947* Dublin 1975.

[3]I succeeded Dr Maurice Moynihan as Governor on 1 March 1969 and was succeeded by Dr C. H. Murray on 1 March 1976.

[4]A Review of the Objectives of the National Pay Agreements 1970-1977, *Administration*, Spring 1977, page 125.

[5]White Paper *National Development 1977-1980* January 1978; Green Paper *Development for Full Employment* June 1978; White Paper *Programme for National Development, 1978-1981* January 1979; White Paper *Investment and National Development, 1979-1983* January 1980; and, finally, a blue-covered paper *The Way Forward* October 1982.

*Government Buildings, Dublin.*

# 5   Instruments of Financial Policy

Governments everywhere are expected to discharge a commendable but virtually impossible task, that of managing an economy so that there will be a steady and adequate growth in employment and living standards without significant inflation or imbalance in external payments. They have assumed this responsibility with good intentions and in response to public pressure but, at the same time, rather incautiously since they are not assured of the continuous co-operation of powerful sections of the community.

The basic problem, which is at the heart of political economy, is the scarcity of resources in relation to aspirations. Expectations constantly run ahead of the capacity to satisfy them and management of an economy is preoccupied with seeing that resources are fully and productively used, that the resultant gains (and no more) are so allocated as both to maintain good progress and advance social equity, and that the whole process of development is protected, as far as possible, against cyclical disturbance, on the one hand, and damaging overstretch, on the other.

In their management role, governments rely on their ability to influence three powerful determinants of the state of the economy – the public finances, the money supply and the trend in incomes. I propose to discuss briefly the efficacy of fiscal, monetary and incomes policies against the background of Irish experience. This will involve describing these three instruments of financial policy and explaining how they can be employed and the need to co-ordinate their use.

117

## Fiscal policy

Fiscal policy is concerned primarily with the level of public expenditure and how it is financed.

Public expenditure is a large and growing component of total national expenditure – in Ireland it now represents 55 per cent as against less than 25 per cent forty years ago – and it significantly influences the level of domestic activity and the state of the balance of payments. This influence derives essentially from the state's power to add to the money supply or reduce it by varying its taxes and borrowings.

Theoretically, one can envisage an economy in which labour and all the other productive factors are fully used, prices are stable and external payments are balanced by current receipts from abroad. In that ideal situation, financial policy can be regarded as being benevolently neutral: the public is freely surrendering through taxes, and providently lending through investment in government securities, just what is needed to cover public outlay. It is in helping to reach this state of full-employment equilibrium, and in keeping the economy there, that fiscal policy is called upon to exercise a positive or negative influence. Indeed, the full employment model is (or should be) used to gauge how much, in any off-balance situation, a government should do to stimulate or deflate the economy.

Upward or downward movements in the public borrowing requirement are the most immediate and direct means by which fiscal policy can influence domestic output and employment. Much depends on whether the public borrowing requirement is financed by monetary or non-monetary means. If savings were available to meet it from the private sector or would be generated by putting idle resources to use, the public borrowing requirement could be said to be financed by non-monetary means and to have a salutary non-inflationary impact. If, on the other hand, savings are inadequate to meet the sum of public and private demands and the residual finance to cover the government's needs has to be created by the domestic banking system (i.e. by borrowing from the commercial banks or the Central Bank) or by recourse to external borrowing, the effect will be to increase demand, enlarge the external deficit and push up prices and costs; fiscal policy will involve the inflationary creation of new money.[1]

While expansion may be justified when domestic activity is slack, it will have an inflationary overspill if domestic production is not fully competitive at the prevailing exchange rate or is already at or near full-stretch.

Experience also shows that the higher the proportion of public spending to national expenditure, the greater is the competition between public and private claims on current production and the more likely is it that new money will be sought by way of credit creation or foreign borrowing to finance the import of extra resources, thus forcing the balance of payments into deficit.

This inflationary competition between public and private claims on current resources reveals itself also in the non-acceptance of taxation as a transfer mechanism. When taxation has to be 'compensated' by higher money incomes, its transfer function is being rejected and the inflationary effects of excessive borrowing are re-inforced.

Interest rates are one of the costs pushed up by pressure of demand on the supply of money; monetary financing of government needs may relieve this pressure but at the cost of inflationary expansion of the money supply, bigger external deficits and strain on the exchange rate.

It will, I hope, be clear even from this highly condensed account that there are close links between fiscal and monetary policies – that one can over-ride or thwart the operation of the other – and that, therefore, their appropriate co-ordination is a pre-requisite of the effectiveness of either. The relevance of movements in money incomes has also been indicated.

I have concentrated on the level of public expenditure and the extent to which the total is financed by borrowing but the composition of public expenditure also matters. There is a significant difference between borrowing for current and for capital purposes. If the state is borrowing, particularly from abroad, it is clearly better to have something to show for it rather than nothing – to have in return public assets, like an improved telephone system, electricity generators, new roads or educational institutions, rather than use the money simply to meet day-to-day expenses. When no productive assets are being created, the burden of interest and repayment charges must impede in future years the economy's capacity to provide new jobs and better living standards.

It can only have been through misunderstanding of Keynes that during the 1970s governments in Ireland adopted on a large scale the policy of financing current deficits as well as capital expenditure by borrowing. Their good intentions on the employment plane were largely frustrated by their having to exert this expansionary pressure against a rising wall of real wage and salary rates. A Keynesian expansionary policy, when appropriate, could have been confined to borrowing for capital purposes and would have depended for full effectiveness on there being no increase in real wages.

Once deficit financing is employed on a large scale on current account, there is, as Irish experience shows, a virtually intractable problem of reversing the policy when the economic situation changes. After the pro-cyclical budget of 1978, there was to have been a reversal in 1979 but the current deficit for that year proved to be greater than ever.

So much for the usual justification for recourse to current deficit financing, namely, that it is readily reversible when economic conditions change. The more general argument concerning its flexibility is equally questionable. It has been possible for years at a stretch to keep public capital expenditure from growing. At least as much flexibility attaches, in practice, to the control of capital outlay – the initiation and pacing of new capital projects – as does to the changing of tax imposts and reliefs and the curbing of current expenditure, which now consists so largely of pay, social welfare and debt service charges. In the 1960s the flexibility of the public capital programme was such that the change in *real* terms from one year to the next varied from an increase of 21 per cent to a decrease of 5 per cent, interspersed with periods of stability.

The fiscal policy instrument nowadays lends itself more easily to expansion than to contraction. Expansion is at times determined in timing and degree more by political considerations than economic. When contraction is inevitable, the watchword quite understandably is 'gradualism' but this unhappily often means 'too little too late'. There have, however, been times in Ireland's past when fiscal policy was less encumbered by pay, tax relief and social commitments and could be more effectively exercised, even in a deflationary direction. I need only mention the 1952 budget and the correction of large balance of payments deficits by fiscal means in 1956 and 1966.

As an instrument of control, fiscal policy has, I fear, lost much of its force and has become entangled in a sort of booby trap. If taxes on expenditure are increased, prices go up and compensatory income increases are demanded. If taxes on income are raised, income increases are sought to restore real take-home pay. In either case, the desired effect of fiscal policy is largely nullified; the public finances are themselves directly upset because of the weight of pay in public expenditure. In National Understandings, increases in government expenditure and/or tax reductions are traded for the uncertain prospect of 'moderation' in pay demands. All this limits the discretionary scope and the effectiveness of fiscal policy.

## Monetary policy

Monetary policy has to do with controlling the supply of money with a view to keeping total national spending within bounds and prices and costs from rising too fast. New money can be supplied from two sources – domestic and foreign. The domestic source is new bank credit. The running down of external reserves or the incurring of new foreign debt provide money from abroad – I leave out of account the rare occasions when new foreign money is earned by a balance of payments surplus. The concern of the Central Bank as the regulator of the money supply is to ensure that there is enough money, but not more than enough, to finance production, trade and investment without serious inflation or external payments imbalance.

When we had a parity relationship between the Irish pound and sterling, and free movement of funds between the two countries, the Central Bank's ability to control the supply of money in Ireland was limited and depended more on its capacity to win obedience than on its disciplinary power. If the Bank had ever tried to impose an intolerable squeeze, many major firms could have turned to British banks to meet their needs and only the weaker borrowers would have suffered. Now, with the sterling parity link broken and exchange controls in force, the opportunity to obtain a supply of money from abroad is hemmed in. The fact that the Central Bank is for the time being prepared to allow foreign borrowing is to be explained by a concern to bolster its external reserves rather than a strictly logical preoccupation with monetary control.[2] In any case, the situation is still not watertight; Irish firms desperately short of domestic credit could still enlarge their external indebtedness, if they judged the exchange risk tolerable or the interest gain worthwhile, by extending the average time gap between trading receipts and payments. In view of the magnitude of these 'leads' and 'lags' – even in one month, as the Minister for Finance has said, they could exceed in amount our total external reserves – and the still liberal supply of various Eurocurrencies on offer, no Central Bank in the free world can operate on absolutely rigid monetary control. Its ability to do so is, of course, thwarted if the home government itself generates vast additions to the money supply by deficit financing and foreign borrowing.

In line with ideas popularly associated with the name of Friedman, a number of Western European countries have in recent years been setting growth targets for the money supply. One of the first was Germany where in December 1974 the Bundesbank announced the desired rate of growth of central bank money. The United States also introduced a money supply target at that time. Subsequently the United Kingdom, France and Switzerland followed. Usually, the specifying of a money growth target is only one element in a broader anti-inflationary programme. Controversy still surrounds the question of the degree of success attained or attainable by monetarist policies.

Smaller countries at any rate, and these include Ireland, prefer to maintain a fixed exchange rate with major currencies and try to ensure that the creation of domestic credit and resort to foreign borrowing will be compatible with maintenance of the exchange rate and adequate external reserves.

Even if monetary control could be fully and effectively exercised, it is difficult to believe that governments in democracies could just set the control (at, say, a 5 per cent p.a. rate of increase) and then walk away with their fingers in their ears. If the current incomes and costs situation were such as to generate the need for, say, a 10 per cent rate of increase in the money supply in order to keep the wheels turning, would a democratic government have the social stomach or political hardihood to ignore the interim cries of distress – the bankruptcies and job losses – and calmly wait for the harsh adjustments to be completed? The monetarists seem better at explaining why things are in a mess than at indicating how to improve the situation with the minimum of social stress. They are not of course alone in this.

## Incomes policy

Finally, a word on the need for money incomes to rise no faster than is compatible with the maintenance of competitiveness at the chosen rate of exchange. Otherwise, sales, output and jobs will be threatened. You will notice I am trying to avoid using the term 'incomes policy'. I find it misleading insofar as it implies that the trend in money incomes is as amenable to official control as public expenditure or taxation or domestic credit creation. It is, however, necessary for good management of an economy that a strong central influence be exerted in favour of moderation of the upward movement in money incomes so that they will not run constantly ahead of productivity and so perpetuate or even accentuate inflation. A rate of inflation faster than that prevailing in competitor countries is the greatest danger of all. The particular aim of a government committed to full employment must be to extend the range of tradable home products and services which have a competitive edge over their foreign rivals. Consequently, the sectors sheltered from the market cannot be allowed to set pay norms which would cripple the exposed sectors.

Government intervention is seen to be necessary as a counterpoise to possible excessive use of power by organised groups of workers in essential industries or services. The intervention may range from the issue of guidelines or the negotiation of a pause or cost-of-living reduction by subsidies to the imposition of a short-term statutory 'freeze'; the latest form in Ireland has been active participation by the government in the working-out of a comprehensive voluntary deal on pay, income taxation, social security and investment with the social partners.

The concept of a 'National Understanding', however good in principle, is exposed to various risks in practice, not least of which is that agreement even on the pay side may be bought at a price which is not only too high initially but tends to escalate thereafter. Commitments on tax reliefs, social improvements or job creation may also gum up fiscal policy and impede its capacity to deal with unexpected developments.

There is, however, no real alternative to continuing to seek genuine moderation through consultation and consent and against the background of national economic and social development needs.

Some flexibility must be allowed for to accommodate such things as changes in demand for particular skills, significant improvements in productivity and the remedying of grave anomalies. But there is a real difficulty in preventing these special increases from spreading indiscriminately as attempts are made to preserve customary differentials.

No democratic country, however, presents a perfect example of a system that ensures a changing pattern of incomes satisfying everyone's aspirations and yet fully conforming to the national interest. In Ireland over the past decade, despite all our efforts, non-agricultural money incomes have risen so much faster than productivity would justify that there have been adverse effects on competitiveness and job stability.

Just as fiscal and monetary policies are interdependent, incomes restraint or the lack of it can supplement or destroy the effectiveness of the other two policy instruments. Pay alone accounts for almost one-half of public expenditure and neither fiscal nor monetary restraint is achievable without moderation of incomes. At present indeed, incomes restraint sufficient to improve competitiveness and gain increased output and employment through exports is the only safe escape from the grim embrace of stagnation and inflation.

## Conclusion

Over the past twenty-five years, governments have been claiming a rising share for public purposes of current production and trade unions have succeeded in claiming for their members a much bigger share of the national income. Both these developments have made inroads into profits and investment.

The maintenance of the high investment and steady growth rates necessary to create adequate employment and support rising standards is thus becoming more difficult, especially in a world of rising energy costs. There will be all the more need, therefore, for a wise and balanced use of the three policy instruments in the attempt to create an environment conducive to the attainment of realistic economic and social objectives. The instruments, though interdependent and interactive, have each their special function. Fiscal policy has such a function in the management of domestic demand, monetary policy in maintaining external balance and the exchange rate, incomes policy in promoting competitiveness and trade. None, however, can operate effectively without the support of the others.

I have spoken broadly of the instruments, not of the tools – of control of the money supply, for instance, rather than of the use of interest rates, liquidity ratios, open market operations or any of the specific means by which such control is achieved. Above all, I have emphasised the limitations to the effective exercise of all three instruments of policy and the paramount need to ensure their appropriate co-ordination if even limited success is to be attained in this almost unmanageable world.

## Notes to Chapter 5

[1]Over the years 1973-79, total Exchequer borrowing came close to £4,000 million, of which 70 per cent was financed by monetary as distinct from non-monetary means. The amount of new money put in circulation to finance government expenditure was over £2,800 million, of which £1,000 million came from domestic credit creation and the remainder from foreign borrowings.

[2]Recently the Central Bank has brought bank foreign borrowing for relending to the private sector within its global credit limitation.

*(The old) Central Bank, Foster Place.*

# 6  Ireland's External Reserves

No doubt because of their apparent adequacy our external reserves have attracted little notice in recent years. Even large balance of payments deficits – once a recurring cause of anxiety and a pressing constraint on policy – have been largely ignored by the general public and treated with lack of concern in official policy documents. It has been left to the Central Bank and to a few individuals to call to mind the fundamental importance for economic growth and employment of a manageable external account and the problems which would be posed by prolonged and heavy reliance on foreign borrowing to shore up sagging reserves and finance artificially high living standards.

The Government's *White Paper on National Development, 1977-1980,* issued in January 1978, while forecasting 'formidable' external deficits and admitting the need for 'continuous monitoring', nevertheless dismissed a prospective £500 million deficit in 1980 as unlikely to pose 'insuperable financing problems'. I was critical of the White Paper's apparent complacency in my comments in Seanad Éireann and stressed the need for reassurance that the deficits would be reduced within a reasonable term of years to levels compatible with a continuing rise in employment and security of progress. The *Green Paper* of June 1978, however, contained only the brief and tentative observation that 'there are as yet no signs that the balance of payments is likely to prove a serious constraint, at least in the immediate period ahead'. Again I deprecated this apparent lack of concern, pointing out that balance of payments deficits could be financed only by drawing down external reserves or by incurring foreign indebtedness and that corrective action, when delayed, has all the greater adverse effect on output and jobs.

In the White Paper entitled *Programme for National Development 1978-81*, published in January 1979, the balance of payments did not receive any special notice.

The Central Bank had, however, brought this problem back into focus in its 1978 Report when it pointed out that the rise in external reserves from £432 million in 1972 to £1,201 million at end-December 1977 had been associated with an increase of about £920 million in government foreign debt, a large part of which was due to mature in the near future. The Bank foresaw that the government's development programme could result in a significant fall in the reserves both as a proportion of imports and of current external deficits. 'A major concern of policy must be to ensure that reserves will be adequate to enable satisfactory progress towards the national goals of increased employment and higher living standards to be sustained'.

The £1,201 million of external reserves at end-1977 rose slightly, amidst wide fluctuations, to £1,252 million by end-December 1978 but had fallen to £994 million by June 1979. Rather less than half of this drop of over £250 million in six months has been ascribed by the Central Bank to the reduction in sterling banking liabilities associated with our joining EMS; the greater part has been attributed to the doubling of the trade deficit. The total external deficit is now expected to exceed £600 million in 1979. The Bank warned in its Summer 1979 Bulletin that 'the deficit is now at an unsustainably high level'. The reserves fell further to £934 million by end-September 1979,[1] despite substantial foreign borrowing by the government and the Bank's Autumn 1979 bulletin warns that 'the external deficit must be reduced significantly if reserve inadequacy is not to become a major obstacle to sustainable national progress'. The Bank calls for a substantial reduction in Exchequer borrowing as a proportion of GNP.

Few people realise that our external reserves, which between 1970 and 1972 represented six months' purchase of imports, are now, though inflated to a higher level by official and other borrowing abroad, of much less value as a protection against adverse contingencies. They now represent less than three months' purchase of imports and, whereas in the early 1970s, they would finance six years of deficits of the then order, they would now be exhausted in less than two years if they were called upon to finance balance of payments deficits of the magnitude we are now incurring. It is no wonder that banks and other institutions are experiencing an acute shortage of liquidity which, like the basic external imbalance itself, can be eased for a time only – not permanently redressed – by renewed resort to heavy foreign borrowing.

The Central Bank's prescription for tackling the balance of payments problem is to keep down production costs so as to enhance competitiveness at home and abroad. An essential basis for this is a moderate trend in money incomes. Such a strategy could reduce the balance of payments deficit and at the same time sustain the growth of GNP. If realism prevailed in respect of pay norms, 'the conflict between growth and employment on the one hand, and inflation and the balance of payments on the other, could be reduced and a solid basis provided for continuing real progress'. The Bank has indicated, however, that current pay developments are not consistent with these desiderata, a view I (and others) have also expressed and which has been endorsed by the EEC Commission.

The balance of payments deficit is bound to claim increasing public attention over the months ahead, since neither foreign borrowing nor drawing down of external reserves could continue for long to sustain it on its present scale. The Central Bank's latest Bulletin expresses its dismay at the tendency for the deficits to reflect increased consumption rather than investment. I cannot suggest any better cure for this problem than a combination of reduced government borrowing (particularly for current purposes), firm credit control (particularly over personal consumption) and more moderate and realistic increases in money incomes. It would spoil the evening to dwell on the unpleasant consequences of letting the situation drift. I shall, therefore, proceed to my main theme: the significant changes effected in the composition of our external reserves over the past decade or so. The diversification achieved in that period has not hitherto been the subject of record.

The appropriate starting point for my story is the devaluation of sterling in November 1967. This second post-war devaluation rang the death-knell of sterling as an international
currency. The sterling area, which had benefitted from the
pooling of scarce dollars and other 'hard' currencies during
the war and immediate post-war period, had become increasingly vulnerable to lapses of loyalty and trust as sterling
staggered from crisis to crisis in the 1950s and 1960s. The co-
operation in dollar economies and payments restraints which
was mustered amongst a dwindling number of members in
what proved to be a vain attempt to avert a second devaluation
gave way in the immediate aftermath to a *'sauve qui peut'*
mentality. If sterling was never again to be dependable either
in value or convertibility, there was no point in holding such
large quantities of it in official reserves.

In our own case apart from a small gold holding (£8 million)
and some £16 million of US government securities, all our
£300 million of external reserves in December 1967 were in
sterling, £147 million of that sterling being in the hands of the
Central Bank. This predominance of sterling holdings could
be justified if sterling were a stable and effective international
currency but the unreliability indicated by two devaluations
and other omens engendered a strong sense of anxiety.
Ireland's pattern of international receipts and payments made
it essential to hold a secure and readily available reserve asset:
the Republic earned a net surplus in its transactions with the
United Kingdom and other sterling area countries, it also
usually earned a surplus with the dollar area, but it consistently
incurred large deficits in its transactions with Continental
Europe. It did not need extra sterling to pay its way currently
with the sterling area: it needed to earn and *à fortiori* to hold
reserve currencies or reserve assets which would secure its
solvency in its economic relations with Europe. As uncertainty
at that time still hung over even the Deutschemark, the solution
seemed to be a movement out of sterling into gold or dollars.[2]

Towards the end of 1967 agreement was reached between
the Department of Finance (where I was Secretary) and the
Central Bank (Dr Moynihan being Governor) on a policy of
diversifying the external reserves. I explained our position to

the UK Treasury: they did not welcome our intentions but could not resist the logic of our argument. It was agreed that, to avoid any undue repercussions on sterling, we would proceed quietly and by stages from March 1968 onwards towards our objective which, as then defined with deliberate modesty and sensitivity, was to change about half the Bank's own sterling into other reserve assets.

While this diversification was proceeding carefully in our case (mostly into gold as a first resort), more drastic moves were being set in motion by some other sterling area countries. The Treasury became alarmed. An arrangement was made, under the auspices of the Bank for International Settlements in Basle, whereby the Treasury obtained a line of credit from a number of lending countries which could be used to support the convertibility of sterling into various currencies in case of need. Armed with this 'last resort' facility, emissaries from Whitehall sped to the far corners of the world in the early summer of 1968 in an effort to induce major holders of sterling not to diversify further into dollars or other reserve assets. The bargain offered was that, in return for committing themselves to hold a minimum proportion of sterling in their reserves, varying from holder to holder but intended to stabilise the June 1968 level of sterling holdings, holders would receive both a guarantee of the minimum dollar value ($2.40=£1) of their holdings and an assurance that, if they needed to draw down their reserves for balance of payments reasons, the proportionate sterling element in the draw-down would be convertible into 'hard' currencies out of the international stand-by credit which Britain had arranged.

In common with most other sterling area countries we decided, though with considerable reluctance, to agree to this bargain but not before we had arranged that £40 million of sterling would be transferred from the Associated Banks to the Central Bank and would be covered by the dollar-value guarantee. By the agreement, the sterling assets in excess of 10 per cent of our total official reserves were guaranteed against devaluation in terms of the US dollar. The minimum sterling proportion we originally agreed to maintain was 65 per cent but this was adjusted later, particularly to take account of the centralisation of the net sterling assets of the banking system in the Central Bank which was completed during 1969 and 1970.

Before participating in the Basle arrangements we had gone some distance in diversifying our reserves. Between March 1968, when the process began and the close down that Autumn the Central Bank reduced its sterling holdings by £33 million (25 per cent) and correspondingly increased its holdings of gold and US dollars and its creditor position in the International Monetary Fund. This creditor position (of £11.6 million) had a gold value guarantee, was repayable on request and yielded a return of 1½ per cent. It was as an interim arrangement that the greater part of the diversification was into gold, held to our account in the US; it was intended to move into more remunerative and mobile reserve assets when a better view could be taken of how the international monetary system might settle down. The 'gold window' through which this gold was bought was closed by the United States in August 1971, and central banks had already (since March 1968) bound themselves not to sell gold in the market but only to transfer it between themselves at the official price (then $35 an ounce). The Central Bank's gold holdings, recorded at $31 million in December 1968, had been halved by December 1969 and reduced to their pre-diversification level by December 1970. I remember we calculated at the time that the realisable price of gold would have to be doubled at least every five years to compensate for the loss of interest on dollar securities. This seemed improbable so long as central banks bound themselves to an official price and foreswore free market sales.

In May 1969, the Bretton Woods Agreements (Amendment) Bill, providing for Ireland's acceptance of and participation in the Special Drawing Rights Scheme, became law. The legislation provided also for the transfer to the Central Bank of the functions previously performed by the Minister for Finance in relation to payments to and receipts from the International Monetary Fund. The assets represented by the gold tranche and by the creditor position were also to be vested in the Bank. All this was in conformity with the principle that the ownership and management of the external reserves should be in the hands of the Central Bank. The Minister had reminded the Dáil in reply to a Parliamentary Question on 10 December

1968, that 'in accordance with the provisions of the Currency and Central Bank Acts, the employment of the funds in the custody of the Central Bank is a matter for the Bank'.

The reduction in the Central Bank's gold holdings during 1970 was amongst the factors which prompted a series of Parliamentary Questions on the Bank's autonomy in this and other areas. There were some members of the Dáil for whom gold continued to hold its time-old fascination, Dr John O'Donovan in particular. He asked several questions about the sale of gold by the Bank in the course of 1970, including a query as to whether the Minister for Finance had been consulted. The Minister said, 'I was not consulted. The management of official monetary reserves is a matter for the Central Bank, acting within its statutory powers'. (Dáil Debates, 10 November 1970). Dr O'Donovan pressed the Minister: did the Minister agree with the decision of the Central Bank to 'get rid of our limited amount of gold'? The Minister's reply repeats the Bank's description of its policy (*Annual Report 1970* pp 52/3) while reasserting the Bank's independence:

> *Mr. Colley:* It is not my function to agree or disagree. The Central Bank is by statute charged with the duty of deciding whether or not our reserves in the form of gold or otherwise should be disposed of. The Bank has set out its general policy in this regard. I might, however, set it out briefly. The policy is that in the management of external reserves their objective is to obtain as large a return as possible on the reserves consistent with, firstly, Ireland's commitments as a member of the IMF and as a participant in the Basle Agreement to safeguard the stability of the international monetary system, secondly, the necessity of keeping a sufficient amount of reserves in liquid form and, thirdly, the maintenance of their international value.
>
> *Dr. O'Connell:* What is the reason on this occasion, or did they tell the Minister?
>
> *Mr. Colley:* The reason is obvious: you do not get interest on gold.

This was not the last we were to hear of gold. The baleful

yellow metal continued to excite covetous instincts. Dr John O'Connell, TD, inquired in July 1973, as to the total value of the country's gold reserves. Deputy Oliver J. Flanagan asked on 20 June 1974 why the Minister for Finance favoured a reduction in the role of gold in the international monetary system and why the proportion of gold in Irish official reserves had declined at a time when the free market price of gold was rising. The questions and the reply are worth reproducing:

*Mr. O. J. Flanagan* asked the Minister for Finance whether, in view of the growing international monetary and financial crisis arising from the deficit with the oil producing countries and of the flood of depreciating paper currency in the world, he will state why he considers that the role of gold in the monetary system should be reduced.

*Mr. R. Ryan:* As I informed the Deputy in the course of my reply on 28 May last to a previous question, there is general agreement in the international community that the role of gold in the international monetary system should be reduced. That is the conclusion of the Committee of 20 on International Monetary Reform, which has just concluded an intensive study of monetary problems, including the gold problem. That Committee has had available to it the services of experts from the International Monetary Fund and from all the member countries of the fund.

The supply of gold available for monetary use is variable and uncertain, depending on the level of world production and the demand for gold for industrial, commercial, hoarding and other purposes. It is now accepted that this does not provide a firm basis for the creation or management of international liquidity in modern economies. Instead, the Committee of 20, with whose report I fully agree in this respect, has opted for the adoption of the special drawing right – popularly known as the SDR – as the primary international reserve asset. In this way the volume of liquidity can be brought under the control of the International Monetary Fund and can be regulated by that body in relation to international need and in the interest of the world community.

What I have said relates to the long-term position of gold.

It does not mean that the substantial existing stocks of monetary gold cannot be drawn on to meet deficits resulting from the higher oil prices or other reasons. This, however, is a complex question which is still under consideration.

*Mr. O. J. Flanagan* asked the Minister for Finance why the proportion of Irish official reserves held in gold declined from 5.6 per cent to 1.7 per cent between 1969 and 1973, at a time when the free market price of gold was continually rising: the manner in which the gold reserves were disposed of: and, if they were transferred or sold to other countries or interests, if he will give details including the selling price. *Mr. R. Ryan:* The proportion of the official external reserves held in gold declined between 1969 and 1973 because of gold sales valued at £5.1 million in 1970 to the United States Treasury at the then official price of US $35 an ounce, an increase in the Irish subscription to the International Monetary Fund of £4.3 million paid in gold in the same year and because total reserves increased subsequently while the volume of gold holdings remained constant. I may add that:

(i) the free market price of gold did not begin to rise significantly until the second quarter of 1972;

(ii) in official external reserves gold is valued at the official price, currently $42.22 per ounce. The Central Bank's transactions in gold in 1970 were carried out in accordance with an agreement of March, 1968, between central banks to conduct gold transactions only among themselves at the official price;

(iii) the Central Bank has received substantial interest payments on official reserves held in US dollars and other foreign currencies.

*Mr. Colley:* Is it true that one of the reasons for the position as outlined in the question and in the Minister's reply is that gold, when held at fixed official price, does not, of course, yield interest as do other forms of reserves, as pointed out by the Minister? Would the Minister further agree that it would be in the interests of this country to establish an international monetary system based not on superstition but on a rational system such as SDRs?

*Mr. R. Ryan:* The Deputy is entirely right.

When the Basle agreements were renewed for two years in September 1971, the Minimum Sterling Proportion was reduced by 10 per cent in each case. Ours, which had earlier gone from 65 per cent to 68 per cent, was thus reduced to 61 per cent. Advantage was taken of this to diversify further.

The incredible revaluation of sterling vis-a-vis the US dollar in the Smithsonian arrangements at end-1971 was predictably short-lived. The floating of sterling in June 1972 further reduced its significance as an international currency. Its dollar value quickly fell from the post-Smithsonian $2.6057 to about $2.35 in the final quarter of 1972. Indeed, one of the matters which came under consideration in early discussions on reform of the international monetary system was the possibility of consolidating reserve currency holdings of central banks into 'modified' Special Drawing Rights in the IMF. This proposal never became operative but we did point out the need, in such a contingency, for an adequate rate of interest on any SDRs which would replace our sterling and dollar holdings. The floating of sterling also caused the UK authorities to suggest modification of the guarantee provisions of the Basle arrangements. The Central Bank was not in favour of a renegotiation, on the view that Ireland should be released from the Basle restrictions as the only sterling area country, apart from Britain, which was acceding to the EEC. If this argument proved untenable, it was thought that we should press hard for a much lower Minimum Sterling Proportion (MSP) in order to have greater freedom to diversify. In the end, while the British never formally conceded the Irish argument that additions to our reserves resulting from foreign borrowing should be excluded in computing the MSP, they did admit that they would no longer insist on applying the MSP to a *rise* in reserves but would be content to agree on an *absolute* limit more or less equivalent to the then level. On this basis, a prolongation of the guarantee and MSP arrangements was again agreed.

To complete the story of the Basle arrangements, this prolongation carried us up to September 1973, and we faithfully maintained the Minimum Sterling Proportion at around 60 per cent. A unilateral proposal was then made by the British authorities to renew the Agreement for six months even though their stand-by credits were being allowed to run out. It was thought that, for such a short period and at a time when sterling was weakening against the dollar, it was better not to forego protection for the bulk of our sterling merely for the sake of the limited further diversification which would have been practicable without accentuating sterling's decline. The offer of prolongation of the guarantee to end-March 1974, was, therefore, accepted. Before the end of 1973 we were being consulted by the British authorities as to our view on the post-March 1974 situation, our opinion being invited on the action which they should take 'to provide stability for holders of sterling pending the devising of a long-term solution to the sterling problem in the context of international monetary reform'. In its consideration of this proposal the Bank still felt that it would be better to seek separate treatment from other sterling holders by virtue of our common EEC membership with Britain. If there were a further extension of the September 1973 declaration – and this would be preferable to a formal bilateral agreement – the Bank would envisage a major reduction over the following three years in its sterling holdings but doubted whether the United Kingdom could concede a *general* reduction of a similar order to sterling area countries. The Bank did not view the improvement in the quality of the guarantee (it was to be related to the effective exchange rate of sterling, not just to its rate with the US dollar) as an acceptable alternative to diversification of reserves. Guarantees were temporary and, under the new régime, at the volition of the guarantor. At their expiration one would risk being left holding reserves denominated in a currency still liable to depreciation.

In the event, a unilateral extension was made by the UK authorities guaranteeing a reduced Minimum Sterling Proportion of about 54 per cent of total reserves for the period ending 31 December 1974. This freed 6 per cent of our sterling for immediate conversion into other reserve assets. The so-called Basle arrangements finally lapsed on 31 December 1974. Ireland received a payment of £3.8 million under the Basle guarantee when in the Winter of 1972 the floating pound fell for thirty consecutive days below $2.40 by more than one per cent. One of the aims of the UK Treasury in suggesting a modification of the arrangements in September 1973 was to be empowered to claw back any such payments if and when sterling recovered again for the requisite period. In fact, the floating pound had strengthened from about $2.48 at end-March 1973 to $2.58 at end-June. It then weakened steadily to $2.16 in mid-January 1974, but recovered at end-May 1974 to almost $2.40. The upshot of all this was that not only did we collect a second guarantee payment, making the total £11.1 million, but, in contemplation of the ending of the Basle arrangements in December 1974 we were able to arrange for substantial switches into US dollars at rates close to $2.40. It also became possible, under arrangements I shall mention in a moment, to switch into Deutschemark and other 'snake' currencies, which were appreciating in relation to the US dollar, at a time when sterling was showing some temporary strength as it did in the Spring of 1975.

Basle, which had been the scene of the support arrangements for sterling, was also the place where the Governor of the Bank of England was informed in late 1974 of our intention to convert further from sterling into other reserve assets and where arrangements were made early in 1975 with the President and Vice-President of the Bundesbank that, within liberal limits, they would countenance our use of the Deutschemark as one of our reserve assets, even though they were opposed to the development of reserve status for the DM. It was also arranged that the Central Bank could hold balances, on a smaller scale, in Dutch guilder, French and Belgian francs, Canadian dollars, Japanese yen and other currencies. The reaction of the Governor of the Bank of England was stoical, as had been that of the Secretary of the Treasury in 1968.

The course of diversification of our external reserves is to be seen in the following Table; diversification began in 1968, was in large part but not wholly arrested during the régime of the

Basle agreements, was resumed at the end of 1974 and was substantially achieved during 1975.

## Official External Reserves (£ million)

| 31 Dec. | Gold | SDRs | Reserve Position in IMF | ECUs | Sterling | Other Foreign Exchange | Total |
|---|---|---|---|---|---|---|---|
| 1967 | 8.0 | - | -3.7 | - | 265.8 | 16.3 | 299.4 |
| 1968 | 31.0 | - | 11.6 | - | 218.3 | 30.6 | 291.5 |
| 1969 | 16.1 | - | 24.2 | - | 183.0 | 64.6 | 287.9 |
| 1970 | 6.7 | 5.6 | 12.6 | - | 191.3 | 74.1 | 290.3 |
| 1971 | 6.5 | 11.0 | 14.7 | - | 217.3 | 131.6 | 381.1 |
| 1972 | 6.9 | 16.4 | 16.9 | - | 264.1 | 127.9 | 432.2 |
| 1973 | 7.6 | 16.4 | 16.9 | - | 259.9 | 134.5 | 435.3 |
| 1974 | 7.6 | 17.0 | 17.7 | - | 208.6 | 244.5 | 495.4 |
| 1975 | 7.6 | 17.2 | 16.0 | - | 128.7 | 506.5 | 676.0 |
| 1976 | 7.6 | 20.0 | 35.2 | - | 174.1 | 718.6 | 955.5 |
| 1977 | 8.2 | 20.2 | 33.2 | - | 174.8 | 964.3 | 1,200.7 |
| 1978 | 7.6 | 21.8 | 29.3 | - | 153.7 | 1,039.5 | 1,251.9 |
| 1979 | | | | | | | |
| End-June | 6.6 | 36.5 | 30.4 | 114.2 | 806.2 | | 993.9 |
| End-Sept. | 4.6 | 36.5 | 30.4 | 90.2 | 771.9 | | 933.6 |

The Table shows that the proportion of sterling in Ireland's external reserves fell from 89 per cent at 31 December 1967, to 19 per cent at 31 December 1975. It has since tended to settle a few percentage points further down the scale. There was not much scope for additional diversification on our part when, in January 1977 as part of a 'package' intended, in addition to advancing internal reforms, to reduce the vulnerability of sterling to 'hot money' flows and to wind down its role as an international reserve asset, arrangements of an entirely new kind were announced by the UK. These arrangements, though also backed by an international credit line negotiated in Basle, differed fundamentally from the original Basle Agreement of 1968. They were directed not towards *stemming* the conversion of sterling into other reserve assets but towards facilitating an orderly *reduction* in official sterling balances. They took the form of a unilateral offer to the major holders of sterling, including Ireland, to convert part or all of their holdings in excess of working balances into foreign currency bonds. These bonds were issued in four denominations – US dollar (with maturities of 5, 7 and 10 years), Deutschemark, Swiss franc and Yen (maturity of 7 years). Purchases of such bonds for sterling were made by the Central Bank. It may be presumed, thereafter, that the amount of sterling held by the Bank represented its view of the working balance appropriate to the size and variability of Ireland's economic transactions in sterling.

This year (1979) the range of diversification was further enlarged by the addition of a new reserve asset in the form of European Currency Units (ECUs), a composite of EEC currencies identical with the European Unit of Account; we acquired £114 million worth of these when, on joining the EMS, we deposited with the European Monetary Co-operation Fund 20 per cent of our gold reserves and 20 per cent of our US dollar reserves to serve as a means of settlement.

It is of interest that, internationally, there has been a growing tendency in the past few years for reserves to be held in the form of foreign exchange (other than sterling) and for currencies besides the US dollar, notably the Deutschemark, the Swiss franc and the Yen (the currencies of the three principal current-account surplus countries in the oil-importing world) to take on the reserve asset function; in other words, many countries have joined us in diversifying their official reserves. Indeed, there is a marked trend, the implications of which I have no time to discuss tonight, towards a multi-currency reserve system rather than towards the IMF desideratum of making the SDR the primary reserve asset of the international monetary system. According to authoritative sources, between 12 per cent and 15 per cent of the world's central bank reserves were in Deutschemarks or Swiss francs at the beginning of 1979. Sterling now accounts for only one per cent of international reserves. The 1979 report of the International Monetary Fund, which criticises 'multi-currency reserve practice' as 'containing the risk of disruptive short-term switches in the composition of reserves' called for 'a larger role for the SDR in members' official reserves' and favoured the establishment of a 'substitution account' by the Fund for conversion of members' foreign exchange holdings into SDRs.

All the reserve figures I have given are in Irish pounds, a procedure which has the perverse effect of increasing the apparent value of the reserves the more the Irish pound depreciates internationally. It is, of course, the foreign purchasing power of the reserves that matters. In recognition of this, the Central Bank began some years ago to publish reserve values in SDRs. This, however, is not a complete safeguard against being misled since even this basket of foreign currencies is itself, in this era of universal inflation, depreciating in purchasing power over commodities. More pertinent indexes are those which express external reserves in terms of so many months' purchase of imports or coverage of external deficits and which show the degree to which reserves are shored up by short or medium-term foreign indebtedness of government, banks and other borrowers. These indicators are now, as I said earlier, much less comforting than a few years ago.

The diversification of Ireland's external reserves, which it has been my main purpose to describe this evening, was initiated by public servants in the Department of Finance and the Central Bank and carried through by them with zeal and determination. The result has been a considerable safeguarding and strengthening of resources essential for the preservation of freedom and discretion in economic policy, though the degree of security afforded has recently been much reduced by large balance of payments deficits. I found it, if I may end on a personal note, very satisfying to have been so placed as to have had an active role, first in the Department of Finance and then in the Central Bank, in the process of diversification of reserves I have just outlined.

## Postscript

The outturn in 1979 was that the official external reserves fell by £277 million because foreign borrowings failed to match the rising external deficit. Between the end of 1979 and the end of 1982 the reserves increased by £619 million. The accumulated deficit in the balance of payments for these three years was £3,300 million but capital inflows, mainly public sector foreign borrowing, came to £3,900 million. Since 1978 no breakdown by currency is available of the foreign exchange component of the official reserves.

With effect from 12 February 1981, the Central Bank's holdings of gold have been revalued to reflect 75 per cent of market value.

The reserves figures for the period from end-1979 to end-1982 are listed in the table below.

## Official External Reserves (£ million)

|         |      | Gold | SDRs | Reserve Position in IMF | ECUs | Foreign Exchange | Total |
|---------|------|------|------|-------------------------|------|------------------|-------|
| 31 Dec. | 1979 | 5.7  | 36.5 | 30.0 | 67.2  | 835.3  | 974.7  |
|         | 1980 | 6.1  | 36.4 | 39.8 | 128.6 | 1135.1 | 1346.0 |
|         | 1981 | 73.8 | 50.1 | 38.8 | 85.9  | 1224.5 | 1473.1 |
|         | 1982 | 68.4 | 54.3 | 38.8 | 125.7 | 1306.8 | 1594.0 |

# 7   Industrial Relations

In opening this seminar, which I do with pleasure and with a word of commendation to the Cork Chamber of Commerce for their choice of such a nationally important topic, I would like to make it clear that I am no expert in the field of industrial relations. I would describe myself merely as a concerned observer of a troubled scene. In a recent speech in Seanad Éireann on the government's *Programme for National Development 1978/81,* I emphasised that 'the bright citadels of prosperity and employment are on the other side of a stormy sound which we do not yet know how to cross' and I suggested that we 'concentrate our endeavours on bringing order and calm into pay and industrial relations so that we can safely make the passage to that brighter world'. This is the purpose to which, with humility but also with earnestness, we address ourselves in this seminar.

Industrial relations is a term which covers many aspects of the relationship between employees and employers, or between workers and managements, and many factors contribute to determining the quality and state of that relationship. Where there is alienation or friction or frustration, it may surface in a special pay demand, in a 'go slow' or in a strike, but the reaction may in reality be directed towards establishing recognition or recovering human dignity where these are being undermined by monotony, repetitiveness, cold indifference, lack of consultation, slowness of response to grievances or other causes. At times there may appear not to be any reasonable explanation for a state of tension or discord and I suppose one cannot rule out the possibility of an element of 'cussedness'; in a world in which the seven deadly sins are powerful motivators, it would be unwise to be too starry-eyed! But there is such a wide range of reasonable causes of conflict, and the consequences are of such significance for society, that great progress would be made if we were able to eradicate even some of them. However much we relish, in the comfort of our living-room armchairs, Wild West scenes in which the hero is the quickest on the draw, we realise, as the frontiersmen also came to realise, the superiority of civilised procedures. Observance of the rule of law saves much time and energy and avoids much destruction and waste.

The economic objective in relation to industrial relations is to reduce the extent and frequency of conflicts which cause stoppage of work and, therefore, loss of output. Before the national pay agreements brought a measure of industrial peace at the beginning of this decade, Ireland's record in terms of work-days lost through disputes was bad, not only absolutely but relatively. We entered this decade with strikes causing an average annual loss of one million man-days. Our experience over the five years 1971-75 was an average loss of 307,000 work-days a year, less than in the UK, Italy and the United States but still, as in the previous five years, much higher than in France, Germany and the Netherlands. In the past three years the losses have grown again, to an annual average of about 600,000 work-days. Two out of every three strikes are unofficial but, in general, official strikes are more prolonged and cause the greatest direct loss of output. Indirect loss through strikes may be of even greater consequence, in terms of interruption and frustration of trading contacts and tilting of the scales against new investment in Ireland. This risk applies particularly to strikes affecting public services such as the post, telecommunications and electricity.

## Absenteeism

To avoid loss of perspective, I might remind you that only a small proportion of workpeople are, at any given time, involved in industrial disputes (3–4 per cent) and that absences ascribed to illness are a big multiple of the days lost through stoppages, official and unofficial. Not all these illnesses, even if medically certified, are genuine. Absenteeism tends to hide under the medical umbrella and there is no doubt it causes much more lost industrial output than strikes. Special attention must, therefore, be given to means of reducing the incidence of absenteeism in any programme directed towards economic and social progress. More attractive organisation of work processes and improvement of the working environment have no doubt a part to play in the reduction of absenteeism as well as in the general improvement of industrial relations.

## Job satisfaction

Having thus introduced the psychological factor, I would like to consider it further for a few minutes under two main heads, job satisfaction and participation, which are not, of course, unrelated.

Job satisfaction arises from voluntary commitment of one's resources to high-quality performance of any task or series of tasks. It is bound up with full use of one's talents, with realisation of one's human dignity. Years ago I read a book by an Australian psychologist called *The Making of a Moron*. One of the main contentions of this book was that a great deal of the discontent, idleness, boss antagonism, truculence and anti-social disposition found amongst certain industrial workers could be attributed to conscious or sub-conscious feelings of frustration and resentment at inadequate use of their talents. They felt degraded. Routine mechanical jobs did not stretch the human capacity of those engaged in them, so the mind sought refuge in other things, including mischief. It was only when a job extended a man fully, and called for the use of his finer faculties in particular, that he was happy. Hence the importance of organising work so as to make it interesting and capable of offering workers of varied interests and capacities an opportunity, in a pleasant environment, to achieve satisfaction through the pursuit of excellence. If this idea of full use of talents in search of quality were more earnestly pursued in Ireland it would not merely provide personal satisfaction on a wider scale but make an invaluable contribution to national progress. If we all were careful to promise just as much as, but only as much as, we could perform, and then made certain to perform what we had promised, this would be a thriving country.

As I was writing this, my eye caught, in the *Observer* of I April 1979, remarkable confirmation from a successful businessman of the theories of the Australian psychologist. The chairman of Marks and Spencer, Sir Marcus Sieff, is reported as saying:

> If people are not treated with respect and do not enjoy their work, but regard it as a necessary evil, then there will be conflict. People will be discontented, organisations inefficient, productivity, profits and wages generally poor.
>
> A policy of good human relations costs time, effort and money, but it can only be implemented if top management have the right mental attitude, which must be based on a sincere respect for the individual.
>
> This results in people working well, less absenteeism, greater staff stability, a more experienced staff and, generally, a willing acceptance of new and more modern methods of production and operation.

To be realistic, one must recognise also that the net loss of disposable family income caused by deliberately ceasing to work for a period, whether by taking time off or downing tools, is much less of a deterrent than it used to be.

## Worker participation

Participation is a general term covering various ways in which employees can have a say, as in principle they obviously should, in determining their part in, and the course of, activities which take up so much of their time and effort and on which they depend for a livelihood. The Commission of the European Communities, in a discussion paper related to the proposed 'fifth directive' on company structures, distinguishes four kinds of participation: negotiation of collective agreements; representative institutions which are informed, consulted and approve certain measures; participation in a company's decision-making bodies; and share (or profits) participation.

## Lessening the conflict

One of the consequences of pay agreements being reached at national level has been a reduction in the scope for collective bargaining at plant and enterprise level, except in relation to productivity. I shall be discussing some of the broader implications of this in a moment. I expect that other speakers will examine to what extent occasions for conflict could be lessened and industrial relations improved by:

1. more effective and widespread arrangements for informing and consulting workers on all matters affecting their daily work and their future;

2. various approaches to involvement of employees in decision-making, whether through membership of supervisory or management boards or otherwise (in Ireland we have not yet gone beyond the Worker Participation (State Enterprises) Act, 1977); and

3. extending industrial ownership through share distribution or profit or value-added sharing schemes.

## Industrial democracy

There is a vast literature on the topic of industrial democracy, including the UK Bullock Committee Report of January 1977, and we are ourselves promised a government discussion document soon. As yet, however, there is little consensus even between workers on what is desirable. Many still think there is a great gulf fixed between workers and employers, a fundamental conflict of interest, and are distrustful of board representation, for instance, as an attempt to secure an unnatural compromise. I will permit myself only two observations. First, wider participation at board level is of little use unless it is founded on and supported by active participation in decision-making from the shop floor upwards. Second, it would be a pity if the enterprise or workplace came to be regarded solely as a centre of power, the principles of democracy being invoked as to how that power should be shared and regulated;

is it not also a centre of production, requiring a co-operative and efficiently functioning assembly of management, financial, personnel and other skills in order to achieve maximum added value for the benefit alike of worker and society?

## Autonomous working groups

There will always, of course, be some inherently disagreeable jobs. Difficulties also lie in the way of securing widespread job satisfaction and participation within the framework of the legal and technical organisation of large-scale production. We must, however, be prepared to experiment and change in order to improve the situation. Attempts to relieve monotony and generate a team spirit have been made in various major enterprises. These are based on the principle of autonomous working groups. The work organisation is changed in the direction of more independently functioning units in which each employee has a more varied task. Significant experiments on these lines are being made throughout the industrial world, notably in Sweden (e.g. Volvo, Saab-Skania), Norway (e.g. Nobo, Norsk Hydro) and in enterprises like Fry's in England. The machine-paced assembly line has been replaced by the giving of responsibility for the completion of particular processes to small groups who organise their own procedures. The resultant job enlargement and enrichment and improvement in relations have raised expectations of what might be achieved not only in the work situation but in wider socio-political processes if this system were extended. Most of you will, I am sure, have observed the greater zeal and interest displayed by small independent groups, such as land improvement contractors, than by those working for large public enterprises. It would seem well worth while trying to simulate in industrial conditions a contract system in which small autonomous groups became responsible for particular intermediate products in terms of quality, quantity and delivery at an agreed price and had themselves the opportunity, through their own efficiency, of gaining and sharing a premium profit.

## The pay–productivity relationship

Since the perceived equity of the rewards system is of vital consequence for industrial relations, our seminar must devote attention to this problem and to the adequacy of the institutional arrangements designed to bring civilised procedures to bear on it. By 'rewards' I mean primarily pay but also the provisions for paid holidays, sick leave, pensions, redundancy and so on. In the interests of brevity I shall focus on pay and begin by raising what I consider to be a fundamental but unresolved issue, the question whether productivity should be assessed and rewarded on a national or on an individual basis. Until this issue is resolved, or at least there is a wide measure of acquiescence as to how it should be solved, I see a never-ending prospect of conflict about pay and relativities.

As I said in Seanad Éireann on 1 March 1979, both the present community sense of fair play and the present organisation of trade unions seem to favour raising the pay of all workers more or less in line, and preserving traditional differentials regardless of differences in individual productivity. This appears to be preferred to a system in which only those whose productivity had measurably increased would have their real income correspondingly improved. From this I drew the following inferences:

> If we want to, or feel we have to, maintain the traditional system, then we must continue to have generalised and uniform pay increases conforming to a norm which allows for the national productivity increase, that is the GNP increase per head, and also, but on a winding-down scale, for inflation. If, however, we want to reward workers for increases in productivity at sub-national or firm level, then we cannot have uniform across-the-board pay settlements and trade unions must abandon their equality principle and their attempts to restore differentials.
>
> Above all, we cannot have it both ways. Doubling up of rewards for productivity is a prescription for accelerated inflation.

If we would settle for a compromise solution, and this depends essentially on trade union acquiescence, I do not think our sense of social equity would be offended by some differential or bonus reward for those concerned in particular enterprises or sectors of the economy which achieve a rate of growth in production well above the national average. But since the national average itself has already taken account of the exceptionally high rates of productivity, anything over and above must be of modest proportions so as to limit its inflationary and, indeed, its disturbing social impact.

Such a compromise would recognise that the growth rate of any particular industry is not determined solely by factors within the industry but is supported by essential external services and, of course, by national policy decisions. In other words, there is no compelling case for saying that differences in productivity growth as between firms and industries are caused solely by differences in the rate of improvement in the skill or effort of the workers concerned.

This compromise approach seems very close to what is proposed in the recent National Understanding. I might add that, where specific and significant productivity improvements occur in a particular enterprise, the Irish Productivity Committee's view is that there should be a three-way split of the benefit between higher pay for the worker, greater profit for the enterprise and better value for the consuming public.

Unfortunately, there is no sign that the considerations I have mentioned have been playing any part in the generality of settlements allegedly related to productivity. It is time we established how we wish pay and productivity to be related in the resolution of particular claims. That they must, in a national sense, correspond – in other words, that real improvements in pay throughout industry and services are governed ultimately by the contribution workers make to increased output – is no longer the subject of argument. Some accepted principle for dealing with individual cases is, however, a necessary basis for the effective operation of institutional arrangements to deal with disputes. I shall now turn to these.

## Institutions dealing with disputes

It is, I believe, unnecessary in this forum to define the functions of the Department of Labour, the Labour Court, the Rights Commissioners, the Conciliation Service and, in the context of national pay agreements, the Employer/Labour Conference. I may, I hope, confine myself to a few comments.

I would like, first, to make the general comment that no system of procedures and institutions, however perfectly devised, will work unless both parties are committed to making it work. There have been many regrettable instances of both concealed and open disregard of the formally-accepted rules of the game. Employers have knowingly exceeded national pay agreement guidelines by conceding spurious productivity increases. Unions have tacitly allowed groups claiming more than NPA increases to go ahead and see how they would fare on their own. Recently, eleven Congress unions accepted a Labour Court recommendation by a large majority but then allowed the dissident tail to wag the dog – they not only supported a suspended union in a 'work to rule' but participated in it, with the result that the members of all twelve unions expected the public, as would-be travellers, to do without bus services and, at the same time, as taxpayers, to continue paying for what they were deprived of. If any group in a particular enterprise earns a genuine productivity increase, claims arise for restoration of relativity even where no productivity element is present. It appears that those breaking the rules of orderly industrial relations do so with impunity. It is as if the frontiersmen gave only provisional assent to the rule of law and still carried guns to use when the court's decisions did not favour them. The use of power is no longer the desperate resort of the underprivileged but is becoming commonplace amongst educated and professional classes and is all the uglier for being the less excusable. I would hope that a strong recommendation would issue from this seminar in favour of honourable observance of negotiated agreements and, in disputed issues, a firm predisposition by both parties to accept, in the interests of order and national progress, the findings of institutions which, in effect, are manned by their own nominees.

As to the adequacy of the industrial relations framework, I might note that there is no relativities board as such, no institution specifically charged with investigating, assessing and making a public judgment where a particular category of workers is dissatisfied with its old pay relationship to others and either considers it has been unfairly left behind or is entitled to a rise in the social scale.

The tension caused by changes in differentials has not been eased in recent times by the belief that workers in the private sector have done better in 'productivity' deals than some of their public service colleagues and the suspicion that the disparity cannot be unreservedly attributed to genuine differences in productivity. Another perennial source of friction is the rarely resolved contradiction between professed concern for the lowly-paid and actual willingness to accept a narrowing of differentials. There is even a disposition to assemble wider categories beneath the sympathetic umbrella, though regrettably this can only make any attempt to remedy the lot of the really low-paid too costly to be practicable.

Relativities are indeed explosive issues. When pressure for a status regrading of particular occupations is reinforced by community need or an accrual of bargaining power, is there, as I asked in Seanad Éireann, any orderly way of dealing with the problem except that recommended years ago in the NIEC Report (No. 27) on incomes and prices policy and reiterated earlier this year by the socialist Prime Minister of Britain, namely an authoritative assessment in full public view by a reputable and representative body? Even then, there will be no peace unless all other categories accept the justice of a particular re-grading and abstain from seeking to maintain the old differentials.

The working of the existing institutions has itself been criticised, on the whole constructively, by both unions and employers in submissions to the Industrial Relations Commission. That the existing institutions have not assured industrial peace is evident; that they have been a significant help in averting worse disorder is not disputed. Neither the largest trade union, the Irish Transport and General Workers' Union (ITGWU), nor the Federated Union of Employers (FUE) is calling for the abolition of the Labour Court or any of the associated institutions. The ITGWU wants to see the Labour Court's independence made more complete, its facilities improved, its staff increased, its work speeded up, its approach less conservative, its awards based on more consistent and rationalised criteria; the ITGWU holds fast to freedom of bargaining and to the need for the consent of the conflicting parties. The FUE would interpose an industrial relations board to take over the conciliation and other non-legal functions of the Labour Court, leaving the Labour Court to make final determinations under relevant statutes and to be a court of appeal in an industrial dispute 'provided both parties agree, in writing, in advance to accept the findings of the Court'. Both the ITGWU and the FUE acknowledge the desirability of developing a code of national standards for good industrial practice. The traditional differences reveal themselves mainly in opposing attitudes to acceptance of arbitration in industrial disputes and, in general, to intervention of the legal system in the field of industrial relations. There must, however, be room for intermediate positions, such, perhaps, as agreed submission to 'final offer selection', where the arbitrator decides which final offer, the management's or the union's, should be accepted.

As for labour law generally, the ITGWU argues for further reform in the interests of employees, and there is possibly a reasonable case for some of these reforms but, in the contentious area of the Trade Disputes Act, 1906, the ITGWU demands extension of a protection which the FUE, and not only the FUE, considers to be excessive in present-day conditions.

## Power of trade unions

Many independent observers consider that the recognition, status and protection necessarily and properly extended by the law to trade unions over the past two centuries, but still being increased and reinforced in different circumstances, have resulted in their having excessive power which, almost unavoidably, is exercisable in negative rather than positive directions. Job security and compensation for job loss, for instance, have been greatly strengthened, indeed virtually guaranteed, by legislation. There has, on the other hand, been no moderation of the statutory protection afforded, particularly for picketing, which now appears excessive and contrary not only to the interest of the community but even of the trade unions themselves. Would it not be reasonable to prescribe a secret ballot, and a 'cooling off' period, before a strike becomes legitimate, at least in an essential industry or service, and to withdraw the 1906 Act privileges where these requirements are ignored or unofficial strikes take place, or negotiation procedures are not fully used? I suggest that the status and influence of trade unions in the community and their internal discipline would be strengthened by such a reform.

Not only their defective internal discipline but various other aspects of the organisation and decision-making procedures of trade unions run counter to the needs of orderly development of the economy. Experienced outside observers, such as Professor Michael Fogarty, have pointed out that the trade union pattern in Ireland has remained far too close to an undesirable British prototype. Reforms have been advocated which would, amongst other things, 1. increase trade union revenue and enable more full-time staff to be appointed at adequate salaries and 2. mitigate the disruptive effects of a plethora of unions in major concerns by having a strong multi-union group, properly staffed, for all negotiating purposes. Our experience since the Ferenka debacle can leave us in no doubt that present trade union numbers, organisation, procedures and attitudes are amongst the greatest barriers to full employment.

Strikes sometimes appear to be preferred to settled procedures because of their 'impact' effect, their superiority as a means of attracting the attention of the media and the public at large, as well as of the employer. They are too often a first, rather than a last, resort. Unfortunately, their consequence and, at times indeed, their purpose is to hurt the community as much as possible. The community has developed a remarkable complacency, amounting to masochism, in these situations, partly because of confusion about the merits of particular disputes. Public opinion might be less indulgent, or at least more effective in pressing for a quick solution, if it were better informed. Would it help if the Department of Labour were charged with making the public fully and clearly aware of the issues involved in every major dispute or stoppage as soon as it occurs or is threatened? Not only are we left in the dark about this at present but there often seems to be connivance in concealing the ultimate terms of settlement, and there is rarely any objective and public post factum review of the causes and effects of damaging disputes.

The community values security against external aggression and internal disorder enough to maintain an army and police force at great expense. It cannot, to my mind, leave itself vulnerable to deliberate and equally damaging coercion of an economic kind. It cannot allow itself be forced to its knees by any group which finds itself in control of essential supplies or services and callously and selfishly uses this power to enforce outrageous demands. It seems to me that the security forces must be trained and used to protect and maintain the life of the community in such extreme contingencies. For public security it is also desirable that monopoly positions be avoided in the public as well as in the private sector.

## Conclusions

The recent clamour for reform of the PAYE system and the growing tendency to link attitudes to pay increases with demands for fiscal and social reforms indicate the need to set industrial relations in a much wider context. The point is made in the ITGWU submission that 'conflicts of interest between employers and employees are only the symptoms of deeper conflicts which arise from the many injustices of our irrational economic and social structures'. Without going quite that far, one can still accept the need for a broad horizon and timespan, providing for adequate consultation and leading, one would hope, to a wide measure of consensus between government and the main economic and social interests on how best to realise our national potential, maximise our output and share the resultant real gains both individually and socially.

As long ago as January 1973, I was writing that acquiescence in the multiple measures necessary to contain inflation and promote progress in employment and output was 'more likely to be obtained in the broader context of economic and social development policy over a period of years ahead than in confrontation over particular pay rounds'. The Central Bank maintained this theme over the years, calling for a resumption of planning on a more flexible and less authoritarian basis and emphasising the danger of making tax relief or social welfare commitments except in this wider framework. I had hoped that the latest White Paper would have been able to report sufficient consultation and agreement on development aims, methods and effects to bring some harmony and order into the associated evolution of incomes, social welfare and taxation. Last week, happily, the consultative process did result in a proposed National Understanding on pay and related issues. This could be, and I hope will be, a significant move towards more orderly economic and social progress. That progress would, however, be quicker and surer and less inflationary if we adopted rates of pay increase less out of line with those of our major competitors in the EEC and the rest of the world. May I also repeat that it would be most unfortunate if fiscal policy, our main instrument of demand management, were to become completely gummed-up in commitments to particular interests. The government must retain adequate discretion in this area, or surrender its capacity to regulate and direct the course of the economy. I was very glad, therefore, to read on 2 April 1979 that the President of the Irish Congress of Trade Unions had declared himself strongly against strikes in pursuance of tax reliefs and had emphasised that such action could easily undermine the democratic system.

As I have said earlier, other valuable conditions of civilised living are also in danger of being undermined by the current preference for force rather than reasonable negotiation. I fear, particularly, for the effect on our young people who are now-adays given little example of devotion to duty or of concern for the common good, but see all around them a work-to-rule mentality, a preoccupation with selfishness, envy and greed and an irresponsible disregard for the progress and welfare of the nation.

The title of this seminar includes the words 'is there a better way?' I hope I have now done my job as the first speaker and that I have indicated various directions in which reform is possible and desirable. We can usefully ask ourselves why are industrial relations better in some firms or industries than in others and what approaches are most likely to improve matters. What contribution do we think could be made by job enrichment, by greater participation of the workforce in decision-making, by profit or value-added sharing schemes, or by more fundamental changes in the present rewards system? It is unlikely that we will find incontrovertible answers or any unique solution. But the problem is urgent and exigent and we must keep on trying. This is why this seminar is so timely and so significant.

*Dr. J. J. McElligott, Secretary, Department of Finance, 1927-53; Governor, Central Bank, 1953-60*

# 8 The Department of Finance

I entered the Department of Finance in June 1938, three years before Dr Ronan Fanning* was born and while most of the dramatis personae of his pioneering work were still in office. My 1938 organisation chart differs little from that for 1926 reproduced on page 522 of the book. Brennan had, of course, gone to the Currency Commission and McElligott was Secretary but Codling, Doolin and Seán Moynihan were Assistant Secretaries, the latter having replaced in 1937 the formidable H. P. Boland, and my first Finance Division superiors were the late Alec Bayne as Assistant Principal and Larry Lynd, brother of the essayist Robert Lynd, as Principal. In the echelons above Administrative Officer there were only about thirty persons; the Department, newly-created in 1922, was still small and compact. Thirty-one years later, after nearly thirteen years as Secretary, I went to the Central Bank. After all this lapse of time, I could note with satisfaction for several years to come that all my predecessors, except William O'Brien, were still alive – evidence, perhaps, that hard work never killed anyone and, certainly, of the youthfulness of the Department as an institution. Dr Fanning, indeed, refers many times to the remarkable continuity of personnel and organisation, centering on McElligott's long tenure in the Secretaryship and his tenacious preoccupation with economy and stability.

Charlie Murray not only had a good idea when he thought of having the Department's history written, but made an excellent choice when he turned to Ronan Fanning. His commendable initiative has been well rewarded by this professional and objective work. All of us who worked with those tattered

*Ronan Fanning, *The Irish Department of Finance 1922-58*. IPA, 1978.

and bedraggled files will marvel at Dr. Fanning's assiduity in blowing the dust off them and his capacity to pick out the matters of abiding interest. He has done a masterly job as a primary producer of history, handling with mature competence the original sources, setting the ephemera aside and presenting the historically relevant material in an orderly and eminently readable fashion. He has not set himself the task of making a final, critical assessment of advice or attitudes. He has provided the basic information and the contemporary background without which any such assessment would be presumptuous. Outside the immediate field of financial policy and administration, his work will undoubtedly be indispensable reading for all interested in interpreting modern Irish history. One hopes that similar histories of other Departments will be commissioned and that note will be taken of Dr Fanning's restrained criticism that departmental records are not arranged by a professional archivist. What is deemed worthy of permanent record should also be deemed worth arranging and cataloguing.

Dr Fanning's book, another jewel in the publisher's crown of the Institute of Public Administration, has a foreword by the Tánaiste and Minister for Finance, Mr George Colley, a preface and a prologue – matched at the end, for good measure, by an epilogue, conclusion, four appendixes and an excellent index. In between there are twelve chapters, fully annotated. Chapter One deals with the historical background and gives a fascinating glimpse of the complexity of the administration of Ireland under the Union. There follow chapters dealing with 'The Department of Finance under the Provisional Government of 1922'; 'The Search for Stability 1923-24'; 'Anglo-Irish Financial Relations 1922–26' – chapters which highlight the magnificent contribution made, in a period of great stress and difficulty, by Brennan, McElligott and their colleagues, with the unstinted help of officers on loan from the British Treasury, towards establishing an efficient, reliable and impartial civil administration at minimum cost. Subsequent chapters are entitled 'Consolidation 1925-31'; 'New Masters: The Department of Finance in the Thirties'; 'Anglo-Irish Financial Relations: The Economic War 1932-38'; 'The Department of Finance and the Emergency'; 'Towards the Post-War World: The Department of Finance in the Forties'; 'The Department of Finance and the First Inter-Party Government'; 'The Emergence of Planning'; 'Functions and Organisation: The Department of Finance from within and without'. Dr Fanning explains in the epilogue why he gives what he describes as 'the merest outline of the more significant events' after 1958. This recent period is too close, in his judgement, for historical perspective.

If Dr Fanning has these difficulties as a trained historian, no one will expect a coldly objective review from one who participated in many of the developments recorded in this book. Having confessed that I have noticed no errors of fact or interpretation, perhaps I may be allowed to continue in the personal vein in which I began, acknowledging first that Dr Fanning's references to me personally have been so generous as to engender strong temptations to narcissism. The Department of Finance was the centre of the best years of my life. For it, as an institution, and for its individual members, my friends and colleagues for over thirty years, I shall always have a very high regard and affection. Whatever may be said of the part played by any of us as public servants, the good fellowship, the sense of shared duty and purpose, the willingness to work long hours, the team spirit which transcended hierarchical distinctions created feelings of personal satisfaction and fulfil-ment which were more than adequate recompense for suffering, as Finance officials often must, the slings and arrows of mis-understanding and criticism. Dr Fanning's book cannot evoke the intensity of the *esprit de corps* which animated the Depart-ment. I would have no greater pride than to think that, in my time in the Department, I had sustained and strengthened this spirit. It warmed my heart as a new arrival to find that everyone was friendly and accessible, that an officer's mess atmosphere prevailed; this was in marked contrast with the 'everyone for himself' attitude which was not uncommon in certain sections of other Departments.

Of the dominant figures of the time, my recollections of Brennan are less vivid and, I fear, less sympathetic than those of McElligott with whom for many years my relationship was very close. The brilliance and effectiveness of Brennan's early work, both creative and critical, command our admiration. His contribution as a public servant during the formative years of the state was outstanding. But by the 1940s, no doubt partly as a reaction to unfair political criticism, he seemed to have retreated into an impregnable conservatism bounded by pre-Keynesian economics and abnormal distrust of the profligate propensities of governments. It is a surprise – but then it was as long ago as 1925 – to see him (p. 177) describe the commercial banks as 'very conservative' and want to deny them a 'reactionary ally' on the first Banking Commission. McElligott, when I first met him, sat in a cold, narrow room, wearing a black linen coat, a model of the austerity he preached. In time I discovered a warm, even emotional man, who could be reasoned with. He might put on a mask of severity in order to say 'no' to new proposals for staff or expenditure, but, if you pushed past his defences, you found he could be persuaded to yield to practical necessity. His tenacity and courage and the classical force and simplicity with which he could express himself are revealed many times in this book. I liked particularly his percipient and trenchant comments on Articles 2 and 3 of our Constitution and his impatient reaction that 'it is no business of the Americans what we do with the loan counterpart funds'.

The training in thoroughness and accuracy I received from Arthur D. Codling (Art Codling, incongruously, in Irish versions of statutory instruments) was gentle, but meticulous. When you lifted the phone and heard 'would you slip across, please' in his Yorkshire accent, you wondered was it a wrong file number on the draft letter you had submitted for signature or something even worse. A man of the utmost probity and of penetrating mind, he gave loyal service of the highest quality to his adopted country. He was one of those persons – fathers are often in the same category – so distanced by years and authority that, to one's life-long regret, one never comes to know fully as a human being.

A classic definition of the function of an Administrative Official is given in a Finance memorandum quoted on p. 255 of the book: 'it is the duty of civil servants to think all round a subject and give Ministers their unbiased opinions on matters referred to them when policy is being considered, and then when policy has been decided on, to carry out that policy to the best of their ability, regardless of their own personal views'.

By and large this prescription has, I believe, been faithfully observed. There are instances in the book of both successful and unsuccessful attempts to have government decisions changed before they solidified. But these were prompted by departmental, rather than personal, motives. There are also, happily, instances of initiatives by public servants which helped rescue Ministers from remaining prisoners of outmoded policies.

In my experience, civil servants held their ministers in great respect; their personal relations might be warm or reserved, but the office of Minister was always treated with reverence. If ministers do not figure much in Dr Fanning's book, it is, as the Tánaiste says in his foreword, because 'politicians are not required to commit their thoughts to paper to the same degree as civil servants'. Their role is to decide rather than to argue and they relate to officials orally rather than in writing. This is not to say that they are unconcerned about the manner of presentation of ideas and arguments. I have often been struck by their deftness and skill in welding scraps of material together into politically effective speeches. Though ministers, of course, are particularly concerned with the political aspects of government, it would be wrong to ascribe to them alone a sense of the politically practicable. Indeed, the economics applied by officials in the Department of Finance could, in my view, be more appropriately described by the older term, 'political economy'. The book instances cases of non-acceptance of the advice of civil servants, but the instances of agreement between ministers and advisers are, in the nature of things, more frequent and less noteworthy. It is sometimes suggested that a new minister, in his early days in a Department, has to show 'who's boss'. I find this a childish misconception; no minister of quality needs to do this, any more than an abbot in a monastery, and no Minister for Finance in my time had any such inferiority complex.

There are many other things in the book to arouse interest – for example, Michael Collins's concern as Minister for Finance with order, efficiency and administrative propriety, the lessening of the influence of the Department of Finance when financial as well as other external relations were politicised in the 1930s, and the discussion of where personnel and economic planning functions should be centred. Some developments could have done with further analysis – the move for instance, from the 'gifted amateur' concept of administration to the professionalism now seen to be necessary. In my own case, though owing, like so many others, a good basic education to the Christian Brothers, I shall be forever grateful to Frank Aiken who kept me at my studies and to Brendan Menton who encouraged me to proceed to the London University MSc(Econ). I feel I would not otherwise have been equipped to make a contribution to national development and believe that those in the upper reaches of Finance should be as well versed in economics and other relevant disciplines as university lecturers.

Some ESRI friends have been critical of the failure to expand demand by fiscal action in the early and mid-1950s. Although it followed external payments deficits of £30 million in 1950 and £62 million in 1951, one may, in retrospect, concede that the 1952 Budget was too severely restrictive. But Dr Fanning has brought into focus the practical constraints to expansionary policies in an era when external reserves in official hands were low, foreign borrowing possibilities were virtually nonexistent, exports depended excessively on erratic British conditions and external deficits of menacing size could arise with little warning. It was not, indeed, until the 1960s and the appearance on the world scene of the Euro-dollar, a product of massive US payments deficits, that foreign borrowing on any significant scale became possible. It was only in 1969 that the sterling holdings of the commercial banks were garnered into the official reserves of the Central Bank.

An intriguing revelation of Dr Fanning's is that Keynes himself, who in Dublin in 1933 commended the Fianna Fáil protectionist policy, might well have been called upon for more general advice later; he was short-listed for membership of the Banking Commission. No doubt there would have been a brilliant and challenging Fourth Minority Report but, with the World War supervening and years of scarcity and external payments difficulties to follow, it is questionable whether his advice would have become effective much earlier than it did indirectly, in any case, in the 1950s. One now reads with surprise bordering on incredulity the observations made in good faith in the pre-Keynesian era. Here are two examples from 1932, in the midst of the Great Depression: 'the balancing of the Budget is not an object of purely academic importance that can be deferred till times are better; it becomes more necessary than ever when times are bad that the State can be shown to be living within its income'; and 'the time has come not to extend the system of public works for the relief of unemployment but to reduce it drastically'. One must remember that Finance was expressing the generally accepted doctrine of the time. We are all, it has been said, the slaves of some defunct economist. In retrospect, the blind spots are only too visible. What, I wonder, will turn out to have been the blind spots of today?

Echoing, perhaps, an editorial preface in *Economic development and planning* (Basil Chubb and Patrick Lynch, 1969), Dr Fanning remarks on the contrast between the views I expressed in 'Finance Attitude' (April 1953) and in 1956 and subsequently. May I meekly suggest that too much is being made of this? Dr Fanning himself quotes the Keynesian concepts of demand management through financial policy which, with Paddy Lynch, I was already voicing in public in 1945 and which inspired the budget speech of 1950 and my comments on the responsibilities of the banks for government financing (June 1953). I underwent no Pauline conversion between 1953 and 1956. The explanation of any apparent difference is that the April 1953 address, which was to an audience of senior officials of other Departments, was written primarily to explain and justify the aspects of financial control which they resented; it was hardly the occasion for a broadminded presentation of expansionary ideas. One thing will be found constant over the past thirty years in the particular brand of Keynesianism which I think applicable to this relatively undeveloped country – a strong preference for expanding demand, when that needs to be done, through increased public borrowing for productive capital purposes rather than to finance everyday needs. It was precisely because my concern for many years was to ensure that the narrow, traditional Finance attitude would be broadened by responsibility for national development that I expressed in Seanad Éireann last Autumn my misgivings about the transfer of the economic planning function to a separate Department. It is interesting that the Devlin Report, as we are reminded on p. 625 of this book, endorsed unreservedly the attachment of this function to the Department of Finance.

Given what is expected of civil servants and Ministers in Irish conditions and the administrative framework, both national and local, inherited from the British regime (as reformed both by them and us in the 1919-22 period), I cannot see that much would have been gained by seeking to introduce some novel system in the early years of the State. I do not know what other models might have seemed appropriate, so I think it rather fanciful to suggest that if there had been no civil war, 'Ministers might have contemplated major administrative reforms' (p. 57).

I am glad that Dr Fanning effectively scotches any suspicion of subservience on the part of Finance officials to the British Treasury. He rightly says that, where their interests differed, 'Brennan and his colleagues proved unrelenting opponents of the Treasury'. The same is true of their successors. Our relations were civilised, often friendly. Our mutual respect was deepened by competent and firm pursuit of our own interests, modified by a willingness in the end to see reason. Dr Fanning mentions the special understanding shown at critical times by Treasury officials who had worked or were born in Ireland. I recall an occasion in the Treasury in the 1950s when all four present – three Treasury knights, Rowe-Dutton, Rowan and Compton, and myself – suddenly recognised that we all came from Ireland.

My last two days as Secretary of the Department, 27-28 February 1969, were spent in negotiations in London. It is an indication of the continuity of the problems traced in the book that it was only then that one of the financial thistles which had been prickling us since 1926 was removed from our bed. We needed a make-weight to balance the trade bargain we were about to conclude and it was I who remembered the Damage to Property Compensation Annuity of £250,000, payable for sixty years from 1 April 1926 under the Anglo-Irish financial agreement of December 1925. Everyone else had forgotten it. McElligott had tried in vain to have it wrapped up in the 1938 settlement. I had the satisfaction of helping to finally get rid of it by urging this on my Treasury counterpart and on the very reasonable Mr. Harold Lever, then a Treasury Minister.

Though Dr Fanning's epilogue is of wider scope than he modestly professes, inevitably there are some developments which have to await a more complete treatment – by himself, I hope – when time has provided the desired perspective. One of the differences to be noted will be the absence in the later period of the virtual identity of view between the Department and the Central Bank which characterised the earlier. The McElligott/Brennan axis was itself coming under strain before 1953, according as McElligott responded to the new influences in the Department. The intellectual independence of McGilligan and the political courage of Ministers like McEntee and Sweetman shine through Dr Fanning's pages. I hope the record of the later period will include, amongst instances of the willingness of ministers to adopt politically unpalatable financial policies, Dr James Ryan's sponsorship of the turnover tax when he had to rely on an Independent vote to carry it in the Dáil.

It is impossible to conclude one's commentary on this masterly work without allowing oneself, on behalf of all the Finance officials since 1922, a brief sigh of relief that we emerge from the record without dishonour. Misguided at times we undoubtedly were, but we obviously did not spare ourselves in striving for what we thought was right. It is a minor satisfaction to see how little there is of officialese in what we wrote; indeed, the clarity and vigour with which views are presented and the good style at times displayed bring many of these yellowing memoranda to life. It is, I believe, with some pardonable pride that we can read this book and, in our imagination, see on it a sub-title corresponding to the inscription on the headquarters of the Royal Dublin Society: *Nostri Plena Laboris*.

*Uimhir 2 de* 1980
*Number 2 of* 1980

# AN tACHT AIRÍ AGUS RÚNAITHE (LEASÚ), 1980

# MINISTERS AND SECRETARIES (AMENDMENT) ACT, 1980

BAILE ÁTHA CLIATH:
ARNA FHOILSIÚ AG OIFIG AN tSOLÁTHAIR.

Le ceannach díreach ón
OIFIG DHÍOLTA FOILSEACHÁN RIALTAIS, AN STUARA, ARD-OIFIG AN PHOIST,
BAILE ÁTHA CLIATH 1,
nó trí aon díoltóir leabhar.

DUBLIN:
PUBLISHED BY THE STATIONERY OFFICE.

To be purchased through any Bookseller, or directly from the
GOVERNMENT PUBLICATIONS SALE OFFICE, G.P.O. ARCADE, DUBLIN 1.

31p

*Ministers and Secretaries (Amendment) Act, 1980.*

# 9 The Department of Economic Planning and Development

My views on whether a separate Department should have been set up to deal with economic planning were expressed in Seanad Éireann on 23 November 1977, when the relevant Bill – the Ministers and Secretaries Bill, 1977 – came before that House. I reproduce them here from the Official Report, with only minor deletions.

In the Dáil on the Second Reading of this Bill the Minister for Economic Planning and Development expressed disappointment at the extent of the consideration which had been given to the Bill 'as a measure, to change, by the introduction of a new Department, the structure of Government as we know it'. I would like to address my remarks to the principle of the Bill, that is, I would like to offer some comments on whether the introduction of this new Department is a good change in the structure of government, whether it will contribute to the smooth and efficient discharge of government functions in relation to economic planning and development, or whether there was perhaps a better way which has been set aside without sufficient consideration.

I hope to discuss this question entirely without reference to personalities. I will be making, perhaps, an unpopular argument, namely, that the Department of Finance should have been confirmed and strengthened in its planning responsibilities. I want to make it clear that nothing I say implies any view as to the relative status or competence of the ministers concerned. They are obviously both such persons as would strengthen any cabinet and I have the greatest respect for their qualities.

The function for which the most appropriate government agency is being considered is that of economic planning in a broad sense. So the first question is: what is a plan?; and the second is: what part does government play in bringing it about? As I conceive it, a plan is a coherent and comprehensive set of policies for economic and social development over a period of four or five years ahead. The plan must be consistent with the availability of resources and its various parts must be well integrated. Since, in my view, a plan is the supreme policy document of the government, it should be settled early in the life of a government. Several projections should be made of economic prospects based on different but not implausible assumptions. These projections, the assumptions underlying them and the conditions for realising them, should be published and used as a basis for consultation with the major economic and social interests.

I was glad to hear the Minister say tonight that that sort of consultation is intended. This would mean that, in advance of the final settlement of a plan and its presentation to the Dáil, objectives of social and economic policy would be considered under the compulsion of necessary choice between alternatives. Since scarcity still obtains, this choice between alternatives is imperative. Not only should the objectives be considered against that imperative, but also with an understanding of the conditions to be observed in order to achieve them. The hope would be that aspirations could thus be brought more into line with the total availability of resources, that conflicts about priorities would be at least lessened, if not resolved, and that at the end of the consultative process a definite plan, which was both realistic and had a wide measure of public support, could be adopted. Otherwise, a plan might merely express wishful thinking and irreconcilable desires and the lack of consensus would in any event tear it apart.

Since a plan may have to be modified because of new developments which falsify the original assumptions or because of failure to realise certain basic conditions of success, a process of review and adjustment is obviously essential. It is my argument that the annual budget is the appropriate occasion for that review and adjustment. This would make its own contribution to the more mature working of democracy by placing the budget in its proper perspective – bringing the shorter term into convergence with the longer term – and so divesting the budget in part, at least, of its traditional Santa Claus connotation. It would also ensure regular accountability of the Planning Minister to the Dáil, a point on which concern was expressed by members of that House.

The preliminaries of a plan, to my mind, are no less important than the end results aimed at. I see great merit in involving the various social and economic interests in considering development potentialities, the conditions on which they can be realised and the uses to which the gains made should be put. This method of educating and persuading the various interests towards an understanding of the trade-offs involved – the trade-off, for example, as between higher incomes and higher employment – of persuading them towards some form of consensus about policies would, I believe, make government easier and better directed and do something to rescue democracy from disorder and the economy from the rather grim prospect of permanently heavy unemployment.

What I am saying is that politics may be the art of the possible but we should always try hard to extend the range of the possible, that is, the area of consensus for action, so that the democratic system will not degenerate into intolerable ineffectiveness. It will be clear from what I have just said that I see a significant difference between a plan and a pre-election manifesto. I consider it is the degree to which the plan's objectives are achieved, subject, of course, to any unavoidable or desirable modifications, which should be the foremost measure of the success or failure of the government's economic and social policies.

If this is what a plan should be, how it should be produced and adjusted and how it can make a contribution to the better working of the democratic system, I come to the second question I asked a while ago, namely, what part does government play in making a plan effective? Discussion of this question should help to decide which is the most appropriate agency of government for that purpose. There are limitations to government action in the economic and social fields. Indeed, it could be said that governments tend at times to assume management responsibilities beyond their capacity. I should like, however, to focus on the positive side. So far as governments *can* influence the achievement of social and economic objectives they do so

mainly through their fiscal prerogative, that is, the right –
indeed, I would think it a duty – to settle the scale, purposes
and method of financing public expenditure; 'method of financing' covers the question of how much by taxation and how
much by borrowing.

There are, of course, other policies through which a government can try to influence the course of the economy, monetary
policy and incomes policy in particular. As we all know, these
are not so readily available. They may be of limited or doubtful
efficacy in particular circumstances. The scope for monetary
policy in an open economy with free outward and largely free
inward movement of funds is restricted, though not insignifi-
cant. The development of incomes in a way helpful to competitiveness and progress is, as we all know, of great importance
but, unfortunately, not as easily influenced by government
action as are expenditure, taxation and borrowing.

The point I want to make, however, is that the execution of
all these policies has rested, and even after this Bill has been
enacted will continue to rest, with the Department of Finance.
The Department of Finance are quite competent to draft a
plan and conduct the necessary consultations. They could do
the whole preparatory job as the government's central agency;
they could do the co-ordinating at government level and, as I
have just said, they will always have the vitally important
executive role. One could see it in this way, that the Minister
for Finance will be the performer on the field of play while the
Minister for Economic Planning and Development gives advice
and encouragement from the sidelines and tries to keep play
within the 'development' rules.

As I know from my Central Bank experience, there can be
a wide gulf, perhaps a wall of silence would describe it better,
between advice and action. The influence that may be exercised through advice and persuasion is a second best, I believe,
to the power of the purse. The role of an adviser or co-ordinator
who has no direct power, no money-allocating function, is not
an enviable one. The Minister for Economic Planning and
Development was careful to spare the new National Science
and Technology Board this particular frustration; yet, surpris-
ingly, he accepts it for himself.

This is the basic weakness of the proposed separation of functions, a weakness that could have been avoided had the Department of Finance been confirmed in their development responsibilities and had that Department's conscience, as it were, been made more sensitive to this overriding obligation by having it clearly assigned to them.

To my regret, this has not been done. The Department of Finance, through this lowering of their sights, this lessening of their responsibilities, is being allowed, perhaps, to slip back into that negative, restrictive role, that preoccupation with candle ends to the possible neglect of long-term national development needs, for which their critics have always loved to pillory them. They equate the Department with the old-time Treasury in order the better to set it up as an Aunt Sally. For someone who, over a long period of years, has tried to bring the exercise of the traditional functions of the Department of Finance – and they are important functions – of critical analysis and control of expenditure and equitable levying of taxation into line with the even more important macro-economic planning functions, this new move is disheartening. The more so as I still vividly recall the enthusiasm and dynamism released in my Finance colleagues of 20 years ago when we turned our minds away from purely critical preoccupations towards a constructive study of national development possibilities.

In the Dáil, the Minister for the Public Service saw 'the establishment of this new Department as part of the evolutionary process first begun when the Economic Development Branch was established within the Department of Finance'. I am bound to say that I had a different vision of the evolutionary process. I saw it as leading naturally to a Department of Finance and Economic Development in which the day-to-day controlling functions and the annual budgetary process would be set in the framework of a longer term development plan prepared and administered by the Department. One of the principal lessons of French economic planning is that the success of a plan largely depends upon the participants believing it to be their own plan. I fear, therefore, that evolution has taken or been given a wrong turn: that it has, as it were, branched off from the homo sapiens route. The development

consciousness of Finance is being diminished but its powers
are not being transferred.

We have been assured that there will be close contact,
consultation, exchange of information, goodwill and co-operation between the ministers involved and, of course, it has
been pointed out that there must be cabinet discussion and
resolution of major issues. As I see it, the situation is such as
to engender doubts and render these assurances necessary. I
have no difficulty in believing that there will be the utmost
co-operation and good working relations between the two
ministers immediately involved and that they will overcome
the risks to which the new structures expose them. But structures should not depend for their viability on the qualities of
particular holders of ministerial office. The new system will
require more co-ordination both between departments and at
government level. Of its nature it opens the door to friction.
The new Department will be another cog in the administrative
machine. I state that as a fact and not with any pejorative
implication. I raise the question whether the arrangement
could be expected to work well if, say, a Coalition were in
power and the Minister for Finance were drawn from one
party and the Minister for Economic Planning and Development from the other. Indeed, what might happen if there were
a personality clash between ministers of the same party in
power?

The Tánaiste has referred to the heavy strain already
imposed on the Minister for Finance who is also Minister for
the Public Service. I appreciate this. But could not one have
tried to ease that strain in other ways? For example, by using
the proposed Ministers of State to assist the Minister for
Finance, on the one hand, with the function of controlling
public expenditure and raising money and, on the other, with
his public service functions, leaving the Minister himself more
time for the all-important development responsibility.

I would concede that, for one reason or another, the Department of Finance have in recent years tended to let slip their
planning function. I think, however, that the Tánaiste was
less than fair to himself and his predecessors when he said in
the Dáil that no Minister for Finance had ever effectively
exercised it. Disenchantment with the more detailed kind of

planning had become pretty general in Western Europe even before the destructive impact of the oil crisis. Then the difficulties of the time were given as a reason for not attempting to take a longer view and the Minister for Finance largely concentrated on short-term problems and devoted much of his time and energy to tax legislation rather than development planning. The growing unruliness of our society – the evident lack of solidarity, of a sense of community inter-dependence – were also inhibiting factors. As I have already explained, I entertain, optimistically maybe, the hope that these difficulties might at least be somewhat eased by the educative and persuasive process of consultation that should precede the final settlement of a plan.

I do not believe that experience, here or elsewhere, establishes the need for a drastic change in planning responsibilities. The Department of Finance is competent, and the Minister for Finance is well placed within government, to discharge these responsibilities. Confirming that they rest with the Minister for Finance and equipping that Minister with the aid and resources to discharge them would, I submit, be preferable from the point of view of logic, order, unity and strength to the creation of a new ministry.

I realise I shall probably not make any converts to this view and I hope that what I have said will not be taken amiss. I feel it my duty to speak here according to my judgment and experience. While I do regard the new structure as a second best, I certainly do not wish it to fail. I am sure that the ministers concerned and the civil service will do their best to make it work. In the interests of national progress I hope the new ministry will successfully overcome the disabilities and strains to which I have been referring and that time will disprove my misgivings.[1]

## Note to Chapter 9

[1] The Department was abolished by the Fianna Fáil Government following Mr. C. J. Haughey's election as Taoiseach in December 1979. Most of its functions reverted to the Department of Finance; some were assumed by the Department of the Taoiseach.

*Lady Lavery as represented on first series of Irish legal tender notes.*

# 10  The Central Bank 1969-76 – A Retrospect

My predecessor as Governor of the Central Bank, Dr Maurice Moynihan, has written the history of currency and central banking since the foundation of the state, stopping short modestly of his own constructive period as Governor (1960-69).[1] I have set down, for the archives of the Central Bank and future historians, a memoir of my term as Governor, from 1969 to 1976. Here, in what I call a retrospect, I offer from my experience some general reflections not likely, I hope, to fall foul of the official secrets code!

I should like first to take stock of the broad changes in the economic, financial and social scene which marked this troubled septennium. The net increase in GNP from 1969 to 1976 was about 25 per cent in real terms, the nominal rise being from about £1,300 million to nearly £3,700 million. Consumer prices doubled; the mid-February index for 1976 being 236 as against 103 for 1969. Agricultural incomes increased by 175 per cent, non-agricultural by just over 200 per cent. The cumulative balance of payments deficit on current account was over £600 million. Government expenditure, current and capital combined, rose as a percentage of GNP from 38 per cent to 49 per cent. The gross capital liabilities of the state trebled from £914 million to £2,660 million; outstanding foreign debt accounted for a mere £55 million in March 1969, had risen to £523 million by March 1976 and had topped £1,000 million by the end of 1976!

The rise in unit wage costs in Ireland relative to Britain and other competitor countries was a critical concern of the Central Bank. Taking 1970=100, unit wage costs in Ireland had risen to 134 by 1973, as against 121 for Britain but by 1975 they had come virtually level (198 versus 196) and for 1976 the comparative indexes were 213 and 221. By contrast, the 1976 index for Germany was 135 and for the United States 142, figures which vividly illustrate how essential for competitiveness was the sharp decline in the exchange rate of the pound in relation to the deutschemark and the dollar.

During the period the population was increasing at the rate of one per cent per annum but employment was not expanding fast enough to absorb both the new additions to the labour force and those still leaving agriculture. The 'flight from the land' exceeded the number of new jobs in industry and services; unemployment increased from 60,000 to 90,000 and emigration continued, but on a moderate scale.

The primary responsibility of the Central Bank is to do what it can to 'safeguard the integrity of the currency' (Section 6 of the Central Bank Act, 1942). The meaning of this phrase was discussed in the first Report (for 1968/9) of my term of office. It was pointed out that, as regards integrity in the sense of stability of internal purchasing power, the Irish pound had shared the fate of other currencies – erosion by price increases. It had not been within the power of the Irish Central Bank, or indeed of other Central Banks, to prevent this depreciation of money, though the obligation to do everything possible must remain binding. The specific provisions of Irish currency legislation placed most emphasis on external stability, in the particular sense of parity between the exchange rate of the Irish pound and the pound sterling. The 'integrity' of the Irish pound in this sense had never been in real danger – effective action had always been taken to correct excessive balance of payments deficits which, had they been allowed to cause an undue loss of external reserves, could eventually have jeopardised the exchange rate.

The Bank never held the view, apparently favoured by some economists, that the parity link with sterling provided an automatic and painless mechanism of adjustment, obviating the need for concern about relative deviations of incomes, prices and costs as between Ireland and Britain, and, therefore, for domestic initiatives to correct them. The Bank acknowledged the long-term influence of the parity link in bringing about a convergence of prices – though this could be disturbed by different policies in the two countries regarding indirect taxes and subsidies – but it never saw the adjustment process as a painless one. If prices tended higher here and, in particular, if production costs were being raised faster here by immoderate pay increases, the 'adjustment' took the unpleasant form of diminished competitiveness, loss of jobs in affected industries, stimulation of imports and widening of the external payments deficit. Restrictive fiscal and monetary measures were then called for to protect national solvency. The form of inflation produced by excessive public and private expenditure, supported by borrowing from the banks and abroad, was in the Bank's view no less dangerous than that which revealed itself directly in price and costs increases; both had adverse effects on the external balance and correcting the imbalance necessarily jeopardised employment. The path of virtue was to keep the Irish trend in prices and costs slightly below the British so as to give a competitive edge to a widening range of Irish goods and services and thus assist the expansion of exports and jobs.

The three principal domestic threats to the integrity of the currency, even in the limited sense of parity with sterling, were picked out for comment in the 1968/9 Report – excessive public expenditure and borrowing, excessive credit creation, excessive income increases. Up to and including the final comment for which I was responsible – that of the Winter Bulletin of 1975 already quoted – the Bank's criticism focussed on the errors or deficiencies of fiscal, monetary and incomes policies.

On fiscal policy, the tenor of the Bank's views is indicated in the following passage from its 1975 Report:

> The course of public expenditure, taxation and borrowing in recent years was the subject of a special article in the 1972/73 Report. The rate of increase in public expenditure has swept ahead even of gross domestic expenditure in money terms. Public finance is absorbing a rising proportion of total national output; total public expenditure, current and capital, which represented 30 per cent of GNP in 1961/62, now represents at least 42 per cent of GNP. This drive to obtain extra resources for public purposes conflicts with private spending aspirations and sets up inflationary tensions. Prices and costs are raised by the need to increase

indirect taxes and by the general effect on wage and salary demands of what people consider to be excessive Government 'take'. In effect, no attention is paid to the argument that price increases due to taxes imposed to redistribute income should not reckon as a basis for further income increases. The private sector in general has shown itself unwilling to yield up the purchasing power which the Government seeks to obtain for public purposes through taxation and borrowing.

The rapid increase in current budget deficits is occasioned primarily by rising pay, social welfare and debt service provisions, not matched by equivalent taxation. The Bank does not accept that current deficits on this scale are justifiable as a means of expanding demand; this need, when it arises, could more appropriately be met by increased capital expenditure. The external indebtedness of the Government and State bodies already exceeds the total of Ireland's external reserves and is mounting fast. There is special cause for anxiety when increased current expenditure, which makes no contribution to relieving the real burden of the debt redemption process, is one of the main objects of such borrowing.

The Bank never entertained extravagant notions about the scope or efficacy of monetary policy in the context of what was a virtual monetary union with Britain. Again, let me quote a typical comment (from the 1975 Report):

The Central Bank has only a limited capacity to safeguard the integrity of the currency in the sense of maintaining its domestic purchasing power as distinct from its exchange value in relation to sterling. The reasons were fully stated by the Bank in its 1968/69 Report. It is appropriate that credit policy, being part of general economic policy, should be aligned with the basic economic objectives of the Government. These objectives are, however, not always mutually compatible and the policies actually pursued do not always result in their being fully realised. The Central Bank has not failed to draw attention to the principal forces which tend to frustrate achievement of the desired aims and, instead, to promote excessive inflation. These forces have been so strong in recent years that an attempt by the Central Bank to suppress excessive inflation by severely restricting the money supply would produce an unacceptable degree of economic and social distress. In such circumstances, the Bank's purpose, having given the best advice it can on policies and objectives, is to try not to aggravate inflation by allowing a larger increase in the money supply than will permit the attainment of the major economic objectives of the Government.

The whole subject was reviewed at greater length in a lecture to the Commerce and Economic Society of UCD on 5 November 1975, which was reproduced in the Winter 1975 Bulletin of the Central Bank. This will serve as a record of the role the Bank then saw itself qualified to fulfil in relation to monetary policy.

The Bank showed that it was prepared to use its limited, but by no means negligible, powers in the qualitative as well as the quantitative sense both to support expansionary policies with which it agreed and in other circumstances to exercise a restraining influence on both the import and the domestic creation of money. The major weakness was not any lack of loyal conformity on the part of the commercial banking system but the possibility of such restrictions being over-borne by the government's financial needs and its discretion to borrow abroad.

In the last resort, of course, and particularly if the Bank were to attempt, even with full government backing, an unacceptably severe restriction on private sector access to credit, a large part of the money needed by Irish trade and industry could have been supplied by British financial sources: only the small concerns and the less well-off individuals would be left out in the cold.

Monetarist doctrine has impressive theoretical coherence but I was always sceptical of attempts to substitute an automatic regulator for management by society of its own affairs, however imperfect at times such management can be. I cannot see how a democratic community could reasonably be expected to accept being placed in a monetary strait-jacket by its own

government unless it were persuaded of the equity and desirability of such a discipline. It is unthinkable that any government would be able to use monetary policy, even if it were so
minded, to grind trade unions or other important interest
groups into submission. I continue to believe that democracy
can be made to work, not through reliance on automatic
regulation or enforced discipline, but through informed discussion of options and objectives, leading to a wide measure of
acquiescence and cooperation. Statutory regulation has its
proper place in 'traffic-sign' situations, where, in its absence,
chaos would rule and where its presence serves to protect an
orderly majority against disruptive and selfish actions by a
small minority. The Central Bank has, for example, always
expressed its support in principle for the underpinning by law
of agreements on pay reached by representative bodies showing
at least some regard for the national interest.

Guided by this socio-political philosophy, no less than by
recognition of the limited scope in an open economy for Keynesian ideas of demand expansion, the Central Bank has devoted
a great deal of its attention and advice to the importance of
general acquiescence in a moderate rate of growth of money
incomes. This is how it understood the rather pretentious term
*incomes policy*. No effort was spared to explain the harm that
could be done by disproportionate income increases in raising
production costs, destroying competitiveness, enlarging balance of payments deficits and in all these ways putting jobs at
risk. A few typical extracts from Bank Bulletins follow:

> The Bank sees national policy as being concerned with
> raising both *real* incomes and the number of acceptable jobs
> .... these aims can be thwarted by the pursuit of unduly
> high rates of increase in *money* incomes. When money
> incomes increase much faster than productivity, costs and
> prices are inevitably raised. If this happens faster in Ireland
> than elsewhere, the market prospects for Irish products are
> curtailed and, since exports are the key to expansion, eco-
> nomic and social progress is retarded. A more moderate and
> orderly evolution of money incomes is seen by the Bank as
> a necessary element of any general policy directed towards
> achieving full employment. The Bank is convinced that

economic expansion and community welfare will be better assured by acceptance of the attainable real improvements in income by way of more moderate money increases coupled with a slower rise in prices. (Spring 1974).

Increased productivity, as indicated by the expected national growth rate, is now a normal element in pay increases. Any further recognition of productivity for pay purposes must tend to raise costs and prices. If a high inflation rate is to be avoided, it is only in genuine cases of exceptional improvements in productivity and even then only in moderation that increases in pay over and above the agreed 'national' norms can safely be allowed. (Spring 1974)

There is no provision for ensuring that collective bargaining is informed or guided by a realistic assessment of the outlook at home or abroad or of the longer-term national interest. Advertence to the prospects ahead, and particularly to the conditions on which maximum progress depends, and a broad consensus as to the social and economic development principles to which Government policies will conform, appear to be essential elements in a process which so largely determines the competitive position of Irish goods and services and, indirectly, the rate of national progress. (Spring, 1974)

The price of job preservation is income restraint. (Spring, 1975)

It is becoming more widely understood that the present rate of increase in money incomes of those at work not only closes off new jobs but causes additional unemployment and makes it extremely dangerous to attempt remedial action by way of further expansion of Government expenditure, requiring more massive foreign borrowing. Granted a lower level of income increases for those still at work, there need be no fear of any fall in total demand; on the contrary, as the Bank has repeatedly pointed out, public and private productive spending could then be expanded in the interests of employment both with greater effect and with less risk. (Summer, 1975)

Real incomes can over time rise only in line with real growth; attempts to secure more than this by way of inordinate increases in money incomes merely add to production costs, damage competitiveness and cause unemployment. To give policy-making perspective and consistency a flexible form of medium-term planning, with full involvement of the major economic interests, is desirable. The course of public expenditure as well as of personal incomes needs to be well ordered in the interests of national progress. (Winter, 1975)

One must conclude that, however important its licensing and regulatory functions vis-a-vis the commercial banks and its power to create and issue money, the Central Bank's main function as a public authority cannot be other than that of trying to influence government policy in favour of protecting to the utmost the value of the monetary unit. The advisory role of the Bank is supremely important. Whether the advice proferred in the 1969-76 period ought to have been better observed, or more largely ignored, is best left to historians to judge. Nevertheless, some impressions of one close to the events may not be out of place.

As to how far advice was listened to, appearances might incline one to take a pessimistic view. There was rarely ever more than a formal acknowledgment of the Bank's written submissions, and views expressed orally were usually heard in silence, though at worst in a neutral rather than a hostile atmosphere. One may, however, suppose that warnings of dangerous trends and reminders of what was right did not fall entirely on deaf ears but had a least some corrective or restraining effect. I need not underline that this is a more qualified hypothesis than Dr Moynihan's conclusion:

However sceptical it might sometimes be regarding the wisdom of Government economic policies, it had no reason to fear any calamitous departure from the paths of financial orthodoxy, and it was supported by the knowledge that its advice had been received with, at least, understanding and sympathy by successive Ministers for Finance.[2]

In the period I am reviewing, the temptations to stray from financial orthodoxy were stronger and not always resisted. The Central Bank's advice, expressed both in private and in public, rarely produced converts in government circles, though it may have heightened a consciousness of guilt and been a safeguard against worse excesses! One salutary factor was the continued growth of the Central Bank's public reputation for independence, efficiency, honesty and technical competence: it may be presumed that this gave its public pronouncements greater weight.

Obviously, the Minister for Finance often shared the same concerns as the Bank. He was not always successful, however, in winning over his colleagues and a not surprising inconsistency can be detected at times between the economic analysis and remedial prescriptions in the opening part of budget speeches and the fiscal decisions announced later. The fact is that neither shortage of money – foreign borrowing on the whole was too readily available – nor any external discipline (such as might have arisen from effective co-ordination of EEC economic policies) operated to limit the freedom of government action.

I take it to be a not infrequent experience of Governors of Central Banks that they should leave office sadder if not wiser men. I am glad, at any rate, that I was able to maintain good terms personally with those whose policies I criticised. There is a great measure of satisfaction in having had a part in bringing the extended functions of the Central Bank into play, in seeing its efficiency increased and its status raised. It is served by a dedicated staff of women and men. In general, I think it can be claimed that a nationally useful relationship with the government was maintained with a high measure of independence, but with due observance of the basic principles of democracy; in other words, the Bank respected the government's final authority but faithfully discharged its critical and advisory functions and was, in no sense, 'the government's creature'.

## Notes to Chapter 10

[1] Currency and Central Banking in Ireland, 1922-60, Maurice Moynihan, published by Central Bank of Ireland, 1975.
[2] Op. cit, page 475.

# 11 Credit Creation for Government

The older Central Banks, like the Bank of England, owed their origin to a monarch's financial need: their first function was to add to the money supply in his favour. But the power of the purse is quickly recognised and comes to be enjoyed with all the greater fervour if clothed with respectability and responsibility. So, as experience grew and understanding deepened, Central Banks came to see themselves, and to be seen, as controllers of the money supply for the public good. They still created money for governments in times of war and difficulty – preferably within a framework of controls over incomes and supplies. But, especially since the First World War, the public have looked to their Central Banks as protectors of the currency, as a brake on the present-day tendency of governments, no less than the kings of old, to debase the value of money by over-spending in relation to resources.

In accordance with this view of the Central Bank as part of a system of essential checks and balances, a great deal of independence had, by the time of the Second World War, been acquired by the older institutions, or been expressly conceded by statute to the more newly established. In the wake of the War, and under the stress of obligations assumed in relation to economic growth and full employment, there has been a tendency for governments to withdraw power from Central Banks. Illusory equations between scarce resources and unlimited aspirations can be written only if the supply of money is elastic and its value is allowed to decline through inflation. Friedman, insisting on control of supply as a condition of sound money, is the great theoretical upholder of the independence of Central Banks but their position for some time has been a tense and uneasy one everywhere, as they strive to carry out a role which is no longer, in the democratic context, unambiguous or fully within their capacity in a technical sense. Are they, in Sir Stafford Cripps' phrase, mere creatures of the government, bound to supply the money required by government policies? Or do they still have some obligation, exercisable within a democratic constitutional framework, to restrain excesses and protect the value of money?

The Central Bank of Ireland has always taken the latter view of its responsibility and, for that reason, has been particularly concerned not to allow governments unduly free access to credit created by the commercial banks or the Central Bank itself. It is not always easy to ward off attempts by the government to ease its residual financing problems by obtaining money from the Central Bank. Originally, as mentioned already, many Central Banks were founded to meet this very need. Moreover, economic theory recognises certain conditions – of under-utilisation of human and material resources – when a higher level of equilibrium might be attained by an expansionary policy. In such circumstances the monetary authority would not only be entitled but in the interests of the economy would be obliged to add to the active money supply either by taking up government paper or in some less direct way.

At the same time, as the explosion in current budget deficits in Ireland in the 1970s shows, a legitimate inch in financial matters may be stretched to an inordinate mile. 'The appetite grows by what it's fed on' and, if a residual source of finance is too readily available to governments, there is every risk of its being liberally drawn upon, whether the economic circumstances justify this or not. So there has been a strongly critical approach in Ireland, as elsewhere, to government representations or demands for Central Bank accommodation.

It had been suggested in *Economic Development* (1958) that future additions to legal tender note requirements should be backed by Irish government securities. This would have allowed only a small annual creation of credit by the Central Bank for the government but would have recognised, to a minor degree, the state's seignorial prerogative to issue notes as well as coin. Dr Moynihan, who became Governor of the Central Bank in 1960, sponsored a more flexible proposition which at the same time protected the Central Bank's discretion, that of making a 'balance in the General Fund' an eligible asset of the Legal Tender Note Fund and thus enabling money from the latter Fund to be siphoned into the General Fund. This Fund had power to invest in Irish government securities and so create deposits for government in the Central Bank. A deposit in the Central Bank can be as effective a base for credit expansion as legal tender notes. Legislative provision was made accordingly. It was, however, with great reluctance that the Central Bank yielded to a government request for some £20 million of short-term funds in 1965/6, a time of difficulty in the dollar capital market.

Indeed, until the Central Bank Act, 1971 became law, there was a first-line protection in that the Central Bank was not formally the government's banker. This function had been the historical prerogative of the Bank of Ireland but it had, since the Second World War, outstripped a single bank's capacity and had, in effect, been shared by the Associated Banks. These participated in government financing, normally by way of three-months Exchequer Bills, according to a deposits-related formula and with a limited right to rediscount these Bills at the Central Bank. The volume of Bills naturally tended to grow and from time to time a funding into medium-term stock occurred. The Associated Banks never displayed any marked eagerness to take up Exchequer Bills – or medium-term stock for that matter – and I have a vivid memory of the difficulties which Frank Aiken encountered, as Minister for Finance in the immediate post-war years (the 'Daltonian Era'), in persuading them to extend cheap credit to the government.

It is largely due to Dr D. S. A. Carroll, first as Governor of the Bank of Ireland and then, from May 1970, as a Banking Director of the Central Bank, that Associated Bank credit for government was fixed in scale, rationalised and largely legitimised. The secondary liquidity ratio, first appointed by the Central Bank in September 1972 at 31 per cent (corresponding to the proportion of Associated Bank resources then held in Irish Government Bills and short-term securities) became 30 per cent for years until November 1979 when it was reduced to 25 per cent. This ratio has fixed, for both Banks and government, the normal proportion of accruing bank resources to be allocated for government purposes. The primary liquidity ratio – the proportion of banking resources to be kept in cash or with the Central Bank – was originally fixed at 12 per cent for the Associated Banks (reduced to 10 per cent in November 1979 and varied from time to time since). Although interest is paid on deposits with the Central Bank it is not as high a return as the banks could earn on other uses of the money and a high primary ratio could, therefore, affect profitability as well as lending capacity. Non-Associated Banks have been progressively subjected to appropriately differentiated primary and secondary liquidity ratios.

The secondary liquidity ratio is thus the automatic regulator of the commercial banks' contribution to government financing. It had been part of the arrangement in 1969 for centralisation of sterling holdings in the Central Bank that the Bank would aim at providing a dealing flexibility in the securities held by the Central Bank comparable to that which they had possessed in relation to British government securities. This was largely achieved with the help of the Department of Finance, who agreed to diversify the choice of securities available in the three-months to five-years range. The Central Bank undertook the task of managing and, where necessary, supporting the market in such securities so that the Associated Banks would be assured of a high degree of flexibility and liquidity as well as reasonable profit opportunities, so far as the securities held as 'secondary liquidity' were concerned.

'Secondary liquidity' can become cash when the Central Bank agrees to rediscount Exchequer Bills or to buy other short-term government securities from the banks. In this indirect way the Central Bank can itself replace the commercial banks as a source of finance for government. Moreover, since it has been since January 1972 the government's banker, it can also directly finance the government by providing it with overdraft facilities or by buying government securities from the Department of Finance.

When I became Governor of the Central Bank on 1 March 1969, I inherited a virtually 'clean sheet' situation: rediscounted Exchequer Bills of only £3.6 million were held by the Central Bank, apart from £20.5 million of 6 per cent Funding Loan which had been raised by the government in 1965/6 and was to be repaid fully before the end of 1969. The amount of

Exchequer Bills held by the Associated Banks grew to £102 million by March 1972 but this was within their secondary liquidity requirement and no Bills were under rediscount with the Central Bank at that date. It was only from 1972 onwards, and particularly after the quadrupling of oil prices at the end of 1973, that government borrowing took a great leap forward and that the question whether the Central Bank should create money for the government or whether the government's residual needs should be met by foreign borrowing became a live and important issue, an issue made all the more difficult by the accepted need for *some* budgetary action to mitigate the constrictive impact of the oil crisis on economic growth.

Even in the course of 1972/3 it seemed for a time that the Exchequer might need more from the banking system than the £50 million which 'secondary liquidity' purchases by the banks were expected to yield but, because of revenue buoyancy, this risk did not materialise.

However, before the end of 1973, Exchequer difficulties, despite large external borrowing, were such as to impel resort to the Central Bank for £25 million (later scaled down to £20 million) for general purposes, in addition to £8 million which the Bank had provided for the Exchequer to enable it to finance the Agricultural Credit Corporation. The Bank agreed to increase its holdings of short-dated government securities but made it clear that it regarded such assistance as temporary and abnormal. The Bank's view was that, in any given circumstances, there was a limit to the total amount of credit compatible with monetary order and the real growth needs of the economy. The financing of government expenditure beyond this limit would have powerful inflationary implications and could entail countervailing and possibly harmful curtailment of credit for the private sector. An easing of monetary policy could serve only to aggravate the inflationary pressures emanating from the rise in oil prices and the operation of the national pay agreement. Reliance on the Central Bank as a major and continuing source of finance for the Exchequer would be at variance with the responsibility which the Bank must retain of regulating the total money supply so that it accorded with national economic objectives.

The Central Bank considered that, in a completely non-inflationary situation (with stable prices and no balance of payments deficit), there would be only one policy reason for adding to the expenditure financed by the community's current earnings and savings, namely, a desire to use national productive capacity more fully, assuming it was not already being fully used. In those circumstances, to pump new money into circulation in a managed way, either through the banking system or by borrowing abroad, would make sense. Provided it did not go too far, it would raise production without significantly raising prices, and any temporary deficit in the balance of payments would represent an import of capital to supplement current domestic savings and generate higher real income. This seemed a reasonable interpretation of Keynesian theory in the circumstances postulated.

The actual situation, however, was quite different. Cost and price inflation was rampant and external payments heavily in deficit. The Central Bank's attitude was that it would play its part in providing liquidity for the commercial banks to enable them to extend credit to the extent necessary to achieve the accepted economic aim of attaining as high a level as possible of domestic production without accelerating the already high and inescapable rate of increase in costs and prices or aggravating the outsize deficit already envisaged in the balance of payments. Monetary policy should be aimed at moderating inflationary pressures while at the some time supporting a sustainable rate of growth of the economy. It would be undesirable and improper that Central Bank credit creation, for government or banks, should itself generate additional inflationary pressure. Because the Central Bank accepts that monetary policy cannot correct the effects of expansionary fiscal policy, it strives all the more to avoid making these effects worse.

So that the financial year might coincide with the calendar year, as in other EEC countries, budgetary dispositions were made in 1974 for the nine months April to December and the financial year was brought into line with the calendar year from 1975 on. The budget deficit on current account for the nine months to December 1974 was the first of a series of very large deficits which had explosive effects on government borrowing requirements. The Central Bank helped towards financing the needs of the 'short year' 1974 by introducing a secondary liquidity ratio for the industrial and other banks (who had hitherto been exempt) and this produced close on £20 million for the Exchequer. There was also a provisional commitment on the part of the Central Bank to purchase some £20 million of government securities from the public in order to ensure adequate domestic liquidity but, in the event, the government's foreign borrowing exceeded original expectations to an extent which obviated any need to create liquidity by direct Central Bank action.

It will be no surprise, however, that the Central Bank should again be seen as a possible source of much-needed government finance in 1975. The Bank found itself in a quandary on valid economic grounds. It could, and did, argue strenuously for what it considered to be the right budgetary policy but once budgetary decisions were taken, and the extent of total government borrowing thus determined, the Central Bank had to consider what were the least objectionable ways of meeting the given requirement. This might well mean altering the balance between foreign borrowing and domestic credit creation. There was little point in the government undergoing the 'discipline' of foreign borrowing when such borrowing was all too easy and had the effect in part of building up external reserves unnecessarily. In 1975 there was a particular tactical reason for wishing to see a reduction rather than an increase in these reserves: Ireland was interested in qualifying for access to the Oil Facility (easy-term loans) organised by the International Monetary Fund.[1] There was, therefore, a case for restricting foreign borrowing so as to avoid increasing the external reserves and to have correspondingly greater recourse to domestic credit creation.

The Bank's report for 1975 recorded that in the previous year, when Exchequer borrowing abroad amounted to about £160 million, the external monetary reserves rose by £60 million. 'Although it would not be inappropriate that reserves should over time increase proportionately to external payments and liabilities, the Bank takes the view that it would not be in the best interests of the economy in 1975 if official foreign borrowing were undertaken to an extent – if practicable –

which would cause a substantial increase in the external monetary reserves. Rather should attention be given primarily to the optimum financing of the economy's external current deficit, official foreign borrowing being limited to such an amount as would not entail any significant increase in the external monetary reserves.'

A restriction of foreign borrowing to the minimum was stated to be desirable on various grounds:

> Rapidly increasing external indebtedness would call into question the economy's continuing creditworthiness and increase the costs of foreign borrowing, including those arising from the appreciation of currencies in which it is necessary to borrow. It could reduce Ireland's freedom of action in regard to economic policy and could give rise to refinancing difficulties when loans matured. Foreign borrowing, in any case, entails a transfer of income abroad in order to service and repay the debt and this burden becomes all the heavier if the original borrowing has not been incurred for productive purposes.

The Bank went on to state that adoption of the policy of not borrowing more abroad in 1975 than was needed to maintain the external reserves at or about their end-1974 level carried with it certain technical consequences. The government's financial needs had to be met to a greater extent from domestic sources but arranging for this presented 'no problem of principle' for the Bank, provided the basic economic objectives for the year were adhered to, public expenditure and borrowing were kept within the June budget framework and at least the incomes restraint proposed in that budget were made effective. It was essential that these aims be realised if a start were to be made in winding down the rate of inflation. So long, however, as these objectives were pursued, the particular financing methods adopted were 'primarily of technical significance'. The immediate effects on the money supply and bank liquidity of financing government expenditure in part through the Central Bank were 'much the same as when recourse is had to external borrowing'. The Bank was, therefore, prepared to help in financing the Exchequer borrowing requirement, though it reiterated that it could not be regarded as a permanent source of finance for the government and 'must ensure that the level of the official external reserves is adequate, in 1976 and later years, to finance the higher deficits which will be associated with a resumption of economic growth'.

In fact the government drew £50 million from the Central Bank in 1975 through increased purchases by the Bank of short-term government securities. Flexible use was also made of the overdraft facility which had first been arranged in July 1974 subject to a maximum of £25 million. To ensure that the overdraft did not become a permanent source of Exchequer finance it was stipulated that the account be in credit for at least 30 days in every year. The Bank's view was that, if the facility were greatly expanded or left open-ended, the finance provided could no longer be regarded as temporary. If the scope for utilisation were greatly increased, it was likely that the average utilisation would rise *pari passu*. This would leave the Bank in the unacceptable position of providing the Exchequer with what would virtually be hard-core finance at a level which it could not anticipate and over which it would have little or no control. The Bank in fact conceded an intermediate increase in the overdraft limit and, as a quite exceptional and temporary measure, allowed the overdraft to run to £70 million to finance 'intervention' purchases of beef and dairy products pending arrangement for the financing of such purchases by the Associated Banks on foot of discountable Bills.

The Bank's grudging reaction to demands for money for Exchequer purposes was a function of its apprehensions about the rapidly deteriorating state of the public finances. The Bank was particularly out of sympathy with the deliberate incurring of massive deficits on current account.[2] The Exchequer borrowing requirement had risen from £151 million for 1972/73 to £601 million for 1975, with the prospective need for 1976 even higher. Foreign indebtedness already exceeded total external reserves.

Under pressure to contribute to an Exchequer borrowing requirement of unprecedented size, the Bank's stand was that it would not make any precise commitment in advance. Otherwise the Bank would be expected to become a regular contributor on a massive and predetermined scale to Exchequer financing, thus losing any discretion as to the circumstances in which a limited amount of assistance might be deemed appropriate by the Bank itself. For 1976, therefore, the Bank would not at the outset commit itself beyond the £50 million contribution of 1975. The Bank had in its Report for 1974 and in its Summer Bulletin of 1975 recognised the similarity, in terms of technical consequences and effect on the money supply, of the residual financing of Exchequer requirements by the Central Bank and through foreign borrowing. Indeed, the Bank has indicated that foreign borrowing carried such disquieting implications that it should be kept to a minimum and incurred only for capital purposes. This required primarily that the total public sector borrowing requirement be curbed and as much of it as possible supplied from domestic non-bank sources. It also required implementation of the 'firm intention' of the government, as declared in the Minister's budget statement on 28 January 1976, 'to phase out the present current deficit over a three-year period'.

It is revealing to put into context with total Exchequer borrowing the contribution which has come from credit creation by the banking system – Central Bank and commercial banks combined. This contribution shares with foreign borrowing the odium of being classified as a monetary rather than a non-monetary source of funds. The non-monetary sources are small savings and net purchases by the 'domestic non-bank private sector' of government securities. These are treated as neutral in the sense that they represent voluntary surrenders of existing purchasing power for government purposes; in other words, they involve no net increase in the money supply and cannot be condemned as inflationary. Monetary sources of finance, by contrast, do involve an addition to domestic purchasing power, whether by creation of credit or the conversion of foreign borrowings into internal money; they must be regarded as inflationary when, as in the period under review, they cause national expenditure to exceed national production and give rise to heavy external deficits. Table 1 shows what happened between 1972 and 1976.

## Table 1: Financing of Exchequer borrowing, 1972-6 (£m)

| | 1972-73 | 1973-74 | Apr.-Dec.'74 | 1975 | 1976 | Total |
|---|---|---|---|---|---|---|
| *Non-Monetary Sources* | | | | | | |
| Small Savings | 23 | 18 | 18 | 39 | 53 | 151 |
| Net sales of securities to domestic non-bank private sector | 42 | 20 | 28 | 101 | 114 | 305 |
| Sub-total | 65 | 38 | 46 | 140 | 167 | 456 |
| | | | | | | |
| *Monetary Sources* | | | | | | |
| *Domestic commercial Banks* (net purchase of government securities and lending to Intervention Agency) | 52 | 50 | 74 | 233 | 81 | 490 |
| *Central Bank* Increase in holdings of Government securities | – | 24 | – | 50 | – | 74 |
| Change in Government held balances* | – | +31 | +29 | −79 | −68 | −87 |
| | | | | | | |
| *Foreign Borrowing* Direct | 22 | 47 | 149 | 164 | 324 | 706 |
| Net sales of Government securities to non-residents | – | – | – | 90 | – | 90 |
| *Other* ...        ... | 12 | 1 | 13 | 3 | 2 | 31 |
| Total | 151 | 191 | 311 | 601 | 506 | 1,760 |

*A positive sign indicates a reduction, a negative sign an increase.

The table is reassuring in so far as it confirms that Central Bank lending to government made a very small contribution to deficit financing over this period; indeed, any inflationary effect it might have had was offset by a more than counter-vailing increase in government deposits with the Central Bank. Credit creation by the commercial banks contributed 28 per cent of the government's borrowing needs, while foreign borrowing in various forms yielded over 45 per cent. The contribution from the non-inflationary source, private savings, was only 26 per cent.

The Exchequer borrowing requirement rose strongly over

the period 1977 to 1982 – from £545 million in 1977 to £1,945 million last year – and its ratio to GNP became much higher. The 10 per cent ratio of 1977 soared to 17 per cent for 1981 before falling back a little last year. Foreign borrowing had to supply over 55 per cent of total government needs while domestic credit creation's share was 14 per cent augmented to nearly 16 per cent when allowance is made for the expansionary effect of net withdrawals from government balances with the Central Bank. The details are given in Table 2.

## Table 2: Financing of Exchequer borrowing, 1977-82 (£m)

|  | 1977 | 1978 | 1979 | 1980 | 1981 | 1982 | Total |
|---|---|---|---|---|---|---|---|
| *Non-monetary sources* |  |  |  |  |  |  |  |
| Small Savings | 102 | 65 | 27 | 52 | 76 | 83 | 405 |
| Net sales of securities to domestic non-bank private sector | 144 | 157 | 256 | 319 | 204 | 504 | 1,584 |
| Sub-total | 246 | 222 | 283 | 371 | 280 | 587 | 1,989 |
| *Monetary sources* |  |  |  |  |  |  |  |
| *Domestic commercial banks* (net purchase of Government securities) | 154 | 67 | 104 | 96 | 120 | 250 | 791 |
| *Central Bank* |  |  |  |  |  |  |  |
| Increase in holdings of Government securities | – | – | 100 | 147 | – | – | 247 |
| Change in Government-held balances* | −66 | +165 | +21 | – | – | −22 | 98 |
| *Foreign borrowing* |  |  |  |  |  |  |  |
| Direct | 71 | 23 | 509 | 566 | 1285 | 1148 | 3,602 |
| Net sales of government securities to non-residents | 140 | 330 | −50 | 17 | −30 | −18 | 389 |
| *Other* | – | 3 | 42 | 20 | 67 | – | 132 |
| Total | 545 | 810 | 1009 | 1217 | 1722 | 1945 | 7,248 |

* A positive sign indicates a reduction, a negative sign an increase.

The circumstances in which the Central Bank lent £100 million to the government in late 1979 are explained in the Bank's Report for that year. Because of the liquidity stringency associated with entry to the European Monetary System earlier in

1979, the commercial banks had been allowed to fall short by about £100 million in honouring their secondary liquidity requirements. The Central Bank made good this amount to the Exchequer by increasing its portfolio of government securities. The further substantial purchase by the Central Bank of government stock in January 1980 was also connected with relieving strain on commercial bank liquidity and so indirectly facilitating their resumption of lending to the government through fulfilling their secondary liquidity ratio. This ratio had been reduced in November 1979 from 30 per cent to 25 per cent for the Associated Banks but without benefit to their liquidity position as they were required to reduce their indebtedness pro tanto to the Central Bank.

It would appear that the Central Bank has so far been able to hold to the principle of not being committed in advance to any contribution to the financing of the government's residual borrowing requirements. Moreover, the overdraft facility which the Central Bank provides as the government's banker has been of a strictly temporary nature and has always been repaid by year-end. The commercial banks, for their part, have not created credit for government beyond that entailed by their secondary liquidity requirements. Nevertheless, the support which excessive government borrowing has received from the banking system as a whole over the period 1972-82 has been substantial – a net £1,613 million, out of a total government borrowing requirement of £9,008 million. Domestic credit creation, however, is dwarfed by recourse to foreign borrowing of the order of £4,800 million. Regrettably, much of government borrowing over this period has been for purposes yielding no asset or future income: deficits on current account have totalled over £3,900 million.

Not content with the large amount of credit provided for them by the commercial banks, and the revenue yielded by normal taxation of bank profits (which are admitted not to be excessive), successive governments in recent years have extracted additional money from the banks through the imposition of levies of an arbitrary and discriminatory nature. These have amounted to £50 million over the years 1981 to 1983 inclusive.

Moreover, because the Banks are paid less than the market rate of interest on the liquidity deposits they must hold with the Central Bank, it can be said they suffer a hidden tax of about £20 million a year, which reaches the Exchequer via the enhanced profits of the Central Bank.

## Notes to Chapter 11

[1]In the event, access to this Facility was not available to Ireland.
[2]See Financial Turning-Points (Chapter 4).

*The first O'Neill–Lemass meeting at Stormont, 14 January 1965: T. K. Whitaker,*
*Seán Lemass, Terence O'Neill.*

# II   Northern Ireland

# 12   Ireland: The Way Forward

**Foreword (Mid-1981):**

*The notes for this article were completed before Easter [1981]. Sadly, in the interval before going to press, the tragedy of Northern Ireland has been aggravated by a further series of premature and unnecessary deaths, including deaths on hunger strike. The divisions in the community have been deepened, the antagonisms sharpened, the ambiguities made more confused and widespread. Fear and violence are being stimulated. The sensitivity and goodwill needed to support a constructive search for a peaceful solution are less in evidence. Yet the urgent responsibility of all in positions of power and influence to find such a solution is all the greater. It is only by clinging to reason, by supporting the democratic process and all in these islands who observe it, by resisting emotional pressures and provocation, and by being prepared to soften rigidities, that progress can be made towards the political settlement which is the only alternative to murderous anarchy. To consider how such a settlement might be approached is no less relevant and even more pressing now than ever before.*

Against a depressing background not only of continuing violence in Northern Ireland but also of worsening economic conditions in the two islands, with output down, inflation high and unemployment rising, the past year has seen political developments of as yet imponderable significance in the triangular relationship between London, Dublin and Belfast.

It is true that the British government's proposals in July 1980, for a revival, under new conditions, of devolved government in Northern Ireland failed to win adequate community consent, Unionists being unwilling to concede an acceptable degree of participation in domestic administration to non-

Unionists. The need to qualify straightforward majority rule in Northern Ireland in order to ensure the essence of democracy – the possibility of a change of government – is not yet recognised. Unionists themselves are at odds as to whether the kind of devolved government which might now be available to them (as distinct from the old Stormont), a continuation of direct rule, or more complete integration in the United Kingdom, would afford them the greatest security. On the other hand, relations between Dublin and London have been given greater potential in the Northern Ireland context by the rapport established in two meetings (in May and December, 1980) between the heads of government, Mr Haughey and Mrs Thatcher.

The viewpoint presented here is that of a peaceful and patient Irishman, born in the North but for long resident in the South, who hopes that the people of Northern Ireland will one day freely decide to join the people of the Republic in a new Irish constitutional framework and who meanwhile wishes the door to be kept open to such an eventuality.

The virtually intractable problem we are dealing with arises from the existence of a double minority in the island of Ireland, based on a conflict of nationality and compounded by differences of religion and tradition. This division is not one solely between Catholic Nationalists and Protestant Unionists. In Northern Ireland, there are Catholics who would prefer to stay in the United Kingdom, just as there are Protestants who would willingly be part of a united Ireland. It seems best to make do with the distinction between Nationalists, who aspire to being in an Irish political system, and Unionists, who wish to remain outside it. This negative formulation is preferable to defining Unionism as unqualified loyalty to a Westminster government or parliament. Dr Conor Cruise O'Brien has drawn a parallel between Ulster Unionists and the Whigs, each prepared to give only conditional allegiance to a Protestant Crown. Nationalists, so described, are a minority in Northern Ireland but a majority in Ireland as a whole, while Unionists are a majority in Northern Ireland but a minority in Ireland as a whole.

No political solution can peacefully endure which is strongly repugnant to either 'minority' or to either of the sovereign states in which they and their brethren live. This seems to rule out, at least under present conditions, both forms of complete integration, whether of Northern Ireland in the United Kingdom as if it were, say, Yorkshire or of Northern Ireland in a unitary all-Ireland republic. The conflict of nationality amongst the peoples of Northern Ireland involves both the United Kingdom and the Republic of Ireland as the sovereign 'motherlands' and no solution which ignores this is likely to be practicable. The United Kingdom government used to contend that Northern Ireland affairs were of concern only to the United Kingdom but this approach has been abandoned. The Sunningdale settlement of 1973 was agreed by both sovereign governments. The joint communiqué issued after the Thatcher/Haughey meeting of December 1980 acknowledged explicitly that the economic, social and political interests of the peoples of the two states 'are inextricably linked but that the full development of these links has been put under strain by division and dissent in Northern Ireland. . . . *In that context, they accepted the need to bring forward policies and proposals to achieve peace, reconciliation and stability. . . .*'

The need for political stability in Ireland, North and South, is not merely recognised by, but is a matter of profound concern to the United States, as well as to the European Economic Community. In the United States, responsible Irish-American political leaders, while supporting the Nationalist cause, have condemned recourse to violence and emphasized their interest in movement towards a political settlement to be reached by agreement. Violence and disorder in any part of the European Community are a threat to its effective functioning and to the harmonious achievement of its aims. In the island of Ireland, there are many potentialities of development which overlap the present jurisdictions and whose realisation requires a co-operative approach of the two administrations and their citizens. There are, moreover, broad areas of economic and social concern, including agriculture, energy, tourism, transport, in which the degree of common interest between North and South in Ireland is greater than between either and Great Britain. Undoubtedly, the European Economic Community would strongly favour a political settlement which would have the assent of the peoples of Northern Ireland.

It is only by setting aside the double minority and conflict of nationality difficulties that a clear case can be made for either form of integration. It is then possible to condemn a system of devolution or local autonomy for Northern Ireland as being much the worst solution because it would concentrate the conflict in a sort of cockpit and focus it forever on differences of nationality and religion rather than diffuse it over the wide variety of political, social and international issues which engage the interest of the citizens of a normal state. Many who favour integration in the United Kingdom assume that those in Northern Ireland who now feel more Irish than British would, at least in time, abandon this idiosyncrasy while their compatriots in the Republic would themselves surrender for ever their aspiration to a united Ireland. Conversely, many who seek integration of Northern Ireland in an all-Ireland republic see no reason why Unionists should not, in time, recognize their true allegiance as being to an Irish state and abandon their British connection. But considering everyone's reluctance to discard patriotic principles enshrined in song and story, and the efforts which extremists on both sides would make to prevent such a loyalty change, integration in either form does not seem to offer an open or safe route to 'peace, reconciliation and stability'.

Whatever route will lead in that direction is more likely to be both long and indirect, affording time for understanding and tolerance to grow in an equitable and progressive environment. Continuance for the time being of direct rule, short of integration, is more widely acceptable and much less dangerous than either the restoration of unqualified Unionist supremacy in Northern Ireland or absorption of Northern Ireland into a unitary system of administration from Westminster. Direct rule in its present form has, however, serious drawbacks for both the governing and the governed; both suffer because the procedures for democratic debate and assent are absent. As a system of administration, it has been authoritatively described as a 'complicated mess'. Direct rule, even if it be tolerable as a short-term second-best, is not a *permanent* solution and opposition to it, both North and South, would grow if it appeared to be so intended.

Complete integration of Northern Ireland into the United Kingdom is not a viable solution. Irrespective of the representation granted in Westminster, the minority in Northern Ireland would feel largely disfranchised since proportional representation does not apply to Westminster elections. They would, in any case, find themselves in an even more acute minority situation. They would be denied unilaterally their long-term interest in the possibility of a majority in Northern Ireland deciding eventually *not* to remain in the United Kingdom. Their nationalism would be suppressed for ever. Moreover, to most people in the Republic so direct a move to repudiate their historic aspirations would be offensive and unacceptable. Violence would become much more difficult to control.

Even Unionists are of two minds as to whether integration would afford them any real security against being thrown at some time by Westminster into the arms of the Republic. They have noted that opinion polls taken in Great Britain show a majority in favour of setting Northern Ireland adrift. They have in the past shown that their British allegiance is conditional on the preservation of their own dominance and way of life in a section of Ireland. So if the old Stormont supremacy cannot be regained – as most Unionists now accept – or, more generally, if their status is gravely threatened, a significant number of them might be disposed to go it alone in an independent 'Ulster', despite the financial and other consequences. To reign in hell could be the Rev Ian Paisley's political doom, though it must be hoped that he nurses higher and healthier ambitions.

The disarray amongst the principal Unionist groupings is brought sharply into focus by Mr Enoch Powell's attack on Mr Paisley as 'the most resourceful, inveterate and dangerous enemy of the Union' and his Democratic Unionist Party as 'a greater threat to the Union than the Foreign Office and the Provisional IRA rolled into one'. Mr Powell alleged that Mr Paisley had 'abjured the Union' by disavowing in 1977 the obligation of obedience to the United Kingdom parliament and that, by his call for a British referendum on the Northern Ireland link, he had 'repudiated for his part the principle that Ulster remains part of the Union as long as the majority of its own people so wish'. The Official Unionist Party, to which Mr Powell adheres, while not as committed to integration as he is, is fearful of the 'unique relationship' now recognised between London and Dublin and of the purport of the joint studies directed to 'the totality of relationships within these islands' in progress following the December 1980 meeting between Mrs Thatcher and Mr Haughey. The head of the Official Unionist Party, Mr Molyneaux, contends that, so long as the Irish Constitution maintains a claim to Northern Ireland, 'it is quite intolerable that the proposed study groups should purport to be finding ways to make relations between the United Kingdom and the Republic closer'.

That the joint studies are to extend to 'possible new institutional structures' as well as to 'citizenship rights, security matters, economic co-operation and measures to encourage mutual understanding' has, indeed, caused a good deal of concern in Unionist circles despite assurances by Mrs Thatcher that 'institutional', not 'constitutional', structures are in mind and that there is no derogation from the guarantee that Northern Ireland will remain a part of the United Kingdom as long as a majority in Northern Ireland so wish.

Claiming to be 'the elected leader of the Protestant people', the Rev Ian Paisley reacted in a Carsonite manner by organising a paramilitary demonstration on a dark Antrim hillside at which he described the joint talks as 'a conspiracy to destroy Northern Ireland' and declared 'we will stop at nothing if an attempt is made to hand the Loyalists of Northern Ireland over to those whom we believe to be the enemies of our country'. Fortunately, not all Unionists are swayed by such rhetoric; there has been open dissent and disapproval.

Despite the differences between them on the relative merits of devolution or full-scale integration in the United Kingdom, and the tendency of some to think even of independence, Northern Unionists have still one thing in common – their predominantly negative attitude to a United Ireland or perhaps one should say to the Republic for they do not seem to appreciate the imprint they could make on the character of a 32-county Ireland. There are some, of course, who feel more Irish than British and who would be quite content to be part of a new Ireland incorporating the changes that would inevitably accompany the transformation of the present 26-county Republic into an all-Ireland state, whether unitary or federal. But these are a small minority which is being alienated by the guerilla campaign of violence in the name of 'unity'. Nor have Unionists generally so far shown signs of being influenced by the consideration that time is against them – that they might within 50 years or so be outnumbered in Northern Ireland by Nationalists – and that they could strike a much harder bargain now with a Dublin government committed to give special consideration to their interests.

In all honesty, it must be confessed that, while the aspiration to unity is strong in the South, we in the Republic are little prepared for such an eventuality, psychologically and financially no less than in the constitutional sphere. Transitional arrangements would be necessary. Even the financial obligation involved could pose a major adjustment problem in the absence of easement provisions.

If the two integrationist solutions are seen as impracticable, the 'Independent Ulster' notion must also be set aside. It lacks broad support even amongst Unionists. The financial viability of such an entity, cut off from London and Brussels and from international recognition, would be doubtful; over 40 per cent of public expenditure in Northern Ireland is financed from Whitehall and Northern Ireland agriculture is supported by the EEC. Above all, Nationalist citizens would view with foreboding a re-installation of unqualified Unionist supremacy, supported by probably sectarian security forces. One is, therefore, forced to the conclusion that, if the dominant fear afflicting both sides in Northern Ireland – the fear of political, religious and economic subjection – is to be allayed, some intermediate solution must be found, and that both sides have a strong interest in seeking it.

Before the elements of such a solution are considered, it is necessary to look closer at the United Kingdom 'guarantee' to Northern Ireland – the constantly repeated assurance that Northern Ireland will remain in the United Kingdom so long as a majority in Northern Ireland so desire. The principal parties in the Republic, and the Social Democratic and Labour Party in the North, believe that the guarantee encourages intransigence on the part of Northern Unionists. The latter, on the other hand, view efforts to undermine the guarantee as no better than attempts to coerce them. Many of them, in any case, regard their own majority position in the North, and their will to defend their interests, as stronger than any paper guarantee; they will not submit to coercion, whatever Britain does about the guarantee. Independence might be their reluctant recourse in a *Götterdämmerung* situation.

It is accepted by the three political parties represented in Dáil Éireann that Irish unity can now come about, or be brought about, only by consent. This means that the people of Northern Ireland who, for historical reasons which we regret, are not at present in union with us, need never join us in a united Ireland of any kind if they do not, by a majority, so decide themselves. Formally, the majority required is not of Unionists but of the voting population of Northern Ireland but no one, with the Stormont experience in mind, would be so foolish as to disregard the majority's obligation to win as much assent as possible from the minority.

All three parties in the Republic, as I understand their position, would answer 'yes' to the following query:

> If you favour a united Ireland in any form – whether a unitary Republic or two States of similar status in a federation or confederation – do you accept that fulfilment of this aim must await the agreement of a majority of the people of Northern Ireland?

Yet this question tends to divide individuals into 'hawks' and 'doves' – those whose desires focus mainly on territorial integrity and political unity, regarding Britain as the chief wrongdoer, and those who hope for constructive accommodation between Irishmen in the ruling of Ireland, recognising the deeper and more complex roots of Partition.

The swing of the balance between these attitudes is, perhaps, most evident in the case of members of the Fianna Fáil Party. The sensitivity and flexibility shown by the leaders of the Party, from Mr de Valera on, have at times reverted to a pristine rigidity of principle. Mr de Valera, Mr Lemass and Mr Lynch recognised that, while the ideal form of re-unification was in a unitary republic, a federal solution, involving a substantial measure of local autonomy in Northern Ireland, would be a tolerable alternative. During their last period in Opposition, however, there was an apparent hardening of the Fianna Fáil line. After their return to power in 1977 the unease continued and, with other stresses, gave rise to the internal convulsion which brought Mr Haughey to the leadership of the party in December 1979. As Taoiseach, however, Mr Haughey has steered a careful course, avoiding explicit reiteration of the 1975 call on Britain for a 'commitment to implement an ordered withdrawal from her involvement in the Six Counties of Northern Ireland'. In the May 1980 communiqué he expressly recognised the need for the consent of the majority of the people of Northern Ireland to any change in the constitutional status of Northern Ireland. He wants the 'guarantee' to be modified by the addition of a positive element – an expression of interest by the British government in the ultimate achievement of unity by agreement and in peace. His repeated assertion that Northern Ireland is not a viable political entity reveals a predominant inclination towards an integrationist solution. He is pursuing a policy aimed at prising the Northern Ireland problem out of an exclusively United Kingdom context into that of the 'unique relationship' between the United Kingdom and the Republic.

This broader context is essential if any acceptable solution is to be reached. There is, however, another consideration of extreme importance. It must be recognised that the views of the majority of the people of Northern Ireland must be respected and that no deal affecting them can be done, or will be attempted, over their heads and without their direct agreement. It is with them that the final bargain must be struck once London and Dublin have established conditions conducive to a settlement. Extreme Unionists must not be allowed to fan the flames of fear, and encourage resort to rebellion or isolated independence, by predictions of a 'sell-out'. All responsible politicians in these islands are committed to peaceful negotiation of an *agreed* settlement.

Is it then a legitimate form of pressure to ask that the British should weaken or withdraw their guarantee to Northern Ireland? It would not be fair in my opinion to ask simply that it be withdrawn. But the guarantee is too one-sided and should be balanced by a clear and positive commitment to ease the transition – and facilitate it financially – if and when a majority in Northern Ireland prefers to disengage from the United Kingdom in favour of a federal or other agreed all-Ireland arrangement. Otherwise, the feeling of security given by the guarantee is matched only by uncertainty and apprehension as to the implications of any alternative. The British Government should spell out the Sunningdale declaration of 'support' in the event of a majority in Northern Ireland indicating in the future a wish to become part of a united Ireland. It would be in Britain's interest, politically, financially and in terms of goodwill and prestige, to commit herself to maintain for a considerable period of years the real value of the net amount now being transferred to Northern Ireland from the British Exchequer for non-military purposes. Unionists and others would then be better informed concerning the options for and against staying in the United Kingdom.

It is not only London that should clarify these options but Dublin also. In the first place, we in the Republic should adapt our unity aspiration to the realities of a complex situation. Too many people in Northern Ireland still think that the people of the South want to dominate them in a unitary and Catholic republic. They need to be assured that our aspiration to unity shelters no desire for domination and would be satisfied by agreed all-Ireland arrangements not involving direct jurisdiction over our fellow-Irishmen. The wording of Article 3 of our Constitution is unfortunate in this respect. This article has been defended as a necessary rejection of British sovereignty over part of Ireland but, even viewing it as no more than an assertion of aspirations, it would be politic to dispense with it if there were any sure and unambiguous way of doing so. It could most easily be dropped in the drawing up of a constitution appropriate to an agreed all-Ireland political settlement. Since we rely on the assent of the majority in Northern Ireland, we in the Republic have a responsibility to create conditions favouring acceptance by that majority of an Irish alternative to continued membership of the United Kingdom. The new joint studies may help to point the way. We already have advantages connected with sovereignty, fiscal freedom and international status which many in Northern Ireland would probably wish to enjoy, and which would offer them more scope for their genius and skill. We need also to do more by a liberalisation of our attitudes and by social, business and cultural contacts (supporting in this context the work of Co-operation North[1]) to provide evidence of our respect and friendship for Northern Ireland Unionists. A sense of community would be fostered by a deeper knowledge of the distinctive and varied cultural heritage we all share on this island. Effective co-operation in economic and social development also needs to be organised. Here again the joint studies may be fruitful. An upsurge in goodwill and confidence and a stimulus to enterprise and investment, both domestically and internationally sponsored, would be the first fruit of political stability based on an acceptable settlement of the Northern Ireland problem.

The open letter recently addressed by Bishop Cahal Daly, himself a Northerner, to a Northern Ireland Protestant expresses well the feelings of concerned Southern Catholics on the political and wider issues involved.

As a Catholic, (he wrote) I have felt enriched by my contacts with your tradition. I have often been inspired by your prayer, your witness, your evangelising zeal, your social and charitable concern. I have seen the fruits of Protestant faith and worship in the tradition of honest work, proud craftsmanship, respect for truth and integrity, honest dealing and a sense of public service, which at their best mark the Protestant farmer and worker, the Protestant business and professional man. Ireland would be impoverished without the truths and values enshrined in the Protestant tradition. . . . As a Catholic, and as an Irishman, I would reject with all my being and would repudiate with any power I had, any 'solution' of the Irish question which would be secured through coercion by physical force or violence of the Northern Protestant community, if such were conceivable. . .

Conversely, Bishop Daly's letter pleads with Northern Protestants to accept that it would be equally immoral, and equally impossible, to coerce Northern Catholics into returning to what for them was a permanent state of second-class citizenship. Please believe that Northern Catholics will never again consent to return to the status of a permanent political minority, excluded as a minority from all share in the making of the decisions on which their future social, economic and cultural welfare depend. . . . Surely some Protestant spokesmen can proclaim publicly that they stand for a Northern Ireland which is shared by Protestants and Catholics in partnership and equality of civic rights and of civic responsibilities . . .

It is not well enough known in Northern Ireland that the Catholic Bishops of Ireland publicly declared in June 1976 that it is not their view that, in the law of the state, 'the principles peculiar to our faith should be made binding on people who do not adhere to that faith'.

The compromise or intermediate solution must contain certain essential ingredients. The most important is that it be open to evolution; only in this way can the overlapping interests of the United Kingdom and the Republic of Ireland, arising from the conflict of nationality in Northern Ireland, be accommodated. The Atkins Proposals were set exclusively in a United Kingdom context. No proposals are likely to succeed which do not leave room for duly-elected politicians in Northern Ireland to try, by way of peaceful persuasion, to influence a majority towards confirming or changing their political allegiance, that is, towards staying in, or leaving, the United Kingdom. Otherwise, the basic nationality conflict would be dangerously suppressed rather than given a controlled outlet. To ensure, however, that disruptive force is not given to the conflict of nationality, every member of the devolved representative assembly and executive should be obliged to swear an oath of fidelity to the constitution of Northern Ireland for as long as that constitution has the support of a majority of the people of Northern Ireland – a question to be tested by referendum only every 10 years, or whenever a three-fourths majority of the assembly should so decide.

Another essential ingredient is the entrenchment of proportional representation as the system of election, a matter on which, curiously, the Atkins Proposals were silent. However desirable, or even necessary, some form of power-sharing or partnership may be as an interim arrangement (for a few years at most), it is difficult to see it as a good *permanent* substitute for majority rule in a democracy. It carries the disadvantage of frustrating the vital role of an Opposition and the risk that a government crisis might bring down the whole constitution. Proportional representation was an immense political advance in Northern Ireland and provides a sounder and more permanent basis for a workable democratic system, even in that artificial area, than direct powersharing. In a less tense political situation, it could produce a more realistic (and therefore, fragmented) representation of the community, opening up the possibility of various parliamentary groups coming together, even across the political divide, to form an alternative government. Northern Ireland might thus cease to be the exclusively one-party regime it was under the old Stormont. It is true that the nationality conflict tends to polarise the community politically but, since it cannot be suppressed, it seems best to contain it and slow it down in the context of a proportional representation system affording maximum scope for diverse shades of opinion.

A third essential ingredient in any intermediate solution is a built-in potential for evolution under appropriate safeguards. The Act devolving a measure of self-government on Northern Ireland – in effect establishing the new constitution for Northern Ireland – would be an Act of the Westminster Parliament but should contain provisions enabling a substantial (say, three-fourths) majority of the Northern Ireland elected assembly to put proposals for change in that constitution to the people of Northern Ireland in a referendum. Changes confirmed by referendum should thereupon legally amend the constitution.

A fourth essential is that the constitution of Northern Ireland should contain provisions safeguarding the rights of the individual and allowing cases of alleged infringement of human rights to be appealed from the Courts of Northern Ireland to the European Court of Human Rights.

This is not the place to attempt to write a detailed prescription for devolution. Control of security would obviously have to rest for the time being with the British government but, since any obtrusive British Army presence would tend to be provocative, and a neutral international military force seems unavailable, it is important to perfect quickly the progress already being made towards the ideal of an adequate domestic police force, acceptable to the whole community.

It may be that the new relationship between Dublin and London will itself engender just enough doubt about the inflexibility of the 'guarantee' to induce a more constructive attitude on the part of Northern Unionists towards an intermediate solution. It is to be hoped that it will do just this and no more – that they will not allow themselves be pushed into needless rebellion or violence but rather be drawn towards negotiating a settlement satisfactory to themselves. No radical change in the constitutional relationship between London and Dublin is likely to flow from the new rapprochement. There may well be an agreement on voting rights or dual citizenship or administrative provision for co-operation in matters of common interest but the possibility of a surrender of sovereignty by Dublin to a British Isles Federation or similar arrangement seems remote. An Anglo-Irish Council is a more likely prospect if it is seen as the institutional expression of a 'unique relationship', a symbol reassuring to Ulster Unionists and concealing no threat to them.

There has been speculation as to whether a defence pact might be one of the new 'institutional' arrangements to emerge from the joint talks. Neutrality, in an unqualified sense, has never been a principle of the foreign policy of the Republic. Its ideological sympathies are with the West. It would be absurd to pretend that it could successfully defend itself on its own against external aggression. No justification of principle – other than unwillingness to aid the United Kingdom to defend the Border – was advanced to explain non-participation in NATO. Agreement was, indeed, expressed with NATO objectives. During the last war Irish neutrality, though scrupulously observed, was benevolent towards the Allied powers; it was declared that any attempt to make the Republic a base of attack on the United Kingdom would be resisted by the

Republic. Tens of thousands from the Republic fought on the Allied side. It has been made clear that, as a member of the European Economic Community, Ireland would participate in any common defence arrangements which the Community might in time evolve.

Within this general framework, it would not be unreasonable that more specific arrangements should be agreed between the two neighbour states in recognition of their particularly close common interest in security. A bilateral military pact is unlikely in present circumstances. Mr Haughey has, however, said (*Dáil Éireann*, 11 March 1981) that, when a satisfactory political solution to the Northern Ireland situation is arrived at, 'we would, of course, have to review what would be the most appropriate defence arrangements for the island as a whole. It would be unrealistic and improvident not to do so. It would also be mandatory that any such arrangements would require the full authority of the Irish people deciding on them as a specific issue'.

If, through all concerned being more reasonable and flexible, an intermediate arrangement can be made which brings peace to Northern Ireland and enables the whole community there to advance in justice and well-being, this would be an enormous gain. To obstruct it would be indefensible. Neither part of the community would have abandoned its nationality or its aspirations but a framework would have been established in which divisive issues could be resolved by free and informed majority decision. The water in which guerillas and paramilitarists swim would have become distinctly colder.

Everyone should be prepared to await patiently the political evolution which must follow a period of constructive living together in a new and more progressive environment. Not only domestic but international investment would be encouraged by an acceptable political settlement, and the Northern community's basic problems – of insecurity, industrial decline and unemployment – could be effectively tackled.

Looking to the longer term, there is much to be said for putting on the table an outline or variant outlines of a new 32-county Ireland. Even if such ideas are at first reviled or rejected, cognisance will be taken of them and in time they will evoke more interest and objective comment, leading, one hopes, to mature consideration.

Agreement by a Northern Ireland majority on a closer political relationship with the Republic seems more likely to come about, and to be durable, when it is based on free choice and near-equality of status. Equalising forces have largely been effective in the economic and social spheres. An approach towards a federal solution could in time develop, by agreement, to meet common needs and aims in such fields as agriculture, energy, communications, use and care of natural resources, tourism, health, culture, the arts and sport. But nothing should be rushed or pushed for purely nationalist reasons. As time passes and the European Community evolves politically in increasing independence, nationality will weaken and allegiance widen. My personal hope, as expressed in an article in the *Irish Times* on 20 June 1978, is that we will move 'towards an arrangement which results in Irish men and women on their own (without a British presence but with their active goodwill) managing the affairs of the whole of Ireland in a constructive partnership within the European Community'.

There may, of course, be neither devolution nor evolution and direct rule may be prolonged until distrust and outrage and violence corrode another generation. This would be a tragic reflection on statesmen and politicians in these islands and also on the ability of Ulster to raise fair and courageous leaders to open the way to a better future.

## Note to Chapter 12

[1]Co-operation North is a non-political, non-sectarian organisation formed in the Republic in 1978 to promote through economic, social and cultural exchanges, a climate of goodwill and understanding between people of different traditions in the Republic and Northern Ireland.

# 13   Postscript (early 1983)

Mercifully, the hunger strike in Northern Ireland was called off in the late autumn of 1981, though not before ten men had died. The main event of 1982 was a fresh British devolution initiative, preluded by a White Paper in April and followed by the election for the Assembly and its inauguration in October last, despite the reservations of Official Unionists, the intended boycott of its proceedings by the SDLP and Sinn Féin, criticism of it as unworkable from the Fianna Fáil government and a less than enthusiastic signal from Fine Gael in opposition.

The only parliamentary debate on the British White Paper in the Republic took place hurriedly in Seanad Éireann, with the transient presence of a junior minister, on 16 April 1982. Not wishing to prejudge the proposals, I preferred to see the Assembly as something with evolutionary potential which ought at least to be tested before it was condemned. The following extract from the debate will explain my approach (a few slight deletions have been made):

> Unless we favour an indefinite continuation of direct rule, or unless we favour integration of Northern Ireland in the United Kingdom, or unless we would consider an independent Northern Ireland desirable, or unless we think we can realistically achieve – and it must be with the agreement of a majority in Northern Ireland – early integration of Northern Ireland with ourselves, then it seems we have no option but to welcome an initiative of an interim or compromise character, involving a sensitive degree of devolution to the people of Northern Ireland, which one would hope

would provide a means for them to work together in a spirit of co-operation and compromise.

I do not understand the exaggerated condemnation of the proposals as being unworkable and unsuitable to the present conditions in Ireland which have been expressed on behalf of the Government. These proposals represent a considerable advance on any we have seen before, certainly on the Atkins proposals. I need only mention a few areas in which that advance is significant. One of these is that there is explicit recognition in this paper of the legitimacy of the aspiration of what is at present a minority in Northern Ireland to be part of a united Ireland – a recognition also of the legitimacy of their pursuing the aim of a change of status and allegiance, democratically and peacefully. I do not know why we are not generous enough to see that that is a substantial recognition of an Irish dimension.

The present proposals also carry within themselves a potential for evolution. How that evolution will take place is vague, but the principles are well established, in particular the principle of no longer relying on a bare majority but of seeking a wide cross-community agreement for political arrangements.

The proposals also, to my mind, have the tremendous merit of providing an effective role for elected politicians in Northern Ireland. They have been deprived of a forum and of any effective role for quite a number of years now and it must be a ground for admiration on our part that so many of them, whether we agree with their views or not, have stayed in the political field and, now that an election is to take place, will have a chance of re-establishing their representative character in the community.

If it is not too immodest I would like to check off the new British proposals against what I thought should be the main elements in any compromise or interim arrangement.

I said in an article in July 1981,[1] that the Atkins proposals, and I said this by way of criticism, were set exclusively in a United Kingdom context, whereas no proposals were likely to succeed which did not leave room for duly elected politicians in Northern Ireland to try by way of peaceful persuasion to influence a majority towards confirming or changing their political allegiance, that is, towards staying in or leaving the United Kingdom. I am glad to say that that first element in my ideal compromise solution is met by the present proposals.

I went on to say that another essential ingredient was the entrenchment of proportional representation as the system of election, a matter on which, curiously, the Atkins proposals were silent. Proportional representation may not be entrenched in the new White Paper but at least it is set down as the basis for the election to the assembly. In fact, I am not particularly keen, otherwise than as a purely interim measure, on power sharing as it has been understood up to now. I do not see it as a good permanent substitute for some form of majority rule. I would prefer the form of qualified majority rule, 60 or 70 per cent majority rule, which is indicated in this paper.

A third ingredient which I specified was a built-in potential for evolution under appropriate safeguards. There is obviously a potential for evolution here in the Prior proposals, an evolution which will depend on a process of negotiation which must secure sufficient across-the-community agreement to progress towards having an executive and having powers devolved from the British parliament.

The fourth essential ingredient of any compromise which I suggested was that, whatever be the constitution of Northern Ireland under new arrangements, it should contain provisions safeguarding the rights of the individual and allowing cases of alleged infringement of human rights to be appealed from the courts of Northern Ireland to the European Court of Human Rights. Possibly the Prior proposals are as yet at too early a stage of evolution to make that particular ingredient relevant. It certainly would become relevant if and when there were any question of the devolution of powers regarding security from Westminster to Northern Ireland.

In the article, and I think it is still relevant, I made the point that if, through all concerned being more reasonable and flexible, an intermediate arrangement can be made that brings peace to Northern Ireland and enables the whole community there to advance in justice and well-being, this would be an enormous gain and to obstruct it would be indefensible. That is why I dislike the over-intensive reaction of a negative kind which we have had. It is not that I am worried because the political parties in Northern Ireland have all seen more of the defects and the alleged unworkability of the proposals than their merits. Paradoxically, I think that is an advantage that will help to get the proposals properly discussed and off the ground. I cannot see that any of the political parties in Northern Ireland can afford to neglect the opportunity to be represented in the proposed assembly. I am very much in favour of a constructive response. The proposals may indeed be found unworkable but they are not unworkable in principle and cannot be so described ab initio. Their practicality remains to be seen and one hopes that every effort will be made to make them work rather than just condemn them without trial. . . .

The Assembly has since met, held together in the beginning by the support of the Democratic Unionist Party and the Alliance Party. Official Unionists agreed only early in 1983 and uncertainly to take part in the committees system. The SDLP and Sinn Féin are so far at least non-participants: for Sinn Féin abstention is a dogma, for the SDLP a compromise reflecting serious disagreement in the party as between outright abstention and participation.

Meanwhile, the toll of violence continues – at times, as at Ballykelly, more bestial than ever. Questions have been raised whether some fatalities in recent months reveal a new tendency towards premature shooting of suspects by members of the security forces. The polarisation sharpens. Violence shows itself as a powerfully disruptive force, tearing at what remains of ordered and civilised life, aggravating the effects of the general economic depression, forcing unemployment to a particularly high level in Northern Ireland and causing hope of economic recovery to recede even further. It would be shameful ambivalence to condemn violence on the one hand yet seek, on the other, to use it as a political lever. A fact, however, must be recognised and, most regrettably, the continued presence of violence in Northern Ireland is a fact.

Another disagreeable fact is the degree of support at the ballot box for Sinn Féin candidates, despite their commitment to continued use of the Armalite rifle. Their gaining of one-third of the Nationalist vote cannot be written off as merely the revelation of a support that already existed. It is a new phenomenon – the product of a deliberate, propagandist cashing-in on the Fermanagh/South Tyrone victory of hunger-striker Bobby Sands in a Westminster election uncontested by the SDLP. That it poses a dangerous threat to the SDLP, and that it has influenced that party to become 'greener' or more Republican, cannot be gainsaid. Indeed, combined with Unionist rigidity, it probably turned the scales in deciding SDLP policy regarding the Assembly.

The most significant political fact, however, remains the immovable intransigence of the Unionists, their refusal to see the need to seek genuine accommodation with the minority, if Northern Ireland is not to become a desert. The SDLP leader, John Hume, constantly and understandably expresses his frustration at the complete rejection of negotiation, and even of debate, not just by the DUP leader, Dr Ian Paisley, but by Mr Harold McCusker of the Official Unionist Party. This is a situation in which those, on the minority side, who wish to use the political process cannot but lose ground to those employing bombs and guns.

Surely, too much is involved here not only for the people of Northern Ireland but for the two sovereign governments for it to be tolerable to allow Unionist intransigence and short-sightedness to hold undisputed sway for ever? I argued in the 1981 article against coercion, putting an unqualified demand for discontinuation of the 'guarantee' in that category. But pressure is avoidable only where reason spontaneously prevails and where selfish interest recognises the need to come to terms with the community's good. It is difficult to avoid the conclusion now that some form of British pressure must be exerted since Unionists refuse to take the path of reason and, through what they might call their steadfastness, put the peace, security and progress of larger communities at risk. They do not live in isolation. They are part of a local community, where their unwillingness to arrange for reasonable political association with the minority is a factor gravely destabilising and impov-

erishing that community and exerting ominous influences on
the whole of Irish society and on Anglo-Irish relations
generally.

British insistence, under James Prior, that a Stormont based
on simple majority rule will not be restored is itself a form of
pressure. It has not worked because direct rule is for most
Unionists a tolerable alternative. The British commitment in
the 1973 Sunningdale Agreement to power sharing (my reservations to which, as a permanency, are explained in the 1981
article – see Chapter 12) was watered down in the Assembly
provisions, though the principle of wide community agreement
was explicitly preserved. There are, of course, various ways of
upholding the principle of adequate protection for minority
interests. Is it not time that Unionists were warned that even
British patience is wearing thin and that the 'guarantee' – and
the financial supports – will remain only on condition that
Unionists come to terms with the need to have a political
arrangement for Northern Ireland which is acceptable to the
minority? It is towards this that I would favour pressure being
exerted, not towards forcing Unionists into a 'united' Ireland.

If pressure on the British side is needed, so also is some
yielding on the part of those aspiring to a United Ireland. It
must be made clear that there is no desire in Dublin to rule
Belfast; that unity can come only when a majority in Northern
Ireland declares for unity in some form; that Dublin is 'easy'
as to whether unity, which is desired as a real and not a
territorial concept, is expressed in integrated, federal, confed-
eral or other form; that, in the words used in my 1981 article,
'our aspiration to unity shelters no desire for domination and
would be satisfied by agreed all-Ireland arrangements not
involving direct jurisdiction over our fellow-Irishmen'; and
that Dublin will fully back a Northern Ireland political entity
that has a wide basis of community support in Northern
Ireland, is ready to co-operate on matters of common interest
and considers it legitimate politics that change may be sought
in the constitutional status of Northern Ireland, with an opportunity being afforded every ten or twenty years for this issue to
be tested by referendum.

The projected Anglo-Irish Parliamentary Council may be a
means of making British politicians more aware of the

Northern Ireland problem and more concerned to solve it, and at the same time, of softening the sharpness of the points of the London – Belfast – Dublin triangle.

Meanwhile, it is a hopeful sign that the SDLP is stressing the need for a restatement of what Nationalists, North and South, would like to see as the shape of a New Ireland. They seem willing to expose themselves to the moderating influence of Southern Nationalists and even of Unionists (if any should be interested) in the preparation of a discussion document. This would be similar to the 'blueprint' recommended in my 1981 article. The Coalition government, with the backing of Fianna Fáil, announced on 11 March 1983 a proposal to establish a 'forum' open to all democratic parties, North and South, which reject violence, in which consultation would take place on 'the manner in which lasting peace and stability can be achieved in a new Ireland through the democratic process'.

Internationally, also, interest in a political settlement of the Northern Ireland problem is increasing. The European Parliament on 9 March 1983 authorised its political affairs committee to draw up a report on the political and economic circumstances in Northern Ireland. The British government has protested against this 'interference' and refused co-operation but, at the same time, has improved significantly the incentives for industrial development in Northern Ireland. In the United States, 28 Senators and 53 Representatives introduced in both Houses of Congress on 17 March 1983 a joint resolution 'to end the conflict in Northern Ireland and achieve the unity of the Irish people'. The text condemns violence and envisages 'a political settlement with the consent of all parties'.

The context in which such a settlement is to be sought is not clear. The term 'a new Ireland' is no doubt deliberately broad and indefinite. At present, many of the SDLP appear to have joined Fianna Fáil in writing off any prospect of political accommodation within a Northern Ireland framework. But constant reiteration that the 'North' is not viable as a political or economic entity amounts to propaganda for the integration of the North in some new all-Ireland creation, with Unionists having to accept that their interests would be fully respected at the negotiating table. The Unionist reaction to such an approach is predictable: the majority of them, given an integrationist choice, would opt for integration in the United Kingdom; a minority might prefer independence. Unionist support even of devolved government in Northern Ireland is unstable. It is a merit of the 'forum' proposal that it appears to envisage a pre-testing, direct or indirect, of the likelihood of the acceptability of any suggested solution to Unionists.

There are those in the Republic who, using the cockpit metaphor I employed in my 1981 article [see Chapter 12], see no point in restoring devolved government in any form. Their argument is that Northern Ireland as a separate unit cannot but be an expression of Protestantism and inevitably a forum for sectarian conflict. Direct rule, in their view, is better from the nationalist standpoint because it denies supremacy to Protestants and focusses their patriotic fervour on Unionism, while bringing home to them as Unionists their second-class role as British citizens and perhaps eventually turning them towards some form of participation in an Irish state. This viewpoint may, however, draw too fine a distinction between Unionism and Protestantism, may require of Northern Nationalists too great and prolonged a measure of patience in conditions of political impotence and competition from extreme Republican activism and may depend too much on the acquiescence of the whole Irish community, as well as the British, in continued exposure to disorder and violence.

It is conceivable that an acceptable *via media* may be found involving some elements of condominium, in which old loyalties would have scope for expression without disrupting the co-operative pursuit of common interests. Personally, I still hope for accommodation in the framework of a Northern Ireland which, if and when a majority so decides, could enter, on agreed terms, an all-Ireland arrangement, unitary or federal. I accept that at least the integral form of an all-Ireland arrangement is not being made easier by the growing disparity between the two parts of Ireland caused by exchange rate and fiscal policies in the Republic. The financial implications of a sudden move to political unity in Ireland are as insupportable as ever without prolonged British aid and liberal international investment – a point which seems to be forgotten by the advocates of 'Brits out and then we'll settle things between ourselves'. I am not one for letting the British government off the hook in this way. At the same time, it seems to me that indefinite continuation of direct rule offers no prospect of peaceful progress.

Time is running out. The drift at present is towards greater division and disruption. No one could exclude the possibility of a civil war of indeterminable scope and unpredictable outcome. Politicians must work fast. Can it be agreed that, for the sake of all in these islands, especially the people of Northern Ireland themselves, priority must be given to the restoration of political and economic conditions favouring peaceful and purposeful working together in Northern Ireland? Old shibboleths and ideals, Orange or Green, cannot take precedence. If politicians do nothing to restore civilised life and order in Northern Ireland or worse still if, by extravagant propaganda, they maintain that a solution in which Northern Ireland is preserved as a political entity is not feasible at all, and yet have no alternative to offer acceptable to all parties, they debase the role of the politician and boost that of the gunman.

Even if an acceptable political arrangement can be reached in Northern Ireland, is there any hope that it will last? Will extreme Republicans not strive to destroy it, as they did after Sunningdale; will extreme Unionists not distrust and frustrate it? Can the middle ground be relied upon to defend and uphold such a settlement against attack from both extremes and, perhaps, internal strains and misgivings? Is there a prospect that there would in this new context be less tolerance, covert and overt, for violence and a transference to the political stage of the pressures for change?

Any political settlement in Northern Ireland must of its nature be a compromise, unacceptable to extremists and constantly irksome even to moderates. Yet it seems on balance to be more likely to restore responsible co-operation and lessen violence than any alternative, whether integration in either of its forms, direct rule, or independence. The choice is really between a confrontation of extremists which threatens to engulf the whole of Ireland in bloodshed and disorder and an accommodation of opposing attitudes and aspirations within a framework of reasonable compromise. It is for all of us in this island to make this choice and it is a particularly significant one for the young persons of Ireland who now constitute so large a part of the population and whose future over the coming decades is critically involved.

The last paragraph of my 1981 article still stands. In particular, we await the arrival on the scene of a Unionist leader of sufficient realism and courage. But none of us can neglect to influence the environment in ways conducive to his emergence.

## Note to Chapter 13

[1]Ireland: The Way Forward *The Round Table* July 1981 (see Chapter 12).

# III Cultural Matters

# 14 The Revival of Irish

When the report of the Commission on the revival of the Irish language (An Coimisiún um Athbheochan na Gaeilge) was published in 1964, I studied it carefully as a deeply interested individual, quite apart from any duty falling on me as a public servant. Indeed, though it was clearly not a matter primarily for the Department of Finance, it so happened that, in the end, the preparation of the government's White Paper in response to the Commission's recommendations fell largely to that Department. At the time, however, when I wrote the following notes, I did so inspired by personal interest and inquiry rather than in pursuance of official duty. The notes were, I recall, the subject of a lively, informal discussion with the Chairman of the Commission, now Cardinal Ó Fiaich.

These notes are not concerned with the recommendations in the Report but with something more fundamental which the Commission itself felt needed to be dealt with if its report was not to be defective, namely, the basis for the Revival Movement. The Commission's reference is:

> Níor iarradh orainn inár dtéarmaí tagartha aon rianú a dhéanamh ar fhealsúnacht na hAthbheochana ná riachtanas na teanga do thodhchaí an náisiúin a shuíomh, ach measaimid gurbh easnamh ar ár dTuarascáil é gan léiriú achomair, ar a laghad, a bheith inti ar an mbonn atá faoin Athbheochan (An Tuarascáil Dheiridh, leath. xiv).

In a short passage preceding this reference, the Commission defined what it understood to be the meaning of *Athbheochan* and in a later passage, explained what it considered to be the

purpose or raison d'etre of *Athbheochan*. This section of the
Report, less than two pages in all (leath. xiii–xv), is to my
mind the most important and requires the most serious consideration because it is the foundation on which the Commission's recommendations rest.

Uncertainty and even apprehension exist as to what *Athbheochan* or *slánú* means and this prejudices the approach to
Irish by excusing indifference or arousing antipathy. The
assumption that the aim is to make Irish the everyday language
of everyone in Ireland to the exclusion, or at any rate the
neglect, of English sharpens the antagonism of those who see
no point in preserving Irish, alienates the sympathy of those
who cherish Irish but value the possession of English, and
discourages even idealists, who recognise such an extreme aim
to be unattainable. Unless there is clarity as to the aim and a
general conviction that the aim is sound and realisable, it is
futile to expect progress. But if this clarity and conviction exist,
the idealism and willpower on which all progress, intellectual
and material, depends will be brought into play. This is the
principle by which we are guided in planning for Irish economic progress and it is no less valid in relation to the Irish
language.

The reference to economics does not imply a cold and
narrow outlook. The heart must play a large part in the
attitude to the Irish language. As Father O'Growney said
about concern for Irish, 'It is sentimentality, and patriotism is
but a sentiment also, and the two sentimentalities are closely
connected'. They are also, as I have said, connected with the
dynamism needed in regard to national progress generally.
But love and admiration for the language may remain virtually
inactive forces unless the mind is satisfied that what is desired
is both reasonable and attainable. That is the core of the
problem.

The Commission explains that it understands *Athbheochan* to
mean that the language will again become the Irish people's
normal medium of communication and intercourse *('go mbeidh
an teanga ina gnáthmheán cumarsáide agus caidrimh ag muintir na
hÉireann athuair')*. The words *'ina gnáthmheán'* could be translated as 'a normal medium' but the reference a few sentences
later to *'an t-athrú teanga sin'* suggests that a change-over from

English to Irish as the everyday language is envisaged. The Commission says that this has been the aim of the Irish movement from the outset and of every Irish government since the state was established.

Some questions need to be raised about this definition of meaning and aim. The purpose of Conradh na Gaeilge (founded in 1893), as indicated on page 14 of the Commission's report, was

> *An Ghaeilge a chaomhnú mar theanga náisiúnta na hÉireann agus a húsáid mar theanga labhartha a leathadh.*

To spread the use of Irish as a spoken language is a less extreme aim than to substitute it for English as the everyday speech of the Irish people.

Again, Thomas Davis, to whose inspiration the revival movement owes so much, expressed the hope in the first of his two articles in *The Nation* on 'Our National Language' that Irish might be restored as the current speech of Ireland but in his second article reassured those who feared that they might be expected to abandon English where it was their mother tongue:

> For you, if the mixed speech called English was laid with sweetmeats on your child's tongue, English is the best speech of manhood.

He also said:

> It is quite another thing to say, as we do, that the Irish language should be cherished, taught, and esteemed, and that it can be preserved and gradually extended.

> What we seek is that the people of the upper classes should have their children taught the language which explains our names of persons or places, our older history, and our music, and which is spoken in the majority of our counties, rather than Italian, German, or French. It would be more useful in life, more serviceable to the taste and genius of young

people, and a more flexible accomplishment for an Irish man or woman to speak, sing, and write Irish than French.[1]

At the time Davis wrote (1843) Irish was, he thought, still the current speech of about half the people west of a line from Derry to Waterford. According to the 1851 Census, which may have understated the position, the total number of Irish speakers was then 1½ million (or 23 per cent of the population); the percentages for the provinces were Connacht 51 per cent, Munster 44 per cent, Ulster 6.8 per cent and Leinster 3.5 per cent. There were nine counties with less than one per cent Irish speakers (Down, Carlow, Dublin, Kildare, Laois, Offaly, Westmeath, Wexford and Wicklow).[2]

In his article, 'The National Language' in the *Irish Ecclesiastical Record* of November 1890 (reproduced in the Record of November 1963), An tAthair Eoghan Ó Gramhna defined 'what those interested in Irish aim at'. He said:

> It is not to banish English – that would be, first of all, impossible, and also absurd. Listen, again, to the words of Canon Farrar:– 'Neither I, nor any man in his senses, dream for a moment of doing anything to hinder the universal prevalence of English. But the prevalence of English is something very different from the exclusive dominance of it. We wish that every child should speak English perfectly, and should also speak ... its native language perfectly.' That this state of education is a possible one is proved by its success in Wales and in other countries. That it is desirable is evident, if the only aim of education be not to make us more English than the English themselves.

The Constitution (Article 8) prescribes that 'The Irish language as the national language is the first official language'. Irish will possess this quality and priority whether the aim be its restoration as the general vernacular or something less far reaching. The latest expression of government policy does not confirm the Commission's assumption as summarised above. Interviewed by a journalist for the *New York Times* on 5 September 1963, the Taoiseach, Mr Seán F. Lemass, replied as follows to the question 'Do you think Ireland will ever be Gaelic speaking?':

> The progress which has been made in the revival of the Irish language, particularly in the schools, is encouraging enough to justify us in hoping that the next generation will be almost fully bilingual. I do not visualise a time when Irish will be the common language of everyday business, but I certainly look forward to the realisation of our aim of giving all our people, through knowledge of the Irish language, full access to our great cultural heritage.

This is quite a different definition of the meaning of *'Athbheochan'* from that of the Commission, though it is in line with the aims of Davis, O'Growney and Conradh na Gaeilge.

It seems permissible, therefore, to dispute the correctness of the Commission's assumptions about the meaning and aim of *Athbheochan* and to put forward a different definition along the following lines.

> To preserve and cherish Irish as the national language; to strengthen the Gaeltacht and extend the use of Irish as a living language, oral and written; and to give everyone growing up in Ireland, through knowledge of the language and its literature, wider access to our cultural heritage.

The merit of an aim so defined is that it is not only attractive and consistent with patriotic tradition but also reasonable and acceptable in present circumstances. It avoids the indifference and even hostility to Irish generated by an extreme aim which is not accepted as being either reasonable or realisable.

On what grounds, it may be asked, does the Commission justify its aim of 'seeking to have Irish spoken again as the everyday language of the people'? *(an Ghaeilge a chur á labhairt athuair mar ghnáth-theanga an phobail)*. It may be noted that this would be a return to conditions which obtained, even outside the major towns of Ireland, only before the plantations of the seventeenth century. The Commission, having instanced a few lesser aims (that it would suffice that Irish be preserved in the Gaeltacht districts or that it be taught in Gaeltacht schools or that it be a subject of study by scholars and experts) rejects *all such* ideas because it believes that Irish would not long survive as a living language if any one of them were adopted – and, even if it did, that it would be too weak to have much influence on the mind of the people or much efficacy in saving and preserving the nation and its individuality, which is the purpose of the Revival Movement. *(Gan mórán tionchair aici ar aigne an phobail agus gan mórán feidhme chun fónamh do bhunchuspóir na hAthbheochana .i. slánú agus buanú an náisiúin gona fhéiniúlacht shainiúil).*

This belief – that having Irish spoken again as the everyday language of the people is essential for the saving and preservation of the nation and its distinctive character – is, therefore the Commission's fundamental philosophy. The Commission itself, however, recognises that it may be a hard doctrine for many. It immediately acknowledges that there can be two views on the subject *(aithnimíd go bhfuil an dá thuairim ann faoi fheidhm teanga sainiúla do bhunú agus do bhuanú náisiúin)*. It confines itself to an affirmation of belief that in Irish circumstances it is necessary to revive Irish as the vernacular if the nation is to be preserved *(ag féachaint dár ndálaí speisialta creidimid go bhfuil sé riachtanach go ndéanfaí an Ghaeilge a athbheochan mar ghnáth-theanga an phobail má táimid chun ár náisiún a bhuanú)*. It is admitted that to prove this to everyone's satisfaction is not easy; it is, indeed, largely a subjective matter *(tagann an intleacht i gceist agus an toil, gan amhras, ach tagann dearcadh an duine, a thaithí phearsanta agus a oiliúint, i gceist chomh maith)*. So far, this cannot be said to be convincing.

In the final section of this crucial part of the introduction to the report, there is a brief explanation of why the Commission believes that the revival of Irish as a vernacular is necessary for the preservation of the nation. The argument is difficult to follow because it relates to an abstraction, the 'native mind' *(aigne dhúchais)*, to which it is claimed the Irish language gives most effective expression, and which is expected never to regain its former vigour unless it is supported by the language, by tradition and the other characteristics of our national individuality and unless the influence of the 'foreign mind' *(aigne eachtraí)* is blunted. The passage is difficult to paraphrase and it is best, perhaps, to reproduce it in its entirety:

Is iad ár dtraidisiúin agus ár gcultúr dúchais na sain-
tréithe a bheireann féiniúlacht dúinn mar phobal.
Slánú na haigne dúchais agus a foirbhiú is cuspóir
deiridh d'athbheochan na teanga, dáiríre, agus maolú ar
róthionchar na haigne eachtraí ar an náisiún. Gheofaí
a rá nach bhfuil in Athbheochan na Gaeilge ach gléas
chun an cuspóir sin a bhaint amach, cé gur gléas riachtanach í. Níor mhór na gnéithe iomadúla dár
bhféiniúlacht a chothú agus a shaothrú – na foirmeacha
sainiúla a chum an aigne dhúchais di féin nuair a bhí
sí lánbheo, agus trínar léirigh sí í féin ó aois go
haois. Má tá an aigne sin le teacht arís ar a lán-neart
beidh gá aici lena dtacaíocht siúd; beidh gá aici, ach go
háirithe, le tacaíocht na teanga ós inti atá a héirim, a
gaois agus a grinneas, agus ós í, dáiríre, an aigne
dhúchais ag feidhmiú. Sin é, i mbeagán focal, raison
d'être na hAthbheochana mar a thuigimidne é.

It is hard to accept that, if there is a native mind, it is being
deprived at present of adequate expression amongst the nine-
tenths of the population whose vernacular is English; or that
our political leaders for nearly two hundred years have neither
understood it nor expressed it properly, having (as the Commission notes on page 6) used English 'mar theanga na
polaitíochta agus an tírghrá.'
    Qualifications may also be entered as to the extent to which,
in modern conditions, making Irish the common speech of the
people could act as a screen against the 'external mind' or
open a way back to traditional culture and literature. The
'native mind' itself, its interests and cultural forms, if a living
must also be a changing thing, affected and often enriched by
external influences. The Irish language too has changed down
the centuries and it would be easy to exaggerate the access to
our literary heritage in the language which even a good knowledge of modern Irish affords.[3]
    Even if it is impossible to assent fully to the Commission's
assertions, and in particular to accept that our future independence as a nation depends on Irish becoming the current
speech of the people, some ideas in the passages I have been
dealing with are undoubtedly sound. But it is possible to hold

that the desired purpose would be achieved more surely by the adoption of the less extreme aim in regard to the Irish language suggested above. No one would deny, for instance, that our sense of national independence and individuality is strengthened by the possession of a national language in which there is a great and ancient literature. But, as a foundation for sturdy self-respect and patriotism, we need not merely to be aware of this fact, and to know something of the language itself, but to be acquainted also with the contribution the Irish people have made down the ages to other forms of learning and culture and, indeed, to every kind of human achievement, spiritual and material. All this – and not just preoccupation with making Irish the vernacular – seem to be required to promote a spirit of individual and national independence. The protection of the individual, and the community, against *excessive* foreign cultural and other influences which might undermine their independence of outlook or their cultural distinctiveness, must, however, depend much more on education in the widest sense than on the Irish language or Irish studies. Must it not be recognised, also, that a wider road to knowledge, as well as to the economic progress on which national independence also rests, has been opened up for the Irish people by the facility with which they speak and read an international language?

The purpose of these notes is to secure full consideration of the future *aim* of policy in regard to Irish, as a basis for deciding on the appropriate action to be taken to achieve that aim. It may be well to say that the notes are not animated by any lack of affection for Irish but rather by concern that an aim be chosen which will be realistic and will stimulate more interest in, and more love and support for, the language than the aim to which the Commission's proposals are directed.

## Notes to Chapter 14

[1]T. W. Moody *Thomas Davis, 1914-45.*
[2]Brian Ó Cuív *Irish Dialects and Irish-speaking Districts.*
[3]From this seed there flowered eventually *An Duanaire – 1600-1900: Poems of the Dispossessed* Dolmen Press, 1981.

# 15   Bilingualism in Ireland

These further notes, also written in the wake of publication of the report of An Coimisiún um Athbheochan na Gaeilge in 1964, deal with the question of bilingualism.

Bilingualism is a difficult term to define. It does not necessarily imply an equal mastery of two languages. It already exists in Ireland in the sense that both Irish and English are spoken as vernaculars. An tAthair Ó hUallacháin has described our situation as one in which there is more widespread knowledge of English than ever before in the Irish-speaking districts while at the same time there is some knowledge of Irish throughout the English-speaking area. The extent of that knowledge of Irish varies. He ventures the generalisation that a considerable number of people in the Galltacht would understand some simple Irish written in the Dinneen spelling and in the so-called Gaelic characters; that fewer would understand Irish in the standard spelling or Roman script; fewer still would be able both to read modern Irish and express themselves on current affairs in it; and very few would be able to understand easily a native speaker at his natural speaking pace. This is a much less developed form of bilingualism that would be found amongst, say, the Swiss or the Finns, many of whom have to know one or more extra languages for economic reasons.

A bilingual person is one who has facility in two languages as a means of communication (see the definitions of bilingual and pseudo-bilingual quoted from An tAthair Ó Dochartaigh on page 243 of the Commission's report). Again, the degree of facility in the second language may vary from equality of competence to ability to make 'complete meaningful utterances.'

235

Bilingualism would scarcely be the natural choice of any community. The use of one language is both sufficient and convenient for normal intercourse and, if it is also a language which provides easy communication with the outside world and ready access to universal knowledge, this is an added advantage. Most individuals, even of high intellectual capacity, find it difficult enough to express themselves fully in their first language. They may become bilingual or multilingual, to some degree, because of need or desire based on economic or cultural grounds. But a community tends to be bilingual only of necessity. Where bilingualism or multilingualism exists in a state it usually reflects the divergent origin or culture of sections of the population; in Switzerland this divergence is cemented over by strong traditional allegiance to the Federation but in Belgium, Canada, France and Spain it tends to be a divisive force.

In Irish circumstances it does not seem possible to suggest sufficiently compelling grounds for the creation of an inconvenient bilingual situation, i.e. one in which there would be large bodies of monoglots unable without considerable effort to understand one another. The bilingualism which it would seem reasonable to promote is one in which:

1. English was still accepted in practice as a general vernacular, though Irish had primacy of respect as the national language;

2. A widespread knowledge of Irish was ensured by the educational system and otherwise;

3. The voluntary use of Irish as a living language not only in the Gaeltacht but by individuals, families and groups outside the present Gaeltacht areas was encouraged; and

4. An awareness of, and pride in, Ireland's individuality was sustained by a general education in Irish civilisation.

A policy of bilingualism, so defined, would be a practical one for the years immediately ahead and would not exclude (indeed, would make possible) the choice of a more radical policy if, on review after a specific period, the community were so minded. Bilingualism needs such careful definition that it is doubtful whether it would serve as an appropriate short description of policy.

It must be anticipated that neither a statement of policy on the foregoing lines nor the related definition of aim in my earlier notes (see Chapter 14) will satisfy the extreme advocates of an Irish-speaking Ireland. These, for the reasons given in my notes, should not, I suggest, receive full satisfaction.

What is the nature of 'the opposition to bilingualism expressed in the past by advocates and critics of the language revival'? As regards the advocates of the language revival, such of them as oppose bilingualism presumably do so on the grounds that parity between Irish and English could not be maintained because English has behind it the weight of a world language, constantly brought to bear through the press, cinema and television. They would presumably argue that in any position short of a monolingual, Irish-speaking Ireland, the greater weight and resources of English would eventually result in the ousting of Irish; therefore the only guarantee of the continued predominance of Irish would be its sole use. This extreme viewpoint finds partial expression on page xiv of the Commission's report. It is to be noted, however, from pages 242-244 of the Report that the Commission itself does not consider bilingualism a bad thing; this section of the Report is headed *Buntáistí an Dátheangachais* (Advantages of Bilingualism).

As regards the critics of the language revival, the same section of the Report indicates some of the arguments they use, related mainly to the inability of many people – particularly those at the lower end of the intelligence range – to use more than one language for the expression of their more complex thoughts and to fears that confrontation at an early age with a second language may in some cases impede mental development. The Commission seems to be concerned to rebut certain views of Rev. Professor Ó Dochartaigh. From the Report it might appear that he is critical of the language revival aim but it may be more correct to say that he is critical of present methods . . .

The notes written in 1964 ended with a list of living authorities
to be consulted on the subject of bilingualism in Ireland.
Fourteen years later, after experience as a member of Comhairle na Gaeilge, introduction to the concept of *diglossia*, study
of the *Report on Attitudes to the Irish Language* and service as
Chairman of the pre-statutory Bord na Gaeilge, my bilingual
contribution to the debate in Seanad Éireann (14 June 1978)
on An Bille um Bord na Gaeilge included the following:

> As our objective is a bilingual society it would be wrong, in
> my view, to have the whole of this debate in Irish as if it
> were a matter only for those already competent or interested
> in the language. *'Sé pobal na hÉireann ar fad, agus ní pobal
> na Gaeilge amháin, pobal Bhord na Gaeilge.* I do not wish to
> repeat what I have said in Irish about problems which have
> beset the board so far but for which this Bill now provides
> a welcome remedy. I hope in particular that from now on
> the board will be assured of the full co-operation of the
> Department of Education and other bodies with major
> responsibilities for the advancement of the Irish language.
> Thinking in particular of that 70 per cent of the population
> who do not claim any competence in Irish I should like to
> put in a few words why the efforts of Bord na Gaeilge deserve
> the full and active support not just of Departments and RTE
> and other official bodies but of every Irish man, woman and
> child.
>
>     The board, like Comhairle na Gaeilge before them, have
> given much thought to the philosophy which should under-
> lie their approach to the public. It is recognised that in
> Ireland there is a very special linguistic problem. In other
> countries the active study of two or three languages may be
> needed to ensure full national communicability and solidar-
> ity, or to promote trade, tourism and converse with one's
> neighbours, or to give access to educational and literary
> advantages. The case for bilingualism in Ireland, however,
> does not rest on any practical necessity. Ninety-eight per
> cent of the population speak English as their mother tongue
> and the remainder speak English as a second language. So
> the Irish people already have a high proficiency in a world

language, and there is no necessity for purposes of communication or wider access to learning to provide a lingua franca, or to promote bilingualism.

The case for bilingualism here rests rather on a recognition that the Irish language is a most precious heritage, the thing that most signifies and maintains our continuity as a distinctive people, the key to a treasure-house of poetry and prose epics, folklore and song, which has expressed the imagination and feeling, the wisdom and humour, all the varied responses of generations of Irish people to life and its vicissitudes from the early centuries down, indeed, to our own day. If Ireland is to become bilingual it will be through the influence of love and esteem for Irish rather than through any linguistic or economic necessity.

Our interaction with other influences, especially the English language, has also enriched us, but English does not carry all our traditions, all the emotions and aspirations we have experienced as a people. The roots of Irish go deeper in our history and culture. Putting it negatively for a moment, if as a result of indifference, the Irish language were allowed to die, the loss would be irreparable. We would have lost one of the most important elements of our identity. We would have cut ourselves off from an invaluable heritage and made ourselves even more vulnerable than we are already to absorption in an amorphous Anglo-American culture. This, if rarely articulated, is the instinct we have about Irish. It is this that leads the majority of the population, including many with very limited knowledge of and competence in Irish, to support a policy of ensuring the future of the language. It is this sentiment that Bord na Gaeilge need to sharpen and strengthen into a will to act, to channel it into practical expression to an ever-increasing extent. The foundations have been laid and the programme announced by the board for 1978 shows the variety of well-considered means by which the board, with the help of continuing research, will be trying to promote competence in and use of the Irish language and also understanding of its value and importance to us as a community.

Whatever degree of appreciation and love may be generated in the public at large, a policy of bilingualism would, I fear, be doomed to sterility if the living source of the language, the Gaeltacht, were to contract further and continue to weaken. The last few generations have seen the everyday use of Irish ebb so fast that there now remain only scattered pools of varying size, mainly along the western seaboard. The smaller Gaeltacht communities are particularly vulnerable to extinction.

The Tánaiste, Seoirse Ó Colla, did much to help sustain the Gaeltacht and its morale when he set up Radio na Gaeltachta, which has since had a rather chequered career, but the need for a whole range of supportive measures and for the development of local self-reliance and initiative remains vital. The life-line of continuity with the past has worn dangerously thin. I suppose that, in my own life-time, the genuine Gaeltacht has shrunk by 60 per cent. I have had the sad experience of visiting and talking to the last native Irish-speakers in Omeath and on the edge of the Burren, and I am familiar, as the Minister is, with areas in north-west Mayo where the only fluent speakers of Irish left are people of our own age or older. What a tragedy it would be to see presented on our television screens the last native Irish-speaker from Carna or Ranafast.

Bord na Gaeilge have a most difficult but also a most important task–the task of keeping Irish alive and ensuring that it will be a strong and active element in a bilingual situation. I must confess I would not have thought it necessary to propose the addition of the words in the Bill 'gnáthmheán cumarsáide'.

There is a lot to be done on the way towards any such objective. The board need and deserve as much freedom and flexibility and as relatively generous access to resources as are conceded to any of our State bodies. I have pressed for this as chairman of the board. I am glad to recognise the greatly increased provision which the Minister was able to make this year and the general improvements made in this

Bill. As regards resources, I should like to urge strongly that these be enlarged soon to enable the board to finance a well thought-out professional publicity programme aimed at promoting understanding throughout the community of the importance of the Irish language and at having it more widely spoken. This is no less necessary in relation to Irish than in relation to health, road safety and similar matters.

*Ag casadh ar an nGaeilge dom, agus mar fhocal scoir, ba mhaith liom a mheabhrú arís gurab é cuspóir Bhord na Gaeilge pobal na hÉireann uilig a spreagadh chun comhoibriú dá ndeoin agus dá dtoil féin chun an Ghaeilge a chur chun cinn mar theanga bheo. Ar eagla go gceapfaí go raibh cuid dá ndúirt mé pas beag gruama, ní miste dhom a bhfuil d'ábhar dóchais againn a lua sul a scoraim.*

*Tá cumas leathan Gaeilge ann nach bhfuil feidhm á bhaint as. Tá lucht labhartha na Gaeilge le fáil i ngach réim de shaol na tíre. Tá cumas léimh sa Ghaeilge níos leithne ná már a bhí sé riamh roimhe. Tá forbairt agus caighdeánu déanta ar an teanga. Tá litríocht bheo dá cumadh sa Ghaeilge. Tá lucht éisteachta agus féachana nach beag do chláracha i nGhaeilge ar an raidio agus ar an teilifís. Tá modhanna múinte teanga ar fáil anois atá níos tarrantaí agus níos éifeachtaí ná mar a bhíodh. Tá tuiscint níos fearr ar fhadhbanna teanga, a bhuíochas sin don Tuarascáil ar Dhearcadh an Phobail. Tá báidh mhórchuid an phobail leis an nGaeilge. 'Sé tá le déanamh againn féachaint chuige go mbainfear leas as na buntáistí seo agus nach gceilfear cabhair nó airgead nó achmhainn gníomha ar Bhord na Gaeilge san saothar neamh-ghnáthach ach fíor-thábhachtach a dhaingnítear orthu sa Bhille seo.*

Recently (and I write in early 1983) the statutory Bord na Gaeilge has prepared an action plan for the years ahead and its publication is awaited, together with an announcement of government policy regarding the Irish language, now ebbing more rapidly from those Gaeltacht areas where parents have ceased to bring up their children through the medium of Irish.

*St. Laurence Gate, Drogheda.*

# 16   Mise agus an Ghaeilge

Is éadóigh go mbeifí ag súil le Gaeilge ó fhear de mo shloinnese. Sé contráilteacht an tsaoil é gurb é sloinne an athar a leanas duine, mar ba de mhuintir Chonchubhair mo mháthair ón dá thaobh agus, ar ndóigh, bheadh cuma i bhfad níos Gaelaí ar an ainm sin. Ach lena cheart a thabhairt do m'athair, ní inniu ná inné a tháinig na Whitakers go hÉirinn. Bhí mé in amhras fúthu mé féin ar feadh i bhfad agus shíl mé gurbh fhearr a rá amach go borb lom gur dóigh gur anall le Cromuel a tháinig siad. Ach thug Eamonn Mac Giolla Iasachta lámh chuidithe dom nuair a dúirt sé go raibh fear de mo shloinne ina bháille ar Dhroichead Átha in 1305 agus gur leathnaigh muintir Whitaker amach i gcríocha na Mí le himeacht aimsire. Sháraigh mé ar an nginealach sin mé féin nuair a léigh mé i leabhar Thurneysen faoi Cheltchar MacUitheachair (sean-leagan de Whitaker, is cosúil), laoch sárláidir – *ein Held von aussergewöhnlicher Starke* – rud a chruthaíonn gur sine sinn ná an Chailleach Bhéara!

Ní shílim gur chnuasaigh muintir Whitaker mórán rachmais riamh ar thailte méithe na Mí. Rugadh m'athair féin i gCill Leamhcáin i gContae na hIarmhí agus, de réir mar a thuigim, b'oibrí de chuid an bhóthair iarainn a athair siúd a d'aistrigh sa deireadh mar mháistir stáisiúin go hIubhar Cinn Trá, áit a bhfuair m'athair a chuid scolaíochta agus a ndeachaigh sé ag obair i monarchain lín. Ba i Ros Treabhair a casadh mo mháthair air – ba é an dara pósadh aige é – agus bhí sise ag obair ann mar bhanaltra, cé gurbh as Contae an Chláir di féin. Is de thaisme, mar sin, is Ultach mé, ach ní raibh a mhalairt le maíomh ag Cú Chulainn féin!

243

Ní fada a fágadh in Ultaibh mé. D'aistrigh m'athair go Droichead Átha nuair a bhí mé sé bliana d'aois. Is saoíthiúil gur mar sin a tugadh ar ais go baile duchais mo mhuintire mé!

I nDroichead Átha, ag na Bráithre Criostaí, a chuaigh mé ar scoil. Gaeilge na Mumhan a bhí i réim sa bhunscoil agus ba ar an mheánscoil a chuir mé aithne den chéad uair ar Ghaeilge Uladh. Togha múinteora, a raibh léann ollún ollscoile air, a mhúin an Ghaeilge dom ón dara bliain go dtí bliain na hArd-Teistiméireachta – Peadar Mac Cana, arbh as Iubhar Cinn Trá dó agus arbh í Gaeilge Óméith is túisce thug sé féin leis.

Bhí mé i gcuideachta scaifte de bhuachaillí thart fá 15 bliana d'aois ag iománaíocht i gcoinne foirne as Dún Dealgan ar Fheis Mhuirtheimhne in Áth Fhirdia nuair a chuir an tAthair Lorcán Ó Muireadhaigh (Grásta ó Dhia air) scrúdú béil orainn ar pháirc na himeartha, bord beag infhillte os a chomhair amach amhail is dá mba chluiche na dtrí cártaí a bhí ar bun aige. Ar an seanláthair chomhraic sin ghnóthaigh mé scoláireacht go Gaeltacht Thír Chonaill – go Coláiste Bhríde i Rann na Feirste nach raibh tógtha ach le trí bliana nó mar sin – agus b'shiúd ar bhealach mo leasa mé.

Ní raibh duine ar bith ó Dhroichead Átha i mo chuideachta ar an turas traenach chun na Rosann. Is cuimhin liom an gheit a baineadh asam nuair a chonaic mé traein bheag na suíochán adhmaid i Leitir Ceanainn agus an t-aoibhneas croí a tháinig orm nuair a bhogamar amach i measc na sléibhte agus na gcaorán. Amanna, agus an traein ag luascadh léi trí na claiseanna nó faoi bhun na mbeann, dá sínfeá amach do lámh d'fhéadfá bachlóg fraoigh a stoitheadh de thaobh na creige. Nuair a stad an traein ag Tobar an Dúin tháinig scaifte ban isteach sa charráiste, seálta dubha thart fána nguaillí, iarracht de bholadh na móna óna gcuid éadaí, agus iad ag stealladh Gaeilge. Ba é seo an chéad uair dom 'caint na ndaoine' a chluinstin agus chuir mé cluas le héisteacht orm féin. Bhí mé i bhfách le páirt a ghlacadh sa chomhrá ach d'fhan mé ciúin ag faire ar m'fhaill. Ag dul thar sliabh mór dúinn, shíl mé ceist a chur. D'fhiafraigh mé den bhean a bhí os mo chomhair

amach i nGaeilge chúramach na scoile: 'Cé'n t'ainm atá ar
an sliabh úd, le do thoil?' Baineadh stangadh aisti. 'Caidé
tá sé a ráit?' ar sise lena comharsain. 'C'ainm atá ar an
chnoc adaí, atá sé a ráit' ar sise. 'Ó, Mucais, a thaiscidh',
ar sise liom. Níor thug mé an dara hiarraidh air!

Ag stáisiún Chroithlí thúirling mé den traein agus i
gcuideachta na scoláirí eile chaith mé tamall ag caitheamh
cloch ar bharr lice 'e dheas don bhóthar fad is bhíomar ag
fanacht le carr teacht inár n-araicis. Tigh Sheáin Mhicí
Óig a cuireadh mé, thíos cois cladaigh, mar a raibh
Gráinne Phroinsís fós faoi réim i mbun scéalaíochta
agus seanchais. Thóg mé síos uaithi leagan den Bhonnán
Buí agus scéal fada fíochmhar faoi Bhalor i dToraigh. Ní
raibh leisce uirthi labhairt faoin dá dhuine dhéag
d'iníonacha ar luigh an laoch oíche leo sa chruth go raibh
dhá dhuine dhéag clainne acu trí ráithe ina dhiaidh sin!

Bliain a '31 atá i gceist agam. Chaith mé mí eile i Rann
na Feirste i 1933, 1935, 1937 agus (mar a bheadh Oisín i
ndiaidh na Féinne) i 1954, nuair a thug mé triúr de mo
chlann féin liom. Ar na tithe eile a raibh mé ar aíocht iontu
bhí Teach Bhrianaí Hiúdaí, Teach Chormaic, Teach
Frainc Bhig, Teach Joe Duffy. Caitheadh go fial liom i ngach
teach díobh agus cuireann sé lúcháir orm i gcónaí
casadh lena bhfuil fágtha ar an tsaol seo dá muintir. Is
iontach an chuimhne, agus an cion, atá ag muintir Rann na
Feirste orthu sin a bhí tráth ar lóistín acu.

Ag siúl siar bóthar na smaointí, is iad na rudaí is mó
a thig chun cuimhne:

Oícheanta na gCéilithe Móra a mhair go maidin agus
an cor seisear déag, a mhúin Séamas Ó Mealláin
dúinn, á chasadh go haigeantach againn;

An Sagart Ó Muireadhaigh ár ngríosadh chun
damhsa le gach búirtheach as – 'Beirt eile anseo';

'Is iad mo chuid Gamhna na Gamhna Geala' nó 'A
Shiubháin Ní Dhuibhir' á chanadh aige féin;

Hiúdaí Mhicí Hiúdaí, go ndéana an Rí a mhaith
air, ag gabháil den phíob;

Hiúdaí Pheadaí ag canadh 'A Bhríd Óg Ní
Mháille';

Na buachaillí i gcomórtas le chéile faoi na cailíní ba

mhaith leo a thionlacan chun an bhaile ach a sáith
cúthaileacht orthu san am chéanna. Ach lámh an
chailín a bheith i do láimhse, na méara snaidhmthe ina
chéile, nó do lámh bheith thart fána com agus,
b'fhéidir, póg amscaí a thabhairt di roimh scaradh
léithe, a Dhia nárbh aoibhinn!

Ansin, ag triall go tuirseach thar charraigeacha loma go
dtí Poll an tSnámha sula dtéimís isteach chun bricfeasta
ag bánú an lae. Codladh trom go headra.

Nó an fuchsia faoi bhláth agus loinnir chorcra i ngream-
har an bhealaigh mhóir agus tú ag rothaíocht le fána go
mall tráthnóna, ar amharc na farraige agus na n-oileán.

Nó ag siúl trasna an deáin agus baill éadaí in airde
os do chionn agat lena dtabhairt slán ón taoide; ag
líonadh na mbucaed ar 'thráigh na gcorr' i ndiaidh rabharta na Féil' Muire; nó ag iarraidh curach cruinn a
stiúradh le céasla ar loch na nduilleogaí báite ('tá
eolas beag air');

Nó ag éisteacht le Johnny Shéamaisín ag aithris scéil
'Fionnbhráid' – 'agus bhí sé canta nach raibh aon
chailín ar an domhan a bhí comh dóighiúil léithe san
am. Ar an ábhar sin bhí ráchairt mhór uirthi. Bhí
prionsaí as an Fhrainc, as an Ghearmáilte agus as
Tíortha Lochlannacha ag tarraingt uirthi is á hiarraidh
le pósadh. Ach sin a raibh ar a shon acu, ar an drochuair
daofa féin agus díthe-se.'

. . . Draíocht agus díogras na hóige . . .
Lena linn seo uilig, bhí dánta, amhráin, béaloideas agus
úrscéalta na Gaeilge ag dul i gcion orm, go háiride
cumraíocht Shéamais agus Sheosaimh 'ic Grianna agus
Sean-Phádraic Ó Conaire, sa chaoi gur tuigeadh go maith
dom an dóigh ar choinnigh an teanga i dteagmháil le saol
agus meon ár sinsear muid.

Dúirt mé gurb as Contae an Chláir do mo mháthair.
Rugadh í sa bhliain 1879 agus tá sí ag dréim le haitheantas
ar leith a fháil ó Chláiríneach cliúiteach – an tUach-
tarán Ó hIrighile – i gcionn cúpla bliain nuair a shroichfidh
sí an céad, más toil le Dia. As deisceart an Chláir di,
taobh ó thuaidh de Leaba Síoda, ar amharc na Sionna. Bhí
an Ghaeilge ag a hathair agus ag a máthair ach, dálta a lán

teaghlach eile ar fud na tíre san am, ní le Gaeilge ach le Béarla a thóg siad a gclann. Mar sin féin, is i nGaeilge is túisce d'fhoghlaim mo mháthair a cuid paidreacha agus cúpla rann páistí. Ní dhearna sí dearmad riamh ar 'Sé do bheatha, a Mhuire' nó 'Bó, Bó, Bó na leath-adhairce'. B'ionadh liom agus mé ar an bhunscoil gur 'Sé do bheatha' in ionad 'Go mbeannaíthear duit' a bhí aici agus gur 'toradh do bhronn' Íosa' a deireadh sí. Ach tuigim an scéal sin anois.

Ní go Rann na Feirste amháin a chuaigh mé agus mé ag tóraíocht na Gaeilge. Thug mé mí ar an gCeathrúin Rua i 1936 agus thaisteal mé thart fá Thír Chonaill ar fad ar rothar an bhliain ina dhiaidh sin, ag tabhairt cuairt ar Fhánaid, ar Ros Goill agus ar Ghleann Cholm Cille.

Sna blianta deireanacha ar scoil dúinn, bhunaigh mé féin agus baicle de mo cháirde cumann beag dár gcuid féin: labhraimís Gaeilge le chéile agus ba é barr ár n-iarrachtaí céilí a chur ar siúl i Seomraí an Mhéara agus cailíní na gClochar a mhealladh ann. Ba rud annamh san am sin i nDroichead Átha déagóirí a theacht le chéile a rince agus tháinig máithreacha go leor ann le súil ghéar a choinneáil orainn! Bhain muid sult as mar sin féin.

Bhíodh tóir againn freisin ar a raibh fágtha den Ghaeilge sa cheantar. Dúirt cara liom go raibh paidreacha i nGaeilge, a thug sí léi ón chliabhán, ag aintín leis a raibh cónaí uirthi ar an Tulaigh Álainn, taobh ó thuaidh den bhaile. Thógamar síos uaithi iad, cé go raibh siad truaillithe go mór agus nár thuig muid an mhórchuid acu. Scríobh mé amach de réir foghraíochta iad agus chuir mé an leagan sin ar aghaidh go dtí an tAthair Ó Muireadhaigh. Ní paidreacha, ach a mhalairt, is mó a bhí fágtha den oidhreacht, faraor. Seanfhear a raibh féasóg ag sileadh go com leis, agus a bhíodh ag thabhairt aire do sheaniarsmaí Mhainistir Buíthe san am, shíl muid gur dhócha an Ghaeilge a bheith aige ó dhúchas. Nuair a d'fhiafraigh muid de an raibh Gaeilge aige sé dúirt sé ar an láthair naofa sin 'tá, póg mo thóin'.

An máistir cuain i gCeann an Chlochair, a chaith tráth dá shaol ar bhád Árann, ní raibh aige ach 'Ná raibh aon

ádh ar do chineál' agus 'Marbhfháisg ort'. Paidreacha agus
mallachtaí – an chuid is buaine de theanga?

I mbliain 1934 bhain mé an Ard-Teistiméireacht amach
agus fuair mé post sa Státseirbhís. Chaith mé dhá bhliain
go leith ag dul go Baile Átha Cliath ar thraein na maidine
agus ag pilleadh tráthnóna. Bhí an turas laethúil seo
tuirsiúil go maith sa tSamhradh; nuair a bhíodh do chuid
caite agat sa bhaile is beag de sholas an lae a bhíodh fágtha.
Is beag, fosta, a bhíodh fágtha de mo thuarastal (£2 sa
tseachtain) nuair a bhíodh costais taistil agus lóin íoctha
agam. Ar éigean ab fhiú dom an stró a chur orm féin! Ach
thug an síorthaisteal seo faill dom leabhair a léamh agus
staidéar a dhéanamh. Lena chois sin bhíodh rang Gaeilge
ar siúl agam i seomraí an Chonartha i nDroichead Átha
agus Fearfeasa Mac Feasa á chíorú agam. I dtrátha an
ama seo, fosta, foilsíodh aiste nó dhó liom ar 'An
tÉireannach'. Lughaidh Mac Céin an t-ainm cleite a thogh
mé – ní mé anois cén fáth. Ní raibh mé ach cúpla
bliain sa Roinn Oideachais nuair a toghadh mé mar Rúnaí
Príobháideach do Thomás Ó Deirg, fear séimh, cneasta,
tuisceanach, a raibh toil mhór agam dó. Bhínn an-ghnaith-
each mar Rúnaí Aire – moll mór litreacha le scríobh agam
i nGaeilge agus i mBéarla gach lá. Ba mhór an chabhair
dom iníon le Seán Mac Maoláin a bheith mar
chlóscríobhaí agus chúntóir agam. Bhí ardmheas agam
ar Sheán de bharr an leabhair sin *Cora Cainte as Tír Chonaill*
a bhí chóir a bheith de ghlanmheabhair agam san am. Is
cuimhin liom i mbun ranga i Rann na Feirste é agus cora
cainte ar bharr a theanga aige – 'bíonn cíocras seacht sagart
ar mhnaoi gan chlainn' . . . 'Sé coigilt na circe fraoigh ar an
fhraoch é' . . . 'Chan scéal rúin é ó chluinfeas triúr é'
. . .


Phós mé i 1941. Chaith Nóra, mo bhean, tréimhsí
míosa i Rann na Feirste sna tríochaidí ach níor casadh
riamh ar a chéile ansin muid. Seisear clainne a rugadh
dúinn, cúigear mac agus iníon amháin. Chaith triúr de
na gasúir agus an ghirseach bliain ar Scoil na Leanbh sa
Rinn nuair a bhí siad an-óg – idir seacht agus naoi mbliana
d'aois. Thug mé an triúr mac is sine liom go Rann na Feirste

i 1954: ní raibh an duine ab óige, Réamonn, ach seacht mbliana d'aois san am agus ní raibh sé riamh sa Ghaeltacht roimhe sin. Bhí an bheirt ba shine cleachta go maith le Gaeilge na Rinne. Bhagair mé ar Réamonn gan dada a rá go dtí go mbeadh sé in inmhe é a rá as Gaeilge. Ní raibh smid as ar feadh cúpla lá. Ansin scairt sé amach i dtoibinne 'Cluinim carr ar an bhealach mhór'. Bhí sé i ndiaidh caidreamh a dhéanamh le tachrán dá aois de bhunadh na háite agus ba ghearr go raibh foclóir agus cumas cainte aige a rinne a ghnaithe dó. An bheirt a raibh bliain caite sa Rinn acu, chloígh siad go dlúth lena gcanúint féin. Tháinig Gearóid isteach de ruathar ón Choláiste lá agus a anáil i mbarr a ghoib aige. 'Tá tú ar ais go luath' arsa bean an tí leis. 'Tá', ar seisean, 'thánag an cóngar.' B'éigean dom a mhíniú di go dtáinig sé an aithghiorra. 'Ó, tchím', ar sise, 'cóngar, is ionann sin agus comhgar: baineann muidne feidhm eile as an fhocal sin' ach ní raibh moill uirthi an gaol a bhí eatarthu a aithint.

Domhnach áirithe ar an Bhun Bheag dúinn, bhí muid thíos ar an ché ag fanacht le muintir Ghabhla teacht ón Aifreann le dul isteach chun an oileáin. Ní raibh ach sean-bhean amháin i gcúl an bháid agus bhí na gasúir s'agamsa ag tarraingt ar théada an bháid agus ag caint lena chéile i nGaeilge na Rinne. 'Tá Gaedhlig mhaith ag na tachráin seo', ar sise, 'ach chan í Gaedhlig na háite seo í.' Bhí ionadh uirthi a chluinstin gur Gaeilge Phort Láirge a bhí acu – agus bhí siad chomh hóg sin á foghlaim gur thug siad leo go beacht na fuaimeanna 'l', 'r' agus 'n' dúbalta. Chaith beirt acu ráithe i gConamara blianta ina dhiaidh sin ar scoláireachtaí Ghael-Linn ach braithim orthu anois go bhfuil siad tógtha níos mó le cúraimí clainne ná le cúrsaí na Gaeilge. Ach tá mé i ndóchas nach rachaidh an síol in éag.

Chaith mé bliain is tríocha sa Roinn Airgeadais (1938-69) agus seacht mbliana ina dhiaidh sin sa Bhanc Ceannais. Ar chúrsaí eacnamaíochta is mó a bhí m'iúl ar feadh an ama sin, cé nár thug mé cúl riamh leis an Ghaeilge. D'fhéach mé féin agus mo bhean chuige go mbeadh sí go maith ag ár gclann. Cheannaigh mé – agus léigh mé – formhór na leabhar nua a tháinig amach. Bhí meas mór agam ar a ndearna Seán Ó hÉigeartaigh agus a bhean ar mhaithe leis an nualitríocht. Go dtí ceann de na Gaeltachtaí a bhíodh ár dtriall go hiondúil fá choinne na laethanta saoire, go Baile an Sceilg, go Múscraí, go dtí an Charraig agus an Bun Beag, go Carna, go hIorras, áit ar bith ina raibh idir Ghaeilge agus iascaireacht, sin ba rogha liom.

Is i 1946, nuair a bhí peitreal an-ghann, a chuamar go Baile an Sceilg le mí a chaitheamh i dtigh ósta an Sigerson Arms, ar le Willie Main an tráth sin é – 'Main by name but not by nature'. Chruthaigh sé sin go healaíonta nuair a shroich muid ceann scríbe an chéad lá de Mheitheamh sin. 'Caithfidh mé an carr a fhágáil sa chlós', arsa mise leis, 'ná níl ach dóthain cúpón agam lenár dtabhairt abhaile.' 'Fóill ort', ar seisean, agus scairt sé ar fhear a bhí ar aimsir aige. 'Thomáis, líon suas é.' Ansin thug mé fá deara an pumpa sa chlós agus níorbh fhada gur chuala mé gliogaíl an pheitril ag brúchtáil isteach san umar!

Lá eile agus mé ag iascaireacht ar an Imleach Mór, gan chead, ar ndóigh, tchím an fear mór ceannasach chugam trasna an phortaigh. Tá mé gafa anois, arsa mise liom féin, mura dtig liom é a mhaolú beagán. Bheannaíomar dá chéile. I nGaeilge a labhair mé agus bhí an chuid ab fhearr di aige. Bhain mé bosca toitíní as mo phóca (bhí siadsan gann san am fosta) agus thairg mé ceann dó. Nuair ba léir go raibh dúil aige iontu, thug mé air an bosca a ghlacadh mar bhronntanas. 'Ca bhfuil tú ag cur fút?' 'Tigh Willie Main.' 'Togha fir.' 'Beidh pionta nó dhó ansin romhat an chéad uair a chasfar ann thú.' B'fhiú go maith é chun an chontúirt a sheachaint agus an comhrá a choinneáil beo. Bhí an náire do mo thachtadh nuair a fuasclaíodh de mo phéin mé. 'Mise an báille, ach ní baol duit mé.' Suáilce í an ghontacht a roinn riamh leis an nGaeilge. Thaispeáin sé na hionaid iascaigh ab fhearr dom: an tráth sin, ní bhíodh aon tseilg ar bhradáin agam ach bhínn ar crith le háthas dá n-éireodh liom breac geal a mharú.

Ní raibh fhios agam an uair sin, ag dul amach go Ceann Bólais dúinn (cé go raibh comhrá breá i nGaeilge agam le bean óg ar bharr aille ann), gur i gCillrialaig taobh leis a bhíodh cónaí ar an tsársheanchaí úd, Seán Ó Conaill.

Sa réamhrá do *Leabhar Sheáin Í Chonaill* (1948) tá an méid seo ag Séamas Ó Duilearga:

Níl le feisgint indiu ar láthair tí Sheáin Í Chonaill ach carn cloch. Tá seilbh tógtha ann ag an neanntóig agus ag an bhfiadhaile agus tá an lus mór agus an liocán ag fás go buacach ar bharr áit na tine go mbímís go léir bailithe tímpal uirthe ag éisteacht leis an nguth atá anois ina thost. Maireann fós na cnuic agus an fharraige, ach cá bhfuil na daoine?

Thit sé ar mo chrann, agus mé sa Roinn Airgeadais, léacht a thabhairt i nGaeilge i 1957 ar 'Forbairt na Tíre Feasta' agus Léacht an Oireachtais ar 'Staid na Tíre' a thabhairt an bhliain dár gcionn. Is fúmsa, dá dhochreidte é, agus ní faoi oifigigh an Roinn Oideachais nó Roinn na Gaeltachta, a fágadh an chéad dréacht den Pháipéar Bán a ullmhú, le cuidiú Shéamais Uí Chiosáin. Is leis an chaibideal tosaigh a chaith mise mo dhíogras agus b'éigean an iomad leagan de a chur i gcomhairle an iomad daoine. Ach tháinig dhá rud slán a mheas mé a bheith an-tábhachtach: nár rún don Rialtas an Béarla a ruaigeadh ach an Ghaeilge a neartú agus a leathnú mar mheán cumarsáide .i. polasaí an dátheangachais; agus an dearbhú nach mbeadh oiliúint cheart ar aon pháiste in Éirinn mura mbeadh an Ghaeilge foghlamtha aige ar scoil. Bhí mé go láidir den bharúil gur mhór a chuaigh sé chun dochair don Ghaeilge i measc an phobail an t-amhras a bhíodh orthu gurb é bhí ón Rialtas agus ó lucht tacaíochta na Gaeilge í a chur go hiomlán in áit an Bhéarla agus an Béarla a chur dá chois – dá dhodhéanta is dá dhíchéillí é.

Dóbair dom dearmad a dhéanamh den eachtra a bhain dom i bhFánaid i 1942 – nó bheadh sé níos ionraice a admháil go raibh mé á choinneáil faoi cheilt go dtí go mbeadh cúiteamh an scéil le hinsint agam. Sa bhliain 1947 cuireadh ar choiste oifigiúil mé le moltaí a dhéanamh don Rialtas faoin chaoi a bhféadfaí feabhas a chur ar an Ghaeltacht mar ionad saoire. Seosamh Ó Casaide, Tadhg Ó Scanaill agus Máirtín Ó Flathartaigh a bhí ar an choiste i mo chuideachta. Thug an obair seo thart ar na Gaeltachtaí uilig muid. Agus sin mar a casadh ar ais i bhFánaid mé, an áit ar náiríodh mé i 1942, an bhliain i ndiaidh mo phósta.

Seo mar tharla. Bhí mo bhean is mé féin ar saoire ar
Charraig Airt agus chuamar ar thuras lae go Fánaid – trasna
na Maolruaidhe ar dtús agus ansin ar rothair go dtí an teach
solais. B'éigean dúinn dul thar chaladh cúpla uair i mbád
farantóireachta – scilling an duine agus sé phingin an rothar,
de réir mar is cuimhin liom. Ar ár mbealach ó dheas go
Portsalon dúinn, tháinig sé i mo cheann go mb'fhéidir gur
san Fhíor-Ghaeltacht a bhíomar agus chuir mé an cheist
seo i láthair mo mhná. Ba chosúil gur chuma léi: bhí
tuirse uirthi. Ansin, thug mé fá deara i gceartlár an bhealaigh romhainn amach fear mór téagartha ag tiomáint
trucaile. Dar liom, cuirfidh mé ceist i nGaeilge ar an fhear
seo agus beidh fuascailt na faidhbe agam. Bhí mé an-
chleachta le Gaedhlig Thír Chonaill faoin am seo agus chuir
mé féin i dtiúin don cheist agus mé ag druidim le fear na
trucaile. Scoith mé é agus thuirling den rothar. In ard mo
chinn scairt mé amach 'Bhfuil muid ar an bhealach cheart go
Portsalon?' agus a fhios agam go maith go raibh. Theann sé
an srian agus thug ar an chapall seasamh. 'É?' ar seisean.
Dúirt mé arís é, ach gan an dánacht chéanna ann. 'If
you keep straight on and take the first turn till the left, you
can't miss it.' Mhothaigh mé mo bhean ag sclogaíl. 'Go
raibh maith agat' arsa mise go tur le fear an Bhéarla. Ghlac
sé trua dom. 'Tá tú ag foghlaim na Gaeilge', ar seisean go
lách. 'Tá', arsa mise, ag maolú beagán. 'Bhuel, bygor,
chan fheil mórán dí agat go fóill.' Bhris mo bhean amach
ag gáirí. Thug seisean croitheadh don tsrian agus d'imigh
leis ar sodar.
    Ach thíos seal agus thuas seal! Cúig bliana ina dhiaidh
sin bhí carr mór Choiste na Gaeltachta ag snaidhmeadh a
bhealaigh trí íochtar Fhánada agus na céadta madaí, a
tháinig chun tsaoil le linn an chogaidh agus nach bhfaca
neach den tsórt sin riamh, ag sceamhaíl is ag drannaíl
inár ndiaidh. Bhí muid imithe ar seachrán. Tháinig muid
fad le teach beag ceann tuí agus, ós é Máirtín Ó
Flathartaigh bhí i ngar don doras, cuireadh amach é chun
aghaidh a thabhairt ar na hainmhithe allta agus fios an bhealaigh a chur. Bhuail sé cnag ar an doras agus d'fhoscail
seanbhean é. 'Ar mhiste leat a inseacht dhom, a bhean chóir,
an dtéann an bóthar seo níos fuide?' Ba léir nár thuig sí

an cheist. 'Gaitse' ar sise le fear, mac léi gan amhras, a bhí
ag tochailt préataí sa gharrdha. Chuir Máirtín an cheist
chéanna air ach níor thuig seisean é ach oiread. Ansin,
dhruid mé féin leis an triúr acu. 'An dtéid an bealach seo
níos fuide, atá sé a ráit', arsa mise. Ba mhór an sólás
croí dom an loinnir a tháinig i súile na seanmhná. 'Ó,
tá Gaedhlig agat', ar sise agus bhí díoltas sa drochbheart
bainte amach agam faoi dheireadh!

Nuair a ceapadh mé i mo Ghobharnóir ar an Bhanc
Ceannais shíl mé gur mhaith an smaoineamh corralt i
nGaeilge a bheith i ráitheachán an Bhainc. Faoi mar a
tharlaíonn go minic, tháinig gach duine liom ach fágadh
fúm féin an chéad alt a scríobh. I gCarna i mí Lúnasa
dom i 1969 scríobh mé 'An tÓr' agus chuir sin tús le
sraith. Sa ráitheachán is deireanaí a raibh baint agam leis
(Earrach 1976) bhí alt eile de mo chuid 'An Ceangal le
Sterling, Ar Cheart é a Bhriseadh?' D'aonturas le spéis sa
Ghaeilge a mhúscailt i measc baincéirí agus lucht gnó a
foilsíodh altanna ar ábhair den chineál seo. Bheadh daoine
ar bheagán Gaeilge chomh caidéiseach sin fúthu is go
n-iarrfadh siad cabhair a gclainne nó a gcarad chun brí
éigin a bhaint astu. Fiú Ghobharnóir Bhanc Shasana,
dúirt sé liom go bhfuarthas oifigeach éigin sa Bhanc sin a
bhí in ann na haltanna a aistriú!

Le linn dom bheith sa Bhanc bhí mé i mo bhall de
Chomhairle na Gaeilge. D'fhreastail mé féin is mo bhean ar
Éigsí in Óméith (An Dall Mac Cuarta), i mbaile mór an
Chabháin (Cathal Buí), i nGaoth Dobhair agus i Rann na
Feirste. Molaim Comhaltas Uladh, agus go háirithe Máire
Bean Uí Ghógáin, ar a fheabhas a bhíodar. Agus cheannaigh muid seanteach scoile in Iorras gur chuir bail uirthi mar
theach saoire. Séamas Ó Duilearga, an fear a rinne cion
céad míle fear ar son na Gaeilge sa chéad seo, a mheall
chun an taobh sin tíre i dtosach muid. Chuir mé aithne air
nuair a bhí mé sa Roinn Airgeadais agus chuidigh mé leis
na socruithe a dhéanamh chun mórchnuasach an Choim-
isiúin Bhéaloideasa a aistriú go Coláiste na hOllscoile,
Baile Átha Cliath; agus is mé tá i mo Chathaoirleach ar
Chomhairle Bhéaloideas Éireann ó shin. Bhí an cnuasach
sárluachmhar seo 'ar a choimheád' i gcaitheamh an chog-

aidh i dteach sábháilte i lár caoráin faoi bhun Néifin
agus níor leisc leis an gcoimhéadaí, An tOllamh Ó Duilearga, éisteacht le fuaim na habhann féachaint an bhfuigh-
eadh sé breac. Thug sé cuireadh dom go Gleann na Muaidhe
i 1970. Bhí lá iontach iascaireachta agam de bharr tuile agus
rabharta; mharaigh mé ceithre bhradán agus thit mé i
ngrá leis an cheantar agus lena mhuintir. Ar na cáirde atá
agam ann tá Mícheál Mac Domhnaill, Na hAchadha, Poll
an tSómais, fear stuama suaimhneach a bhfuil léann air
agus toil mhór aige don chomhrá is don cheol; teanga bhreá
Ghaeilge aige agus croí maith mór. An chéad chomhrá a
bhí agam leis i nGaeilge cois cladaigh bhíomar ag caint ar
na hathruithe a tháinig ar an aimsir leis na cianta agus rinne
mé tagairt do Dhóiteán Mór Londain agus don abhainn
bheith siochta lena linn – agus féach, bhí dáta na bliana
aige i bhfaiteadh na súl! Is i ngeall ar theach cónaithe a
bheith againn in Iorras a tharraing mé an t-ainm cleite sin
chugam féin nuair a d'aistrigh mé scéal de chuid na
hÍoslainne go Gaeilge mar chaitheamh aimsire bliain ó shin
– An tSeanchruach Fhéir (*An tUltach* Márta 1977).

Ansin, bliain sular fhág mé an Banc Ceannais, iarradh
orm bheith i mo Chathaoirleach ar Bhord na Gaeilge. Nuair
a ghéill mé d'achainí seo an iar-Aire, Tomás Ó Domhnaill, ba in éadan mo thola é, mar nár mheas mé go raibh
na cáilíochtaí ná an t-am agam chuige. Ach chuir sé crua
orm agus d'aontaigh mé fanacht fad is bheadh an bhunchloch
á leagan. Mar a dúirt mé san am le hAire na Gaeltachta,
Donncha Ó Gallchobhair, níor shíl mé riamh go mair-
feadh an tréimhse thosaigh sin trí bliana gan Bille a bheith
rite fós chun bonn reachtúil a chur faoin Bhord. Níor shíl
mé ach oiread go mbeadh sé chomh deacair is chomh
malltriallach foireann a earcú de bharr laincisí Choimis-
inéirí na Státseirbhíse, ná go mbainfeadh oiread sin
moille le cinneadh a fháil ar chuid de mholtaí an Bhoird.
Aithním go bhfuil a bheag nó a mhór den mhoill sin
inmhaite as siocair an Olltoghcháin. Sa tréimhse thosaigh
seo b'éigean dom cur i gcoinne dianchóras smachta a bheith
ar airgead a chaitheamh. Ba cheart, dar liom, go mbeadh
iontaoibh as stuaim agus díogras agus taithí na mball den
Bhord. 'Má theipeann ar an mBord aon ní fónta a

dhéanamh taobh istigh de thréimhse réasúnta, tá sé de cheart ag an Rialtas bata agus bóthar a thabhairt dóibh. Ach ná cuirtear laincisí orthu a bhacfadh orthu na trialacha cuí a dhéanamh.' Tá mé lán dóchais go mbeidh sé ar acmhainn an Bhoird clár fiúntach oibre a fhógairt agus a chur i gcrích. Bhí orm féin imeacht as an chathaoir óir tá sé toirmeasctha ar Sheanadóirí agus ar Theachtaí Dála a bheith ina gcomhaltaí de Bhoird Stáit.

Maithfear dom, mar sin, focal nó dhó a rá faoin tromaíocht atá déanta ar Bhord na Gaeilge. An té a iarrfas leas na Gaeilge a dhéanamh go stuama tá a fhios agam go gcaithfidh sé neamhshuim a dhéanamh den tsearbhas. Faraor, ní bhíonn ar bun de shíor ag an chuid is fíochmhaire de lucht tacaíochta na Gaeilge ach gearáin agus géarchaint; ní fhéadfadh Dia féin iad a shásamh. Ní raibh an Bord ach tagtha ar an saol go raibh siad á rá gur cur i gcéill a bhí ar siúl ag an Rialtas, nach raibh siad 'dá-ríre' i dtaobh na Gaeilge, agus nach mbeadh aon rath ar Bhord na Gaeilge. Ní raibh siad sásta riamh cothrom na féinne a thabhairt don Bhord; níor thuig siad gur ar phobal na hÉireann agus nach ar phobal na Gaeilge amháin atá an Bord ag freastal; agus ghéaraigh ar a ndrochmheas nuair ba léir go mbainfeadh moill le toradh a theacht ar shaothar an Bhoird mar gurbh fhearr leis an Bhord an staidéar agus an réamhobair chuí a bheith déanta acu chun clár gníomha éifeachtach a eagrú sula scaipfí díogras agus maoin. Caitheadh an t-achasán leis an Bhord nár chaith sé iomlán an airgid a bhí ar fáil agus ní fada go raibh bréag á scaipeadh i dtaobh céad míle punt (!) a bheith ceilte ar chúis na Gaeilge. Sé an fhírinne go bhfuil caiteachas an Bhoird ag dul i méid go tapa. An té atá cleachta ar charr a thiomáint tuigeann sé go dtógann sé tamall air an lánluas a bhaint amach, fiú má bhíonn an t-umar ag cur thar maoil le peitreal. I dtaca leis na clamhsáin seo de, tá an Bord mar a bheadh sé teannta idir an dá thine Bealtaine, é féin ag iarraidh rudaí áirithe a áiteamh ar an Rialtas (maidir le foilsitheoireacht, mar shampla) agus ag coinneáil srian ar a mhífhoighid chúns nach bhfuil a mhacasamhail de smacht ar lucht a cháinte – clocha ceangailte agus madaí scaoilte!

Ag fágáil slán agus beannacht ag Bord na Gaeilge dom, ní raibh mé ag tréigean na Gaeilge, ar ndóigh. Admhaím nach ndearna mé riamh gaiscíocht ar a son ach bhí mé dílis dí ar mo dhóigh féin – 'I have been faithful to thee, Cynara, in my fashion'. Sa chuntas a thug mé in óráid phoiblí sa bhliain 1977 ar na nascanna cultúrtha idir an tír seo, an Bhreatain agus an Fhrainc, tá míniú ar an dílseacht sin. Cúitíodh go maith liom é; is saibhride go mór an spéis agus an sult a bhain le mo shaol an bhá sin leis an Ghaeilge a musclaíodh fad ó shin i nDroichead Átha. Go dtuga Dia slán í, mar Ghaeilge!

# Note to Chapter 16.

[1] Fuair sí bás ar 24 Feabhra, 1979 — suaimhneas síorraí dá h-anam.

# 17   Cultural Links

It is a great honour for someone entirely outside the field of medicine to be invited to give the nineteenth John Snow Memorial Lecture. No one could fail to be impressed by the pioneering achievements which, despite ill-health, this York-shireman crowded into his short lifespan of forty-five years. But I am not competent to assess his contribution to the science of anaesthetics and, in any case, I was encouraged to talk about something altogether different. So I have chosen to address you on some cultural links in the past between the principal countries represented here — Great Britain, France and the host country, Ireland. I do so without any malicious intention of taking revenge on anaesthetists by putting them asleep. Accidents may happen but I shall try to sustain your interest, without any pretence of original scholarship, and inspired less by reverence than by that light-hearted spirit which made Lady Longford say of the use of chloroform at the birth of one of Queen Victoria's children: 'Even the names of the Queen's attendants seemed to share the aura of purity which her royal participation had given to the subject: Mrs Lilly and Mrs Innocent the midwives, and, of course, Dr Snow.'

It seems only fair, since I shall be making scant reference to medicine, which is your competence, that I, for my part, should avoid economics and finance, which you might consider mine. So, with a quick and tantalising reference to our first coins, struck by a Viking King – Sitric III of Dublin – in the tenth century and virtual replicas of the more widely-used coins of the Saxon King, Aethelred II (foreshadowing by a thousand years our choice of a parity relationship between the Irish pound and sterling!), I shall forego financial matters and

257

engage you on the common but rich ground of culture. Even
there I must be selective. Time would not permit me to go
over the already well-trodden ground of the influence in the
twentieth century of Irishmen such as Yeats, Joyce and Beckett
on Anglo-Irish and indeed, world literature. Nor can I do more
than remind you of the contribution to the English drama of
Congreve, Sheridan, Goldsmith, Wilde, Shaw, Synge, O'Casey
and many others; and of the fresh source of poetic enrichment
and inspiration provided by translations from the Irish language in the nineteenth century. I shall confine myself to some
of the lesser-known interactions of the literature and music of
the three countries from early historic times to the end of the
Elizabethan Age, when, in Ireland, the old Gaelic order col-
lapsed and Irish began to be replaced by English as the
language of poetry and politics as well as of trade and commerce. The visual arts I must leave out of the picture. I shall
be a magpie – an Irish magpie – picking up some curious and
interesting facts which may divert you for a while from the
scientific preoccupations of this conference.

May I recall, first, the origins we have in common as
inhabitants of Ireland, Britain and France. At the time Caesar
was writing about his campaigns – indeed, probably for centuries before – the chief ruling peoples in our three countries
were Celts and we shared the same heathen gods, the same
language and nomenclature, the same social and political
institutions, the same general way of life.

There is no time for detail about that way of life, in which
not only warriors but poets, seers and druids were held in high
honour. But, with tonight's banquet in view, it may be timely
to quote an ancient writer's description of the eating habits of
the Celts:

> . . . the nobles shave the cheeks but let the moustache grow
> freely so that it covers the mouth. And so, when they are
> eating, the moustache becomes entangled in the food, and
> when they are drinking the drink passes, as it were, through
> a sort of strainer. When dining they all sit not on chairs, but
> on the earth, strewing beneath them the skins of wolves or
> dogs. At their meals they are served by their youngest
> grown-up children, both boys and girls. Beside them are

hearths blazing with fire and cauldrons and spits containing large pieces of meat. Brave warriors they honour with the finest portions of the meat. . . . (Diodorus Siculus)

The Romans subdued Gaul and most of Britain but never came to Ireland. Tacitus's father-in-law, Agricola, who commanded for a time the Roman army in Britain, never put to the test his boast that Ireland could be taken and held by a single legion and a few auxiliaries. In fact, when the Roman grip on Britain and Gaul was loosening, Irish raiders were active on the fringes of the decaying empire. This was our only colonial period. Irish kingdoms were established during the fourth century in Wales and at the end of the fifth century in Scotland. Between the Saxons and ourselves we squeezed some of our P-Celtic cousins out of south-west Britain and forced them to take refuge in Armorica (present-day Brittany) where a Celtic language, Breton, still lives on. In Scotland our early gains were extended and consolidated, so that by the ninth century, the Picts having been overcome and assimilated, the whole of that country was Gaelic-speaking and ruled by an Irish dynasty. Indeed, for a further four hundred years Irish (or Gaelic) was the language of the Scottish Court; Ireland and Scotland shared a common literary tradition until the seventeenth century; and there is still in both countries a widely-held desire to preserve the individuality and distinctiveness associated with the threatened but tenacious Gaelic language and its literature.

One of the slaves taken from Roman Britain by an Irish raiding party came back to us with the Christian message. Some of us Irish cannot quite reconcile ourselves to having been evangelised by a Briton. We preferred to think of Patrick as coming from Gaul, sent to us direct by Pope Celestine in AD 432. This theory is no longer accepted and we now content ourselves with the thought that we have repaid the debt to our neighbours by sending Colmcille to Iona and Scotland and Aidan to Northumbria!

Writing, and access to Latin literature, came with the monastery, which was the administrative and cultural centre of early Irish Christianity. The ancient secular schools of poetry, genealogy, topography and law no longer had to rely entirely on mnemonic tradition, though for centuries afterwards they clung to the oral, in preference to the written word. Kings, poets and broad-minded clerics worked together to preserve this tradition by committing it to record. 'It is an interesting thought that had it not been for the tolerance and intellectual curiosity of the monastic *literati*, very little of the old literary heritage would have been ours now to enjoy.' (MacCana).

There were only three nations beyond the sway and influence of the Roman Empire whom, as Kuno Meyer said, 'letters reached early enough to leave behind some record of their pagan civilisation in a vernacular literature. These were the Irish, the Anglo-Saxons and, comparative latecomers, the Icelanders.'

Reproducing in Latin, with intricate and loving ornament, the Gospels, the Epistles and the writings of the Fathers was, of course, the first and special care of the monastic scriptoria but Irish itself was used from very early times both to record the prehistory, the great epics, the Brehon law and poetry and also to write 'glosses' on the Latin texts. There is a 1,200-year-old fragment of a St Matthew Gospel in Irish in the Stiftsbibliothek at St Gallen and the 'glosses' in Irish manuscripts at Wurzburg, Milan and elsewhere in Europe are important sources of our knowledge of the vocabulary, grammar and structure of Old Irish. At St Gallen, too, one can see the neumatic notations made by Irish monks at the Carolingian Court as a guide to the intonation of chant. These intricate squiggles on top of the Latin words of the Psalter preceded the invention of stave notation.

From the sixth to the twelfth century there was much coming and going between monks and scholars in these Western European islands and a great exodus from Ireland to the European continent. This was our age of pride, when this 'island of saints and scholars' carried the torch of faith and learning back to a Europe engulfed in darkness and barbarism. Admittedly there were Irishmen, then as now, who were neither saints nor scholars – sham pilgrims and turbulent itinerants – but those with a genuine claim to fame were numerous and spread themselves widely. As the newly-appointed Archbishop of Armagh, Tomás Ó Fiaich, says, the Irish went mainly to Britain during the sixth and early seventh centuries, to France and Belgium during the second half of the seventh century, to the cathedral towns of north-eastern France and Belgium (Laon, Liège, Aachen, Rheims, Cambrai, Soissons) during the ninth century, to the border territory of Lorraine and the Rhineland from the middle of the tenth century into the eleventh, and to southern Germany (and Austria) from the twelfth century on. Colmcille and Aidan, the evangelisers of Scotland and Northumbria, I have already mentioned. The Venerable Bede tells us of a Northumbrian king (Aldfrid) who, shortly before he ascended the throne in 671, 'cultivated study among the Irish, submitting to a voluntary exile for the love of learning'. To undergo the penance of separation from homeland and kinsfolk in order to evangelise the new pagan tribes who had overrun the Roman empire was the driving force behind the *peregrini pro Christo*. Amongst the most famous were Columban, who towards the end of the sixth century founded monasteries as Luxeuil in France and Bobbio in Northern Italy; Gall, his recalcitrant disciple, who stayed on in the wild country around Lake Constance rather than accompany his master to Italy; Kilian who evangelised the Thuringians and Franconians during the second half of the seventh century; Fursa and his brothers who made Péronne the 'Monasterium Scottorum' (*Scotti* being the then current description of Irishmen) and an important entrepot for the distribution of manuscripts from Ireland throughout Western Europe; Virgilius of Salzburg (second half of the eighth century) whose views about the cosmos incurred the same Papal disfavour as those of Galileo later; Colman of the High King's family, who was murdered on his way to the Holy Land in 1012 and is specially commemorated at Melk in Austria. I myself have noticed, when visiting the shrines of some of these saints, that a local saint shares the honours of the altar with them – thus Otmar at St Gallen and Ruprecht at Salzburg. I suppose Irish initiative and devotion needed eventually to be underpinned by German organisation and method!

Many Irish scholars were attracted to the Carolingian Court towards the end of the eighth and during the ninth century; amongst them Sedulius Scottus, Clemens Scottus, Dungal, Dicuil the geographer, and the philosopher you see represented on our new £5 note, John Scottus Eriugena. He has been described as the enfant terrible of contemporary churchmen and theologians. The following story is told of him by William of Malmsbury, the twelfth-century English historian. Charles the Bald was entertaining and had, like his guests, imbibed well. Mischievously he looked across to John Scottus and asked *'Quid distat inter Sottum et Scottum?'* ('What is there between a Sot and a Scot?'). The Irishman replied *'Tabula tantum'* ('Only the table').

Ordinarily a visitor to Dublin could see in Trinity College library the Book of Kells, a ninth-century manuscript in majuscule containing supreme examples of Irish illuminative art. (At the moment half of it is on loan to the Metropolitan Museum, New York.) In the Book of Armagh and in less ornate and later Irish manuscripts one may notice the distinctive style imparted by the Irish hand to the Latin letters, a style of calligraphy carried by Irish schools into England and many parts of Europe. Vellum was scarce and dear and as Crump and Jacob say in their *Legacy of the Middle Ages* the obvious way of saving vellum was to write more on a page.

> One way of getting more on a page was to make narrow instead of broad letters, to write a smaller script, in short, to use minuscule. It is this forced economy which made the Irish, probably an impecunious race even in the seventh and eighth centuries, squeeze more writing into a page than a decent regard for the reader's convenience would warrant, or good taste dictate ... and it is perhaps not a mere coincidence that the two centres from whence come most of our Latin palimpsests are both Irish foundations. How thoroughly the lesson of thrift had been inculcated in the followers of St Columban and St Gall, and how badly in need they were of writing material in the seventh and eighth centuries may be surmised from the frequency with which the monks of St Gall and Bobbio made use of membranes that had already been written upon. It was not out of contempt for the classics that Cicero's *De Republica*, Fronto's letters, Lucan and Juvenal were erased – for biblical and patristic texts suffered a similar fate – but out of sheer need of writing material.

These authors describe minuscule as the medieval contribution par excellence to writing and 'to Ireland belongs the credit of having been the first to develop a minuscule in the true sense of the word.'

It would, however, be a pity to pass from these widely dispersed manuscripts without a glimpse not only at their beauty of form but also at the literary treasures almost hidden away in their content. If space could be found for it, a poem or even a snatch of verse in Irish might be written on fly-leaf, margin or end-page of a psalter or gospel. Various non-Irish experts have remarked on 'the extraordinary sincerity and directness of feeling' in this early personal poetry (Robin Flower), on the love of nature, even its tiniest phenomena, which it reveals – the 'natural magic' of Celtic poetry, as Matthew Arnold called it – and on the freshness and beauty of this 'earliest voice from the dawn of West European civilisation' (Kuno Meyer). It would be tantalising not to give some instances.

Here is one of those 'little poems that jet forth as suddenly as the song that prompts them and are as suddenly silent' (Robin Flower's comment and translation):

The tiny bird
Whose call I heard,
I marked his yellow bill.
The ousel's glee
Above Loch Lee
Shakes golden branches still.

There was a singular intensity of devotion in the early religious poetry. This is a translation by Kuno Meyer of part of a short poem on the Crucifixion:

At the cry of the first bird
They began to crucify Thee, o cheek like a swan,
It were not right ever to cease lamenting –
It was like the parting of day from night.

Ah! though sore the suffering
Put upon the body of Mary's Son –
Sorer to Him was the grief
That was upon her for His sake.

In the following quatrain the call of ascetic duty prevails over temptation of the flesh:

The clear-voiced bell
On chill wild night God's hours doth tell;
Rather in it I'll put my trust
Than in a wanton woman's lust.

The hermit monk in his lonely cell could enjoy a cat's companionship. Over a thousand years ago one such monk wrote this delightful lyric and Flower's translation catches the rhyme and rhythm of the original Irish:

I and Pangur Bán my cat
'Tis a like task we are at:
Hunting mice is his delight
Hunting words I sit all night.

I cannot quote all eight verses, though the harmony and counter-point are perfect. Suffice it to cite the last:

Practice every day has made
Pangur perfect in his trade;
I get wisdom day and night
Turning darkness into light.

The peace of the monasteries was, however, being shattered at this time by Viking raids, as the following quatrain in the St Gall Priscian recalls:

The bitter wind is high tonight,
It lifts the white locks of the sea:
In such wild winter storm no fright
Of savage Viking troubles me.

In this early poetry – as in the prose and verse of the epic tales, especially the *Táin* – we see that 'sharp and homely brevity of epigrammatic speech' which Flower considered to be the special ever-present characteristic of Irish literature 'from the earliest records down to the tales and popular sayings current among the peasantry today.'

The Vikings had started to plunder and sack the Irish monasteries on coast and river bank before the end of the eighth century. They established settlements at Limerick and along the eastern coast. Norse place names such as Skerries, Holmpatrick, Howth, Wicklow, Arklow and Lambay bear testimony to their presence. For over 150 years Dublin was a Viking city, ruled by Olafs and Sitrics, until their power was broken by a combined force of native Irish and Limerick Vikings in a battle on the north side of the Liffey in 1014. Since this Address commemorates a man born in York, it is a curious coincidence that Dublin and York were ruled for a period by members of the same Viking family which, alas, like other families before and since, was rent by internal strife.

In the interval of 150 years between the defeat of the Norse-men and the arrival of the Normans much constructive work was done in the literary and ecclesiastical spheres; the great books were written which have survived to this day, including the Book of Leinster and the Book of the Dun Cow, with their compilations of Irish heroic tales and the poetry of the *filí*; a beginning was made on reform of Church organisation and dioceses were set up with defined territorial limits under epis-copal jurisdiction. But political unity was not consolidated and the Norman conquest was made easier by divisions among the Irish. The new methods of warfare and defence employed by the Normans enabled them to establish and consolidate sig-nificant areas of feudal sovereignty in the east and south and later in the west. The leaders spoke French but their followers were a mixed lot of Welshmen, Saxons, Flemings and other opportunists. Before long, however, they were all assimilated into a mainly Irish-speaking community.

The arrival of the Normans, and hard on their heels, the continental (French-speaking) religious orders – Cistercians, Dominicans, Franciscans – reinforced the influence on Irish culture of the contacts which saint, scholar and vagabond had already forged with the European continent. The Normans themselves were interested primarily in music and dance as forms of light recreation, and the new orders were not as scholarly and cultivated as the monks of old, but both influences 'readied the road' to northern France where the literature in the thirteenth century continued to be the richest in Europe. To northern France had spread from Provence and Limousin the songs and dances of the troubadours, and romantic love became the principal subject of poetry in western Europe from the thirteenth century on. Our own Irish folk songs in their present form belong mainly to the period 1600-1850 but some of them have roots as far back as the thirteenth century.

If I may turn to medicine for a moment, you are doubtless aware that in medieval times the medical schools of Montpellier, Padua and Paris were international centres of learning. From 1350 or so onwards students from Ireland attended these schools and it is not perhaps too fanciful to suppose that they brought home not only a knowledge of the Arabian medicine taught there but also much non-medical Arabian lore and a repertory of the new songs and dances, the Pastourelle, the Chanson d'Amour, the Chanson de Jeune Fille, the Carole and the Reverdie.

Their studious zeal is, however, confirmed by the vast amount of medical lore translated into Irish in the Middle Ages. In the Royal Irish Academy alone there are thirty-six medical manuscripts, mostly Irish translations from the works of Avicenna, Aurelius Celsus, Hippocrates, Galen, indeed a whole range of medical authorities then in repute. Occasionally no Latin original can now be traced for the Irish translation. The *Rosa Anglica* of John of Gaddesden, who was physician at the Court of Edward II, was written in Latin and translated soon afterwards and many times into Irish; yet it was only in this century that it was translated into English – from the Irish version!

A similar zeal ensured the continuation of the old Irish tradition of translating and adapting Latin and Greek texts. The versions in Irish of the *Aeneid* and other classical texts are the oldest in a Western European vernacular and these and other tales and romances helped to provide the inspiration for Irish analogues of the Orpheus legend, for visions of hell and

heaven – there were Irish precursors of Dante – for accounts
of the pursuit of hapless lovers and so on. In the later Middle
Ages and during the Renaissance, the translations extended
not only to medical texts but to works of philosophy and
astronomy as well as to religious works, moral and immoral
tales, poetry, romance and travel like the tales of Mandeville
and Marco Polo. Horace and Ovid found their way into Irish.
Aesop travelled to Ireland with his fables, and Erasmus
appeared in Irish garb in *Pairlimint na mBan*. The traffic was
not one-way; an echo of an Irish song is heard in Shakespeare's
*Henry V* where Pistol replies to the Frenchman he has defeated
on the battlefield: 'Quality! Calen O custure me'. *Cailín ó
chois tSiúire mé* – I am a girl from beside the river Suir – was
the name of a popular Irish song of the time. Indeed, since
music knows no boundary and travels further and faster than
the written word, many Irish tunes were internationally
known. They are well represented, for instance, in the *English
Dancing Master* published by Playford in 1650 and in other
publications prior to Bunting's organised and systematic collection, begun at the end of the eighteenth century.

In old Irish literature women like Maeve and Gráinne are
seen using their power and beauty to advance their own
interests. Romantic love was a rare otherworldly affliction.
'The loves of the heroines of the old sagas are like swift and
terrible visitations' says Robin Flower. The love commemorated in the medieval songs, however, was a special, indeed
heretical, kind of love, *amour courtois*, developed under the
influence of Arabian philosophy in southern France. It was
certainly not the relationship of man and wife. The concept at
that time was that no woman was ripe for love until she was
married and few were allowed to commit the indiscretion of
loving a husband. It was an illicit and insatiable desire, a
sentimental passion in which the woman was idealised. As the
art form became more popular the love itself became less
courteous – the rendering of homage and service to the loved
one gave way to blandishments intended to ensnare her.
Indeed, in some of the Pastourelles, the young man boasts of
his forceful conquest of the fair country maid. This poetic form
spread from French into English, Welsh, Irish and most of the
languages of the European mainland. It was inevitably

moulded to suit the Irish temperament and to conform to
bardic metrical rules. The courtly poems could be spiced with
a light touch of irony:

> They lie who say that love must be
> A sickness and a misery;
> He that ne'er loved woman knows
> Never anything but woes.

> .   .   .

> Clad in flesh and blood I move
> Though a swan-like maid I love;
> Though I love, I eat and sleep
> Music's service still I keep.

A lover's farewell to his mistress has these lines:

> And if we meet, as we may do,
> At church or on the plain,
> You'll pass me by as I will you
> Nor turn your head again.

> We'll ne'er admit that it was I
> That did you so adore,
> And both of us will soon deny
> We ever met before.

The theme of renunciation is expressed with skill but I fear
dubious fervour in a poem attributed to the priest-historian
Geoffrey Keating:

> O woman full of wile
> Keep from me thy hand;
> I am not a man of the flesh
> Tho' thou be sick for my love.

> .   .   .

Take thy mouth from my mouth
Graver the matter so;
Let us not be skin to skin
From heat cometh will.

'Tis thy curling ringleted hair
Thy grey eye bright as dew,
Thy lovely round white breast
That draw the desire of eyes.

Every deed but the deed of the flesh
And to lie in thy bed of sleep
Would I do for thy love
O woman full of wile.

Apart from the studied compositions of the bardic schools, the
love theme in all its aspects has been cherished, down to our
own time, in popular poetry and song. The best of these love
songs, says Professor MacCana, 'in their intensity, vivid colour
and dramatic simplicity are no whit inferior to the early lyric
verse. . . . Small wonder that Douglas Hyde's *Love Songs of
Connaught* was Synge's constant companion and one of the
dominating influences upon his writing.'

Let me quote one of the songs Hyde collected, which is a
poignant expression of loneliness and longing:

My grief on the sea,
How the waves of it roll!
For they heave between me
And the love of my soul!

Abandoned, forsaken,
To grief and to care,
Will the sea ever waken
Relief from despair?

My grief and my trouble!
Would he and I were
In the province of Leinster,
Or county of Clare!

Were I and my darling –
Oh, heart-bitter wound! –
On board of the ship
For America bound!

On a green bed of rushes
All last night I lay,
And I flung it abroad
With the heat of the day.

And my love came behind me –
He came from the South;
His breast to my bosom,
His mouth to my mouth.

The first Norman Earl of Desmond wrote courtly love poems
in French; but by the end of the fourteenth century, his son
(the 3rd Earl), Gerald the Rhymer, was writing them in Irish.
Indeed, this FitzGerald caught the imagination of Irish
story-tellers and according to them he never died but lies
enchanted below the waters of Lough Gur, wakening every
seven years to ride the white-capped waves. Another
FitzGerald, the ninth Earl of Kildare, had early in the sixteenth
century a library containing 34 Latin books, 36 French, 20
Irish and 22 English. The linguistic situation of these centuries
shows how close, amongst the educated at least, were the links
between Ireland, England and France. Three vernaculars,
Irish, French and English, were currently spoken over large
parts of Ireland, 'although in the battle of tongues the victory
inevitably inclined to the Irish side'. In Scotland the position
was similar, but with English gaining ground. In England too,
the linguistic situation from the Norman conquest to Chaucer's
time showed much variety. Amongst the nobility, and indeed
largely amongst the common people, French was the principal
spoken language up to 1250 – it was probably the foremost
vernacular at Oxford University in the thirteenth century –
but English had gained the upper hand by the end of that
century. Nevertheless, French singers and musicians were
prominent at the English Court even in the fourteenth century.
Professor Seán Ó Tuama has described the people of

England and France, as well as the Anglo-Normans of Ireland, as sharing, in this era, virtually one culture. But this cultural community was in time undermined by political division. Language was ever associated with political allegiance. As early as 1366 an English-dominated Parliament in Kilkenny tried to outlaw the use of Irish by Englishmen in Ireland, but the Anglo-Irish lords paid little heed to this enactment and, curiously, French remained the language of Acts of Parliament until 1472.

The real change began with the Tudors and culminated in the destruction of the old Gaelic society at the Battle of Kinsale in 1601, after which the principal native chieftains fled to the European continent, leaving Irish literature virtually without patrons and dependent on the loyalty of the common people and the desultory support of the Big House – 'a sort of oasis in a desert of poverty'. Ironically, as Professor Brian Ó Cuív has remarked, only sixty years before Kinsale, when Henry VIII was proclaimed King of Ireland by his Parliament in Dublin, the business had to be transacted in Irish. Of the Lords present only the Earl of Ormond, who acted as interpreter, could speak English!

I do not wish to go beyond the Tudor Age when, as I have said, a sadder fate befell the Irish language, though it has shown remarkable resilience and imaginative force, particularly in poetry and story-telling, down to our own day. We kept up our contacts with Europe, through the Wild Geese, through the scribes of religious and secular patrons on the continent, through our scholars at universities in Paris, Louvain, and Salamanca. We have, as I recalled at the outset, made a distinctive contribution to English literature. In turn, both France and England have shown a scholarly interest in Celtic studies: it is over a hundred years since the *Révue Celtique* (now *Études Celtiques*) was founded for this purpose in France and exactly a hundred years since the Chair of Celtic was established at Oxford.

As a general observation about the period I have so rapidly surveyed I suppose one could say that the Norsemen founded our towns and the Norman-French and English consolidated them for defence, trade and administration. No large town ever became fully Irish. Gaelic society remained essentially rural and reached its highest artistic expression, not in city architecture or painting but rather in minute artistry on vellum, metal and stone and in the fresh poetic vision of monk or scholar in the quietness of monastery or bardic school.

I have already touched on the interest of Irish monks in religious chant and on the interaction of Irish and continental airs and dance tunes down the centuries. Dancing in fact was a popular medieval import into Ireland. Irish harpists saved many of the best Irish tunes from oblivion. The blind Carolan, who died in 1738, was well acquainted with the music of Vivaldi and Corelli and was a composer in his own right. His skull, by the way, like that of Haydn later, suffered a macabre fate; it was believed that milk boiled in it, or water containing powdered fragments of it, was a cure for epilepsy. Such was the level of superstition, or dare I say, medical research in those days! Bunting's systematic collection of Irish airs began with the last convention of harpists organised by him in Belfast in 1792 and it was published in parts over succeeding decades. This and the work of Petrie and other collectors made traditional Irish music accessible to a wide public in these islands and beyond. Ireland received as honoured visitors Handel (whose Messiah was first performed here in Dublin), Arne, Francisco Scarlatti and, in the last century, Franz Liszt. Handel, indeed, is supposed to have wished that he, rather than the seventeenth-century Cearbhall Ó Dálaigh, had composed the Irish air 'Eileen Aroon' which popularised those well-known words of welcome *Céad míle fáilte*. Beethoven and Schumann were interested in Irish music and Mendelssohn wrote Fingal's Cave under the inspiration of Macpherson's version of the Irish poetic cycle recounting the heroic deeds and hunts of Finn, Oisín and the Fianna. Michael Kelly from Mary Street, Dublin, sang in the first performance of Mozart's Figaro – a worthy operatic predecessor of John McCormack and Margaret Burke-Sheridan. An Irishman, John Field, was the first to compose the nocturne and Balfe and Wallace made their contribution to the Opera in The Bohemian Girl and The Lily of Killarney. Thomas Moore, Byron's Irish friend, through his Lalla Rookh and Irish Melodies, became well-known as a poet throughout Europe. The 'Melodies', which were Moore's words set to Irish airs taken from Bunting and other sources, are said to have sparked off music in composer after composer, Berlioz being particularly influenced by Moore as a 'source of musical quotation and verbal inspiration over decades'. It was Moore, the Irish nationalist, who made the rather malicious comment that 'music is the only talent for which our English neighbours ever deigned to allow us any credit'.

But the Irish magpie has now hopped on to controversial ground, and he had better return to his nest before any discord enters to spoil our sense of shared origins and culture or cast a shadow on the pleasant atmosphere of this international gathering. So I bring this Memorial Lecture to a close in the hope that what I have brought to your notice may do something to make you feel more at home in Ireland and add interest to your visit.

*Campanile, Trinity College, Dublin (above); University College, Cork (below).*

# 18  Third Level Education –
## Essential Public Safeguards

As Chancellor of the National University of Ireland it was natural that I should ask myself what were the principal responsibilities which fell to the University as distinct from the constituent colleges. The latter had a large degree of autonomy and, in particular, were not financially dependent on the University. It was clear from the terms of the Charter and legislation, as well as from experience of the business of the Senate of the University, that the University's primary concern was with two issues: the adequacy of degree standards and the suitability of appointees to posts as lecturer and professor.

The *Report of the Commission on Higher Education,* whose major recommendation was in favour of the splitting of the NUI into independent universities, had recommended a Council of Irish Universities which would have mandatory powers in regard at least to the following matters:

> entrance and degree standards, schemes of extern examining, conditions for transfer of students, exchange of information on policy, development and research, and participation in post-graduate student-ship and fellowship schemes.

The Commission saw the function of a Council as being not just to serve its members but to 'serve the community by ensuring that the member institutions would co-ordinate their activities for the common good'.

Discussions between NUI and TCD had resulted in 1970 in agreement that the powers of a Conference of Irish Universities should include: approval of the appointment of external examiners and the right to receive an annual report from each external examiner on the adequacy of standards; ensuring reasonable uniformity with regard to appointments, promotions, salaries and pensions of academic and other staff.

The Higher Education Authority (HEA) in 1972 thought that some of the powers suggested in the NUI/TCD Agreement would amount to a serious encroachment on several principles of university autonomy – for instance, the power in relation to external examiners 'would appear to violate the right of a University, in our tradition fundamental, to make its own appointments and to set its own academic standards'.

What seemed to be compatible with the views of universities and HEA was a merely ad hoc experimental, informal, advisory or consultative non-statutory body. It seemed to me as a citizen that there was a public interest, as well as a university interest, in the maintenance of the highest standards in relation to degrees and appointments of staff. If there were a lapse from such standards, the corrective process might be unduly protracted and expensive on the national level if it depended solely on the reaction of a particular university to public awareness and criticism of deficiencies.

It was on this basis that I wrote to successive Ministers for Education urging that legislation creating independent universities should prescribe in the public interest procedures designed to ensure adequacy of degree standards and impartiality and excellence in appointments to posts as lecturer and professor. An opportunity of pressing these points in Leinster House arose when the Bill dealing with the National Institute for Higher Education, Limerick, came before Seanad Éireann on 2/3 July 1980. The following abridged version of my interventions will outline and explain the views I hold regarding this important area of public interest.

My remarks on the Second Reading on 2 July 1980, ended:

*Is é m'achaine ar an Aire go ndéanfaí cúram níos deimhne sa Bhille den dá ní a luaigh me cheana – an fhoireann teagaisc is foirfe a roghnú agus caighdeán na gcéimeanna agus na dteastas a bheith cothrom, ar a laghad, nó níos airde, más féidir, ná mar tá sa Chomhphobal i gcoitinne. Beidh mé ag moladh leasaithe dá réir ar Chéim an Choiste.*

While I wish to see NIHE Limerick established on a statutory basis, I am not enamoured of this Bill in its present form because it treats NIHE Limerick as if it were a State corporation rather than a pioneering third-level educational institution needing special freedom and flexibility if it is to succeed in the urgent national objective of promoting technological studies and skills in a country still too biased in favour of the purely academic.

Instead of so many strict and detailed ministerial controls, I suggest that what should above all appear in this legislation, and in any other legislation concerning third-level institutions, are provisions establishing a system or procedures to reassure the public that two essential criteria will be met. One, that staff appointments will be on merit only, with no room for canvassing or favouritism; and two, that the degrees and diplomas awarded will be of an adequately high standard, bearing favourable comparison with those in other EEC countries.

The second of these criteria requires not merely that standards should satisfy the NCEA[1] but an effective system of external examiners or advisors as well.

The first criterion – regarding staff appointments – would be satisfied by legislation requiring, not only in NIHE but in every university and third-level institution, an appointments system directed towards ensuring the pre-eminence of excellence and quality. I believe the best way of doing this is to prescribe assessment by a board comprising at least as many extern as intern assessors with an independent Irish person as chairman, and making the judgment of such a board virtually final. If any concession has to be made to the over-riding authority of a governing body, a two-thirds or larger majority of such a body should be needed to overturn the assessors; even that might, I fear, still leave some room for the undesirable personal canvassing which has occurred in the present NUI appointments system.

I am sorry that the Minister's approach is based more on a view of NIHE Limerick as a State-sponsored body to be tightly controlled rather than as a pioneering third-level institution in the technological field, meriting a high degree of flexibility of action, subject to the two public interest qualifications on which I have focused as being particularly important. I intend to submit amendments on these two matters on Committee Stage.

On the Committee Stage the next day (3 July 1980) I put forward two amendments. The first was to insert a new sub-section in Section 9 to read:

(3) The following provisions shall have effect in relation to any appointment to the academic staff of the Institute:

(a) Whenever such a appointment is proposed, applications from duly qualified persons shall be invited by advertisement in media of wide circulation in Ireland and at least two other member countries of the European Economic Community.

(b) A board of assessors shall be appointed by the Governing Body, after consultation with the Academic Council, to examine the applications and recommend, having stated the grounds for their choice, the candidate whom they, by a majority, consider the most suitable for appointment.

(c) The board of assessors shall consist of five persons of whom not more than two may be members of the Institute and not less than two shall be nationals of member countries of the European Economic Community other than Ireland, and of whom the chairman shall be an Irish national who is not a member of the Institute.

(d) Should the board of assessors decide to indicate, in addition to their first preference, their second or later preferences for appointment to a particular post, they shall state the grounds on which they have determined their order of preference.

(e) The recommendation of a board of assessors shall be approved and given effect by the Governing Body unless a majority of at least two-thirds of the membership of the Governing Body shall decide otherwise, in which event another candidate regarded by the board of assessors as qualified for the appointment may be appointed.

This amendment is an attempt to give more explicit expression to one of the two major proposals I made last night on the Second Reading.

I would like first to draw attention to the fact that section 9 refers only to the appointment of officers and servants. It makes no specific reference to academic staff. It makes no distinction between staff of any kind, catering or teaching staff – a point which does lend some support to the impression that the model is a state body rather than an educational establishment. The amendment I am sponsoring does make the distinction between academic and other staff. It relates only to academic staff and is an attempt to lay down a statutory procedure for the appointment of academic staff, building into that procedure an assessment board system of a certain kind with external as well as internal representation and an independent chairman and according a preponderant weight in regard to appointments to the decision of the assessment board.

I explained last night that I thought a statutory procedure of this kind is a necessary public interest safeguard which should apply not only to the National Institute for Higher Education in Limerick but to every university and third-level institution. The purpose is to safeguard excellence and impartiality in appointments to senior teaching posts and this is a matter of vital importance to the public which is called upon to finance these third-level institutions and which relies on them for the highest qualities in their teaching staff and the highest standards in their courses.

Assessment boards are commonplace in present appointment procedures but they are not always mandatory. The National University is a case in point where recourse to assessment boards was not prescribed originally in the Act or charter but where this procedure is in fact used voluntarily because of its efficacy in examining objectively the merits and achievements of candidates. The Minister told us last evening that the assessment board procedure is also used in the NIHE. In neither case, however, in neither the National University at the moment nor in the NIHE, is it necessary to have recourse to such a procedure. In neither case does any special weight have to be given to the recommendations of an assessment board. In the case of NUI, it has sometimes happened that the unanimous recommendation of an assessment board has been overturned by a small majority of the appointing body – in the case of the NUI, the Senate – as a result of, or following canvassing of the statutory recommending and appointing bodies by candidates who were not recommended as a first choice by the assessment board.

I am not saying that assessment boards should never be overturned but I do think that efforts to do so by canvassing should be discouraged. The proposal in this amendment is that it be discouraged by making a two-thirds majority of the appointing body necessary to overturn it. This would preserve the final authority of the appointing body, in the case of NIHE the governing body, and would enable it to correct an eccentric decision of an assessment board, should such occur, however rarely. Also in the amendment there is a provision that assessment boards should state clearly the reasons for their choice of candidate and for any preferences they may indicate.

I am putting forward this amendment because I regard an appointments procedure based on assessment boards as not just a desirable but a necessary element in the constitution of third level institutions of all kinds. I hope the Minister will be able to revise the initial negative reaction he expressed last night. He did say that assessment boards are common and are being used by NIHE but he would be the first to recognise the distinction between what is (which may not be permanent and could be changed) and what ought to be, which is what I am concerned about in this amendment. This is why I am suggesting that this sort of provision is an appropriate part of the constitutional framework of third level institutions.

While this proposal received some support, it was also criticised as being restrictive and unnecessary. The Minister's rejection was, indeed, based not on principle but on the existence already of voluntary arrangements to the same effect. My final comment before the amendment was defeated was that I did not consider such an important arrangement ought to be left to good sense and goodwill when an opportunity existed to make it a statutory requirement.

On the other major point of public interest – adequacy of standards – my proposal was to add a new section to the Bill as follows:

The Governing Body shall, following consultation with the Academic Council, appoint external advisors from member countries of the European Economic Community other than Ireland to report at least once every three years on the adequacy of the standard required for each degree level and diploma level courses of the Institute having regard to standards for corresponding degrees and diplomas in their respective countries.

Again, by way of this amendment I am raising a point of principle which is relevant not only to NIHE but to universities and other third-level institutions. As things stand under this Bill, the standard of degree and diploma courses followed in the NIHE will be determined by the National Council for Educational Awards. I said last night that I had respect for and faith in the NCEA. I am, however, dealing with what I consider to be a principle of fundamental importance from the point of view of safeguarding the public interest, namely, the principle that the constitution of third level bodies, the Act providing for their establishment, should provide for a check on the adequacy of the standards of the qualifications they offer or for which their courses prepare. I mean adequacy not only by domestic comparisons but, now that we are a member of the Community, by reference to the standard of corresponding qualifications elsewhere and particularly in the EEC.

. . .The NUI is obliged by its charter to have external examiners in connection with each of its degrees. . . . However, the NUI is to be disbanded in due course and new independent universities are to be set up under fresh legislation. That is why it is important that, at this juncture, we should not lose sight of a requirement which was thought to be necessary and desirable 72 years ago when the NUI was founded. Therefore, I propose an amendment which requires at least periodic consultation, that is every three years at least, with appropriate external advisers on the adequacy of the standards required in the degree level and diploma courses of NIHE.

Last night the Minister said this kind of amendment, strictly speaking, should be to the NCEA Act itself. I submit that the principle is of general relevance to third level institutions. The Minister said that this Bill will be a model for the constitution of other third level institutions and, *faute de mieux*, I have had to phrase the amendment so as to apply to the standard of courses rather than to the degrees and diplomas themselves.

Again, this proposal was supported by Senator West and others but was not accepted by the Minister for Education who was content to rely on the applicability to the NIHE of the provisions of the National Council for Educational Awards Act, 1978 in regard to standards of courses and degrees. My concern, of course, was with what might happen in the case of the *universities* when legislation to give them independent status was introduced. In my reply to the debate I reiterated my concern – and there, for the present the debate rests:

At least this debate emphasises the importance we attach unanimously to there being very strict standards, very high standards, for degrees and diplomas in all institutions which we finance out of public funds. I would hope that the Minister's disposition to rely on the national authority, whatever it might be, always to do the right thing, with which I go a long way, will not be generalised by him so as to free the new universities when he sets them up from any monitoring by way of external examiners. I would emphasise the importance of this safeguard which has been present, as has been said by me and others, in the case of NUI for 72 years. It has proved its worth over that time and has at times proved somewhat of an embarrassment in certain faculties but has brought the national institution very quickly to set matters right. The experience of a responsible institution such as the NUI would suggest that it is desirable to have some public safeguard in legislation dealing with higher level institutions so as to ensure not only that there is an external check on the standards but also external support for efforts which the native institution will always be seeking to make to improve things.

Even in the financial field we find that it is a great help to the country to have a critical body like the World Bank or the European Investment Bank, the EEC or the IMF standing outside objectively to advise us on what needs to be done. I think the Minister would agree that Governments often find this a great help in strengthening their own resolve to steer a true course at home.

## Note to Chapter 18

[1] The National Council for Educational Awards, established by Act of 1978.

*Seán S. Ó hÉigeartaigh.*

# IV Commemoration

## 19 Seán Sáirséal Ó hÉigeartaigh

Baineadh as mo riocht mé Dé Déardaoin nuair a leag mé súil ar an ngiota sa pháipéar faoi bhás Sheáin. Ba é an scéal céanna ag a chuid comrádaí uilig sa Roinn é. Ba dhoiligh agus ba leasc linn a chreidbheáil go raibh fear cumasach lúfar mar é, a bhí ag obair ar theann a dhíchill san oifig go dtí a sé tráthnóna Dé Chéadaoin, sciobtha uainn ar shlí na fírinne.

Ba léir ariamh go raibh mianach a athar ann: a dhílseacht don náisiúntacht, a bhá leis an chultúr Gaelach, fiú an toil a thug sé don rothar agus do Rugby, thug siad sin i gcuimhne é. B'fhurast a mheas go raibh an do-chloíteacht chéanna ag baint leis agus nár bhaol go dteipfeadh an tsláinte air. Is cosúil, faraoir, go raibh ball éigin dá chorp a bhí so-ghonta, dálta laochra na seanscéal, ach gur i ngan fhios dó thárla an laige seo air.

Ró-fhuinniúil a bhí ar dhóigh. Ní dhearna sé ariamh aon dá chuid dá dhíograis. Is eol don saol go raibh saothar beirte á dhéanamh aige le blianta fada – sár-obair ealaíonta sa Roinn a ndéanfaidh mé trácht uirthi ar ball – agus, ar dhul abhaile dó, sclábhaíocht i mbun clóphreasa go dtí an meán-oíche nó fiú go teacht an chéad-sholais, chun leabhair Gaeilge a chur ar fáil.

Chaith Seán a shaol oifigiúil go léir sa Roinn Airgeadais seachas tréimhsí sa Roinn Soláthairtí, sa Roinn Tionscail agus Tráchtála agus mar ionadaí na Roinne Airgeadais ar chúrsaí pinsean sa Roinn Cosanta. Ba shaineolaí ar dhúrúnta na bpinsean é. Chaith sé tamall ag gabháil d'idir-réiteach agus eadráin sa Státsheirbhís, an chuid ba thaitneamhaí ar bhealach dá dhualgaisí oifigiúla óir thug sé caoi dó a bhuanna díospóireachta a chur i bhfeidhm. Ba bhreá le haon duine a bheith ag éisteacht leis agus cúis á plé aige os comhair an Bhoird Eadrána – na fíricí bailithe le chéile go paiteanta aige, an argóint go loighciúil agus an sruth cumasach cainte. Is fada go sárófar é.

Ba é ionadaí na hÉireann é ar bhuíon eadarnáisiúnta a bhí ag dréachtadh rialachán do Státsheirbhís na hEorpa agus cáil mhór air dá bharr.

Chaith sé lán a dhúthrachta le gach ní a thóg sé idir lámha. Bhí sé ar dhuine de na Státsheirbhísigh ba mhó léann, díograis agus éifeacht lena linn agus bhíothas ag brath ar chuidiú mór uaidh ag tabhairt aghaidh ar an gComhargadh dúinn. Is tubaisteach an chaill don Stát é Seán a bheith cnagtha ag an mbás agus é in ard a réime is a mhaitheasa. Duine bríomhar, diongbháilte a bhí ann, a raibh barúla aige nach réiteodh cách leo, ach duine séimh, sibhialta chomh maith, nár chleacht ariamh aon chaimiléaracht ná cos ar bolg. Idéalaí ab ea é gan amhras, ach níor fhan sé i muinín na bollscaireachta: ba mhó go mór aige an beart ná an chaint. Níl aon áireamh ar a ndearna sé le litríocht na Gaeilge a chur ar aghaidh. Chaith sé iomlán a chuid saor-ama agus maoine leis.

Ní háibhéil a rá go dtug sé a shaol ar son na hÉireann agus ar son na Gaeilge – saol a giorraíodh de bharr a dhíograise. Ní beag sin de theist air.

Sonas síoraí dó agus sólás croí dá bhean is dá mhuirín.

# 20 Dr J. J. McElligott

On Wednesday afternoon last J. J. McElligott attended as usual the board meeting of the Central Bank and made, as was his form, some terse and critical comments on matters that arose. Although he had become very frail recently, his mental alertness showed no decline. He died in his sleep that night. There is no doubt but that is how he would wish to go, quickly and quietly, with no contraction of the range of his intellectual interests.

From an Honours BA in Classics at UCD in 1912 he proceeded, despite exciting adventures in the interim, to an Honours MA in Economics in 1917. He had already, in 1913, entered the civil service at administrative level, being assigned to the Local Government Board. On his way back from the races in Fairyhouse on Easter Monday, 1916 he gained admittance to the GPO to take part in the Rebellion. Afterwards he became exceedingly reticent and even caustic about this and other facets of Irish nationalism. But the legend is that his experiences included kicking his way through Clery's plate-glass window to open an escape route to Marlboro' Street; seeking refuge behind a pillarbox there only to find Seán McEntee already installed and drawing unwelcome fire from all quarters; winding up in Stafford Jail beside Michael Collins; and being arrested a few years later for reconnoitring Chequers when Lloyd George was in residence.

In 1923 he was recalled from the managing editorship of *The Statist* to become an Assistant Secretary in the Department of Finance and he succeeded Joseph Brennan as Secretary in 1927, a post he held for 26 years.

When he left the civil service in 1953 it was to become Governor of the Central Bank for seven years and then to continue to serve as a director. Indeed, the continuity of his membership of the boards of the Currency Commission and its successor, the Central Bank, was unbroken, extending over the whole 47 years of the life of these institutions. This close identification with the evolution of the currency and credit system in Ireland was reinforced by his membership of both Banking Commissions, that of 1926 and that of 1934-38.

J. J. McElligott's long tenure of office as Secretary of the Department of Finance was marked by tenacious adherence to the classical principle of curbing public expenditure and taxation, though this was moderated by recognition of the need for major productive developments, such as the Electricity Supply Board. He was more in sympathy with Adam Smith and Gladstone than with Keynes or Dalton. It now seems incredible that there was a reduction in government expenditure during the 1920s, that it was only £25 million in 1930, and we were taken through World War Two with an aggregate of only £16 million in budget deficits. The formative work done in the early years by men like McElligott did much to establish the respectability and viability of the new state. His talents and influence were devoted unreservedly to the service of that state. He was a member of all the important economic and financial commissions and committees of his time and represented Ireland at many international conferences. He was president of the Institute of Bankers in Ireland in 1956 and the first president of the Economic Research Institute. The National University of Ireland honoured him in 1946 with the degree of Doctor of Laws.

My first recollection is of him sitting in his austere corner room in the Department of Finance, dressed in an alpaca coat and casting a cold eye on those who came to argue for more staff or bigger budgets. Ireland, he would remind us, was a small and poor country and should not entertain imperial notions of expenditure. Yet this forbidding exterior was, in reality, a protective crust he had built around the inner fires of emotion. He was upset for a long time when a versatile and lovable colleague, Walter Doolin, died. He concealed his deep and genuine patriotism under a cover of sarcasm. But when one broke through the artificial defences, as the brave and fortunate did, no man could be more reasonable and considerate or more entertaining company.

Tenacity of purpose and fearlessness in expressing his views were amongst his great qualities. He had a penetrating mind and a most enviable capacity to present his thoughts in perfect order and with classical precision. Even his handwriting bore testimony to these gifts, which some will ascribe to his education in, and feeling for, the classics. A man of simple tastes, he liked nothing better than to read in the evenings, smoking endless pipes.

He had married in 1927 Miss Ann Gertrude Fay of Edenderry, who predeceased him, and he found great happiness in his home life, in his family relationships and in the company of friends. His memory will live as one of the greatest of our public servants. We offer to his daughter Ann, her husband and children, and to his other relatives, our sympathy in their sorrow.

*Dr. J. P. Beddy.*

# 21   Dr J. P. Beddy

When the history of Irish industrial development comes to be written, the name of Dr J. P. Beddy will have the prominence and honour due to a pioneer. It was his quiet genius that brought from infancy to strength the financial and promotional institutions on which our industrial progress has been based.

For four decades, ever since he left the inspectorate of taxes in 1933 to join the newly-established Industrial Credit Company, as its first secretary, his gentle but authoritative hand has guided the evolution and expansion of Irish industry. He had become much more than secretary of the Industrial Credit Company before he succeeded the late J. P. Colbert as its managing director in 1952. Already he had equipped himself academically, as well as through experience, to perform a public service of the highest quality. The mature articulation of theory and practice which informed his analysis, assessment and organisational decisions was indicated even in the title of his thesis on 'Profits – Theoretical and Practical Aspects' published in 1940 and for which he received his Doctorate in Economic Science. He lectured for many years in UCD on economic geography.

When the Industrial Development Authority was established in 1950 as the official promotional agency he was the natural choice as its first chairman. He was also the first chairman of the grant-giving authority – An Foras Tionscal – set up in 1952. He was then at the apex of the institutional system for both the promotion and the financing, through loans, share issues and grants, of Irish industry. He exercised his acuteness of judgment and gave his fair, well-considered and cogent advice on all the major projects of the fifties and sixties. He retired as chairman of the IDA in 1965, remained chairman and managing director of the ICC until 1969, staying on for a while afterwards as part-time chairman.

A shy man, he was yet the best of company, with a keen sense of humour, and discriminating taste. He preferred the excellent in moderation to the good in abundance – a single Corona a day, a thimbleful of the best brandy at night.

Born in Cobh in 1900, he was later in the same class at O'Connell Schools in Dublin as Sean Lemass. He lost his heart to Kerry when he was an inspector of taxes in Tralee. He made his name on the Kerry bogs as one of the sharpest of snipe shooters. He was interested in sailing, too, but fishing was his most abiding love. Some of my happiest days were shared with him on Lough Inagh, where he would fish a purist's wet fly despite his rival's greater success with the 'dap' and would meticulously prepare tomato soup for lunch in the fishing hut.

Jim Beddy lived for his work and his family and his wife's death a few years ago created a great void. An expression of sympathy with his daughters, son and their families must contain a special word for his granddaughter, Maeve, whose companionship and love were always, and particularly in the latter years, a great comfort to him. A public servant who achieved much for Ireland, yet shrank from any praise or recognition for it, has gone to his eternal reward.

# 22  James Hamilton Delargy

The man I commemorate tonight was one of yourselves – a man from these parts. He entered life here on the Antrim coast where, reputedly, the first men entered Ireland; he lived as a child in the Glens – but a child who 'knew the grace for light';[1] and he went forth to harvest the rich but fast perishing oral tradition of simple Irish folk whose way of life had changed little over thousands of years.

James Hamilton Delargy was born in Cushendall on 26 May 1899. His father died when he was only two and, a few years later, his mother brought him and his brother to live in Glenariffe. As he himself said:

> . . . we left the old house which my grandfather, Captain James Delargy, had built in the intervals spared from seafaring. . . . I was between four and five years of age at the time, but I can still hear the grating of the wheels of the 'long car' on the gravel outside my father's door, and the crack of the whip of Davy Johnston, the driver, as the long unwieldy vehicle lumbered off, and the look we gave across our shoulders at the past we were leaving behind.

He also described to me the view from the little house in the Glen.

> In front of us was the sea, and on stormy winter days the spray came whirling in before a north-easter to rattle on the window-panes and the rain-squalls shut out the as yet unspoiled vision of sheer beauty – Red Bay and the long sandy beach (An Tráigh Bhán), the ruined castle of the

MacDonnells at Uaimh an Deirg, and in the far distance
the islands and the headlands of Kintyre.

These quotations, and others I shall use later, which reveal
Séamas Delargy's poetic feeling and love for the past and its
people, are taken from the typescript of interviews I had with
him during 1974, when he was already 75 years of age. Fearing
that he would keep on postponing an account of his remarkable
life and achievements, so intent was he still on bringing edited
records of Irish folklore into print, I, with others of his friends,
sought a way of coaxing from him a mémoir of his early life
while relieving him as much as possible of the effort involved.
So I turned to the device of interviewing him, taking a tape
recording of the conversation, and having it typed. He willingly
co-operated in this turning of the tables on himself – our
foremost collector of folklore – and we spent many agreeable
hours together in his home, with a hospitable glass of whiskey
within reach, initially recording his reminiscences and subsequently checking and editing the typescript. One evening he
produced a short piece of autobiography, mainly of his boy-
hood years, which he had already committed to paper. It was
agreed that I should thread this into the record at the appropriate points. The resultant typescript of forty-six pages leads
up to his return to Dublin from Scandinavia and his vision, as
the mail-boat came in, of his life's vocation.

> I went right out to the bow and I saw the Irish hills. That
> is a long time ago – 1928 – and I said 'the tradition of
> Ireland is behind those hills and we've got to rescue it before
> it's trampled into the dirt' . . . , because it was a jewel of
> great price and one had to see that it was given a refuge and
> an appreciation by the Irish people.

The little boy in the Glens heard his first folktale from the
village part-time barber. But let me draw upon his own
account:

> He was a very knowledgeable man. He could build a boat
> and shoe a horse, and dance a jig, and had many other
> accomplishments. He was a friendly man and had a way

with children, and my mother sent for him when she made the great decision to have my red hair cut for the first time. He came with a smile on his face, and a big pair of scissors in his hand, and he frightened the life out of me, for I knew that something terrible and irredeemable was going to happen, and that I was drawing away from my mother's apron-strings and about to take my first step forward into a strange world. So I cried, and howled, and poor Jimmy stood there with the scissors in his hand, and looked at poor mother who felt half-resentful herself and was on the brink of tears. I forget now which of them solved the difficulty, and stopped me from howling my lungs out. Anyhow the upshot of it all was that if I stayed quiet and let him cut my hair he would tell me a story. That's how I heard my first folk-tale.

What might have become a nightmare became a longed-for ritual, for every time Jimmy came to cut my hair he brought with him a new story. It might be a tale about the fairies in Tiveragh, the fort on the hill above the village where the 'wee folk' lived, and rode around the country on the yellow ben-weed which made the finest horses that ever you could see, much finer than the shaggy 'shilty' ponies which we children saw the farmers driving in flocks off the hills of Glenariffe and Garron to the fair at Cushendall. Or it might have been the story of the 'grógach' a wee hairy fairy who used to help the farmers in old times to thresh their corn but had a great dislike for anyone who offered to reward him.

When I look back on the road that I have travelled and count the milestones, and think of some of the strange things that have happened to the litttle red-haired boy who lived long ago – and long ago it is – in the Glens, I think that these tales told by the long dead part-time barber gave a twist to the road that lay ahead. If that be so, soft may the sod lie on Jimmy's head, and God give him peace, for those tales have indeed brought me into pleasant paths and friendly company, not only in the Glens of Antrim but through most of Ireland and many another land besides.

The school in the Glen, with a mossy well beside it on the roadside, had the distinction of being No 1 on the official lists, the school in the native glen of Sir Alexander MacDonnell, Commissioner for National Education, the No 1 school of Ireland to its proud pupils.

> The school is gone now but the well remains. It was there when I visited the Glen in 1944 after almost 20 years' absence, the same mossy well, the same limpid ice-cold water, the same violets and primroses. And my mind went back to the days of my youth, and to my own people who sleep in the only land I own, the graves in the churchyard at the End of the Bay.

In 1907 the Delargy family left the North for ever. The two brothers were sent first to a convent school in Kilcool, Co. Wicklow and later to Castleknock College, near Dublin, 'from which in due course my brother went to sea, and I, a transgressor to tradition, to the University, where I stayed'.

It was at Castleknock that the young Delargy fell in love with the Irish language. The Irish teacher was Frank Fahy, many years afterwards Ceann Comhairle (Speaker) of Dáil Éireann, who encouraged his interest, gave the boy extra lessons and threw open a cupboard of Irish books for him to read. Then, on holidays with his aunt, Mrs McDonnell, in his native Cushendall at the age of sixteen he made his first trip to the Gaeltacht. His aunt had given him a half-sovereign to bring him to Rathlin Island to attend a summer school of Coláiste Comhaill in Belfast, which was in charge of a Miss Haverty, a 'good woman and a true Gael'. His account of the voyage is amusing but would take too long to tell. He remembered that it was Paddy McQuilkin from Rathlin who owned the ferry, a sailing boat, and that he paid a shilling to go across. The rest of the fare was paid in kind – passengers had to pick up big stones from the foreshore and put them in the boat as ballast. He saw the irony of the pupils being taught at the summer school from the Munster Irish texts of An tAthair Peadar (Fr Peter O'Leary) although the language of the islanders was much closer to Scottish Gaelic than Irish. He describes a pamphlet called *Scéaltan Reachreann* as a not very reliable collection of tales by an eccentric Gaelic Leaguer named Aoidhmín Mac Gréagóir 'who wore only Gaelic League clothes, Gaelic League boots and all that'. It was, however, this little book which gave him the longing to visit Rathlin.

I have beside me as I write ten pages of notes in a careful schoolboy hand taken down during that first visit to Rathlin, when he stayed with Dan and Jane Craig for three shillings a week. Some of them are proverbs in Rathlin Irish: *Mar san is téinne an gad, san is dóiche a bhriseadh* (the tighter the knot, the nearer to breaking-point); some are common expressions – *chan fhiach duit do shaothar ag teacht* (it's not worth your while coming) – but, even at this early stage, differences of pronunciation, grammar and idiom are being noted. He returned to Rathlin in 1916, 1918 and, possibly, in 1920.

The interest awakened in Castleknock and nurtured in Rathlin brought him to the Aran Islands and Donegal in 1918 and to the Hebrides in 1919 and 1922. Meanwhile, the Glens were not forgotten. On holidays with his aunt in Cushendall he searched out the last speakers of the Antrim Irish of which he was unaware when he went to school in Glenariffe. Irish had been ebbing out of the Glens – out of Glenballyeamon and Layde and Glenariffe – but a brother of the last great storyteller of Glenariffe was still living in Waterfoot, Jimmy McAuley. Every evening Jimmy went to Red Bay pier to fish and the young man from Dublin, whose grandfather was himself a native Irish speaker, went with him to fish and listen. It was on Red Bay pier that he took down his first tale in Antrim Irish in an 'exercise book' with 1920 on the cover which I have by my side. It begins

*Innsidh mé scéal beag dúit a chuala mé vón tsean mhúintir tiomailte air rud a thachair uair amháin ann áite a bheir siad Cloch Corr air. Bhí coinfheasgar amháin agus bhí sé éagsúil ceodhach: Chan fhaiceas tú do fhaid féin roimhe leat agus díreach an t-am is measa a bhí sé shiubhal duine beag asteach 'un a taighe agus ghuidh sé orra fasgadh na h-oíche dó . . . .*

Another story, recorded in September 1920 from the same man, deals with the hunting down of the last wolf in Ireland – *'mhairbh siad an faolchú fá dheire a bhí in Éirinn ann garrdha*

*m'athar ... stróich (na madaí) é óna mhullach go dtí a shál'.*
In 1920 and 1921 also he took down stories from Barney
Bhriain MacAuley of Glenariffe and visited Maire Mhór
MacCormack on the road to Cushendall and the McKay
sisters and brother at the top of Glenariffe. He had photographs
taken of them all and encouraged Éamonn Ó Tuathail, later
Professor of Irish at Trinity College, Dublin, to record their
voices on the old Ediphone. He mentions with respect Father
Dan Tohill who was himself interested in all these old people
and their heritage and who brought out an edition of the
Imitation of Christ in County Down Irish. This priest had
once asked the Delargy boys, as they played on a low wall in
Glenariffe, whether they knew Irish and, when they said 'no',
told them they should be ashamed of themselves. Apparently,
the rebuke had a good effect!

My typescript contains some hero-tales concerning the
Delargys themselves – the sea captains whose vessels were
familiar with Shanghai and San Francisco and the tea-trade
and the voyage or *immram* of one such ship which was becalmed
somewhere in Polynesia and whose captain and crew 'ended
up in a stewpot and were eaten by cannibals'. There is also an
account of an earlier confrontation, averted only by the intervention of a Yankee Clipper, between this reckless Captain
Delargy and a British gunboat in Shanghai harbour over the
flying of a Fenian flag.

But the bravado always tends to subside into nostalgia.
'Tradition's voice was stilled when Gaelic died in the Glens.'
'The dead words on a manuscript page are a poor substitute
for the haunting beauty of the language which lingered and
died on the lips of my old friends.' A stanza of William
Rooney's was often cited:

For the olden memories fast are flying from us
O, that some kind hand would come and bind them in a
garland
Ere the present hardens and the past grows cold and dumb.

In his Sir John Rhys memorial lecture to the British Academy
in 1945, entitled 'The Gaelic Story Teller', Delargy has a
footnote deploring the loss of the oral literature of the counties

of Antrim and Down of which only a few fragments have been preserved. This area of east Ulster, he recalled, had ancient traditional links with the Isle of Man, and through Galloway and the west of Scotland with the culture of the Norse Kingdom of the Isles. In his conversations with me in 1974 he mentioned the preservation of a lost link in the pedigree of the O'Neills in the memory of an old woman of Glenariffe – Peggy Carnegie – and the value placed by that other scholarly Glensman, the late Professor Eoin MacNeill, on this crucial supplement to the genealogical records.

I have dwelt on Delargy's affection and respect for his native place because this was an integral part of the character of the man and I am certain he would wish me to convey something of his life-long *Heimweh* for the Glens.

After Castleknock he had entered the Vincentian Fathers' novitiate in Blackrock and begun his university studies. He did not stay long as a novice and, indeed, suffered his first major illness in his second year at University College. Depressed and short of money he was about to give up his studies and look for a job when, through the kind and discreet intervention of the formidable but shy Professor of Old Irish, Osborn Bergin, he was enabled to stay on. After gaining his MA in Celtic Studies in 1923 he was engaged as an assistant to Dr Douglas Hyde, then Professor of Modern Irish at University College, Dublin. In 1923 also, on Bergin's advice, he went to Ballinskelligs in West Kerry and there met the seventy year old monoglot Irish speaker whom he describes as follows in his Rhys Memorial Lecture:

The first story-teller I ever met in the south was a certain Seán Ó Conaill, a farmer-fisherman of the tiny mountain-hamlet of Cillrialaig, in the south-west corner of Co Kerry. Seen from the sea one has the impression that this cluster of six houses hangs between sea and sky, clinging to the precipitous slopes of Bolus Head, 300 feet above the sea. It is a lonely, wind-swept place where man has formed here and there out of the rocks and boulders and rough mountain land a crazy quilt of tiny fields to grow his oats and rye, hay, and potatoes. Past the houses the rocky road winds like a ribbon along the side of the hill to reach here at journey's end the last of all inhabited places on this edge of the known world. The little village of Cillrialaig will never fade from the fond eye of memory, for here I met the man in whose tales and traditions I found the inspiration to collect or have collected, in so far as in me lay, the unwritten traditions of the people of Ireland. . . .

In the collection of folk-lore which I took down from Seán Ó Conaill, there is for the first time in one book all the material recorded from a single Irish story-teller. The book contains 396 pages of Irish text alone, exclusive of notes and English summaries, divided as follows: 51 *märchen*, (197 pages); Irish Finn and hero tales 7; shorter anecdotes of mythological, religious, historical, or social-historical character 42; fairy-tales 45; tales of eighteenth- and nineteenth-century Gaelic poets 41; a few songs and song-fragments, and a collection of various smaller items of prose and verse conclude the volume.

This one book alone would stand as a monument to Delargy's prescience and perseverance as the guardian of a dying heritage.

Seán Ó Conaill was, however, only the first of a line of revered story-tellers at whose fireside Delargy sat and this Kerry collection was only the beginning of a life-time's work for which he equipped himself by acquiring further competence in the Celtic and French languages, by learning German and by gaining access, through learning Swedish and Icelandic, to the scholarship as well as the rich folklore of Scandinavia. 'The scientific collection, classification and comparative study of folklore is an offshoot of nineteenth-century German linguistic science, and reached maturity after 1885 in the work of the Finnish and Scandinavian schools' (Professor Michael Tierney). From being interested in oral tradition primarily from a linguistic and literary standpoint, Delargy was drawn to it as a scientific study in its own right and an indispensable aid to social and historical studies when, by good fortune, he was introduced in July 1927 at a lecture given by Reidar Christiansen of Oslo to a Swedish folklorist who had been learning Irish on the Great Blasket. The unlettered countryman, Seán Ó Conaill, and the erudite Swede, Professor Carl Wilhelm von Sydow, share the credit for transforming enthusiasm into a sustained and ordered zeal which, in the nick of time, brought safely into a scholarly archive an incalculable wealth of tradition doomed otherwise to oblivion.

Delargy himself, having referred to the written literature of medieval Ireland, goes on to say:

> In the unwritten literature and traditions of the Gaelic-speaking countryman are echoes out of the vast silence of a still more ancient time, of which hitherto the archaeologist has been the only chronicler. This venerable body of tradition survived in most parts of Ireland until the Great Famine of 1846-47, and the succeeding period of unprecedented evictions and emigration. . . . The scholars and literary men of Ireland, both Irish and Anglo-Irish, who wrote exclusively in English, were in the main completely ignorant of Irish, and contemptuous of the language and the people who spoke it . . . the loss of the language over most of Ireland brought about the destruction of the oral literature enshrined in it, leaving a gap in our knowledge of Irish folk-lore which can never be filled ('The Gaelic Story Teller').

The foundations of a co-operative effort to save as much as possible of that dying oral tradition were laid as early as 1927, when the Folklore of Ireland Society was formed and the publication of *Béaloideas* commenced. Delargy was to edit this Journal for forty-six years. In 1930 the Irish Folklore Institute was established with a small state grant and was later materially helped by the Rockefeller Foundation and the Carnegie United Kingdom Trust. The Institute gave way in 1935 to the Irish Folklore Commission, more securely endowed from public funds, and Delargy continued as its honorary Director on the basis of his lectureship and (from 1946) professorship at University College, Dublin. He assembled a group of distinguished and dedicated collaborators, including Seán Ó Súilleabháin, Caoimhín Ó Danachair and Máire McNeill, and a team of able collectors with modern recording apparatus. Delargy himself continued to collect – in Clare, Connemara and Kerry – as well as to direct and assess. He helped Robert Flaherty to produce in 1934 the first-ever sound film in Irish, 'Oíche Sheanchais'. Even as 'the eleventh hour chronicler of an older world', as he described himself, he achieved wonders. The *meitheal* he directed brought home a rich harvest – two million pages or more of manuscript, together with sound-recordings, photographs, sketches and numerous other reminders of tradition.

Delargy's successor in the Chair of Irish Folklore, Bo Almqvist, has described in a 1977 lecture the achievement and legacy of the Irish Folklore Commission. The Commission as such was wound up in 1971 when, with its library and garnered treasure, it was subsumed into the Department of Irish Folklore of University College, Dublin. An Chomhairle Bhéaloideas Éireann, of which I am Chairman, now has the particular duty to promote, in association with the Department of Irish Folklore, the cataloguing, editing and publication of material from the collections. It has already, under the sign of the Harvest Knot, published a number of books and pamphlets and republished the famous *Leabhar Sheáin Í Chonaill*, of which an English translation by Máire McNeill will shortly appear.[2]

I was privileged to become a friend of Séamas Delargy in his later and lonelier years, when his wife had died, his son had become a priest and his daughter was married. I was glad to play a part in arranging the transfer of the archive to University College, Dublin. We travelled to Iceland together, he for his farewell visit, I for my first. I spent happy days fishing in Erris and pleasant nights chatting with him by his fireside at 28 Kenilworth Square. I accompanied him on a last sentimental journey along the course of the River Inny, near the lodge in the Mayo bogland where the folklore collection was housed for safe-keeping during the war years. We revisited house after house, finding inevitably that many of his friends had gone on '*slí na fírinne*'. It was brought home to me that his life task had more than its share of sadness, as, indeed, is evident from his poignant introduction to Leabhar Sheáin Í Chonaill. In my few remaining words I shall be drawing on the appreciation I wrote for the *Irish Times* on the morrow of his death on 25 June 1980.

I referred to the Pauline zeal with which he travelled widely, bringing his gospel and encouragement in person and by letter to remote parts – the Hebrides, Iceland, Corsica, the Shetlands, the Faeroes. He tried in vain to interest the Vatican in organising the collection of folk-life material in mission lands. Invitations crowded on him to lecture at eminent universities. Honours for the pioneer came in numerous doctorates and in decorations from the King of Sweden and the President of Iceland. An emotional man, he appreciated this acclaim and treasured the thousands of letters from those he helped and inspired. His greatest respect and reverence was, however, always reserved for those who had confided to him their immemorial and treasured lore.

So I salute, here in his native place, a remarkable man who had the vision, the training, the warm humanity, the unflagging zeal and the organisational capacity to collect and safeguard the dying heritage of Ireland's oral tradition before it was too late. By very few in our history – apart, perhaps, from the scribes and illuminators of our greatest manuscripts and that other Northerner, Bunting – has as great a cultural service been rendered to Ireland.

## Notes to Chapter 22

[1] Moira O'Neill in one of her Songs of the Glens of Antrim laments time's change: 'Nor a child in all the nine Glens that knows the grace for light'. The traditional prayer on the lighting of the lamp in evening, even in my mother's Co. Clare, was 'the light of Heaven to our souls'.

[2] Seán Ó Conaill's Book, translated by Máire McNeill, was published by Comhairle Bhéaloideas Éireann in 1981.

*Liam Stack, J. H. Delargy and Walt Disney in Stack's house near Waterville, Co. Kerry, November 1946.*

# V  Envoi

## 23  My First Salmon

Economists say profit is the reward of risk-taking: no less a reward of risk-taking is an interesting holiday. In my case the risk consisted in venturing beyond my experience. I had never fished for anything more exciting than brown trout and that only desultorily and without spectacular success. This time my target was the salmon, often described as 'lordly' in the books I consulted. I gazed with fascination at a photograph showing A. H. E. Wood of Glassel – the master of greased line fishing – with the thirteen salmon taken to his rod on part of one day on the Dee. Even one such fish in a fortnight would make me happy. So I got a friend's advice about rod and tackle and my first large mouthful of holiday atmosphere was the hour or more spent shopping hopefully. I had to stop spending sometime and felt I had been reasonably careful when I decided my old leather coat would do instead of a new fishing jacket and confirmed that there would be a discount on the total bill – a point I hoped would earn me credit at home.

The same feeling of economy sustained me, though less surely, in accepting a smaller collapsible net than seemed certain to hold the salmon of my ambition. But I had an uncomfortable moment when I displayed all my new equipment and my wife remarked that she could buy a dozen salmon for what it cost.

The end-of-season licence was taken out, the permit to fish on the local river paid for and we were off to Donegal. Then something happened that everyone but a psychologist would consider strange: I became suddenly reluctant to try out the new rod. Instead, I explained, I would like to make a reconnaissance – to see what the river was like, where the good pools were – and I took out my old trout rod and clambered over the slippery rocks with the children. I even helped them unravel their lines and advised them on how and where to cast. Enough trout were caught within an hour to satisfy me that this humble sport was no longer interesting enough for me. I was justified in moving on to bigger game.

Not without some further reconnaissance, however, Having taken furtive stock of what others did and asked where were the best pools, I eventually got going with the new rod, finding it at first quite a tiring handful. My river, fortunately, was so tortuous that it was almost always possible to find somewhere one could stand and let the wind help to carry the line across stream. For some days hope was kept alive only by positive evidence that there were salmon in the river. I saw them jump now and then but they seemed to be wary creatures and I had begun to devote more attention to the beauties of the Donegal countryside – the long narrow hay fields, with the odd patch of oats or vegetables, in the valleys; the infinitude of greens on the slopes; the fuschia hedges and heather-crowned walls; the white or light-green cottages with thatched roofs snugly pegged down – when, unexpectedly, I took several fine brown trout and one white trout on the new rod one afternoon. Never before had I caught anything that could not be swung on to the bank without a second's delay. Now suddenly I had fish on the line that needed to be manoeuvred into a net. But how was I to perform this dexterity, balanced precariously on a rock in mid-stream? Fortunately, sixteen-year-old Raymond was at hand and with much fuss and excitement managed to bring the net over their heads.

For the first week, however, the salmon remained aloof. There wasn't enough water or else there was too much, according to the local experts. There was some rain almost every day and then it rained heavily a whole night through. The river was in spate the next morning and a host of fishermen appeared with spinners and worms. I waited until the following morning when the water was clearer and was tumbling less to try my Bloody Butcher in the run above Johnson's Pool. I hooked a larger and livelier sea-trout than I had ever handled and, being without a ghillie and still inexperienced with the net, I tried to beach him but he came off the hook at the last moment. When I had recovered my poise and called up Raymond to act as ghillie, I tried again with the same fly and shortly was into a salmon. I knew by the whine of the reel as the line was torn out in his first frightened rush that it was a 'fish'. The curve of dark blue as he jumped confirmed it.

Now I had to remember in a flash everything I had read – dip the rod as he jumps, keep a sideways pressure on him, let him tire himself out. I thought if I pulled him gently downstream that (according to the books) he would forge upstream and encounter the pull of current and line. But this was a cleverer fish. He decided to make a dash downstream through a curving stretch of rocks and brown foaming water. I followed hard in his wake, trying to keep within feel of him. Clambering up the bank of the pool I could still feel him on the line and, having allowed him another couple of runs and jumps, I began to think of leading him in to the net. At his first sight of Raymond crouched over the bank he panicked and I had to reel him in again slowly. Just as Raymond swooped at him, a second time, he did a quick roll and the line went suddenly loose. Only when I raised the rod and saw the fly whirling in the air did I realise I had lost him. I heard myself ask 'what did I do wrong?' and then I became cold, sad and tired all at once. Is there any other sport in which failure can be so poignantly disappointing? In golf, for instance, you have a chance of recovering with your next shot. But a salmon lost is gone forever.

All the resources of reason and psychology were needed to preserve even a semblance of equanimity. It was only as we were taking down the rod later than Raymond (bless him) noticed that the hook was broken off at the barb and advanced the consoling theory that this had happened as I tried to beach the white trout, so that I was holding the salmon only by a curved pin. I made a mental note to use a proper salmon fly the next time and also to be less impatient about the business of hauling in.

But would there ever be a next time? Only a few days of the holidays were left and failure seemed more probable than success. Raymond reminded me that luck is on the side of the confident and we set off the next morning saying we would have a salmon before midday. In flagrant disregard of the theory that lightning never strikes twice in the same place we

went back to the same run, a little higher up. Within a quarter of an hour I had hooked a salmon, or rather a salmon had hooked himself, and it was a No 8 salmon fly this time and I was determined to play it cool. After a couple of jumps and zig-zag runs the fish decided to dig himself in, so firmly that I could not budge him and began to fear I was caught in a rock. I had to pull dangerously hard to get him moving. We timed ourselves as an insurance against impatience. Only at the end of twenty minutes of play did I draw him into the shore, where Raymond netted him skilfully and ran with him up the bank to safety. It was ten minutes to twelve. I had to stand then holding the fish to have my photograph taken. I fear that, when it is shown to visitors next winter, I shall be neurotically deprecating about the smallness of the salmon. But *that* moment was sweet. So also was the moment when the cooked fish was set before me to serve all the family and, by common consent, I awarded myself the *curadh-mhír* or hero's portion.

Lest I should become too proud, I was subdued again before the week was out when a much larger salmon swung round unexpectedly and broke my cast with his tail. This was a fiercely acrobatic fish which I held for quite a while and I have yet to consult the experts on what went wrong. However, the incident established a kind of natural balance – in favour of the salmon and of personal humility – which I feel to be right and proper.

The sense of duty and purposiveness with which I am sometimes overburdened had drained away. So interested was I in fishing that I ignored rain and wind and could not bring myself to read or write. It required resolution even to make a short tour of the countryside, beautiful and varied though it is, with mountains, enclosed inlets, caves and high grey-white cliffs.

To be away from the river was a deprivation. This devotion brought other rewards. There was the evening when an old man joined the children and myself on the river bank and then, as I rested against the hedge with the hay field behind, recited for me a long story in Irish about a gambler who sold his soul to a beautiful she-demon for the certainty of winning at cards and how he was rescued from the jaws of hell by the clever help of an apostate priest, himself saved in the end. A stranger, indeed even an Irishman, might pass through the whole district without being aware that any language but English was spoken and this old man would have kept talking to me in English if I had not expressed an interest in Irish and invited him to speak it. Where else in Western Europe would a visitor have the good fortune of hearing from an old man by fire or riverside a stylised tale which had been transmitted orally from generation to generation? As a form of entertainment it is no longer fashionable. I regarded my experience as a rich reward for intermittent and minor fidelity to tradition.

I packed the boot of the car in the early morning in the quiet village street as the bell rang for Mass and the strong-smelling turf smoke swirled about in a breeze that was already lifting the rain clouds and revealing a blue sky. The river would be about right. But another year must go by before I could fish it again.

# Appendix 1

## Author's Notes on Items

### Ireland's Development Experience

A paper read to the Annual Conference of the International Development Studies Association, Dublin on 24 September 1982 and published in *The Irish Times* 28 September 1982. In effect this is the latest of various attempts, including the inaugural Louvain Lecture, 1981, to summarise the economic history of the state since its foundation.

### Capital Formation, Saving and Economic Progress

The publisher suggested the inclusion of this 1956 paper to the Statistical and Social Inquiry Society of Ireland which compared significant features of the Irish economy with those of countries in which there was a more favourable trend in real incomes. It was a step towards the comprehensive survey, national and sectoral, of deficiencies and potentialities which appeared in November, 1958 under the title *Economic Development*.

### From Protection to Free Trade – The Irish Experience

The inaugural Seán Lemass Memorial Lecture, delivered at the University of Exeter on 17 January 1974, and first published in *Administration*, Winter 1973. I was closely involved, as Secretary of the Department of Finance, in the final stages of this transition, from the period of the First Programme for Economic Expansion (1958) to the 'crunch' period 1959-61, the joining of GATT in 1960, the conclusion of the Anglo-Irish Free Trade Area Agreement in 1965 and other steps leading to entry to the EEC.

311

### Financial Turning-Points
A paper written especially for this collection and benefiting from my direct association, in the Department of Finance and the Central Bank, with the developments reviewed.

### Instruments of Financial Policy
The inaugural Dillon-Malone Lecture sponsored by The Marketing Society and delivered in Dublin on 6 November 1980. Published in *Management* 1 January 1981. Theory is set in the practical framework of experience.

### Ireland's External Reserves
Text of an address to the Dublin Centre of the Institute of Bankers in Ireland on 22 November 1979, published in the January 1980 issue of the journal of that Institute. First account of the diversification of Ireland's external reserves following the sterling devaluation of November 1967. A postscript brings the position up to date, in the light of Ireland's membership since March 1979 of the European Monetary System.

### Industrial Relations
Text of opening address at a Seminar entitled 'Industrial Relations – Is There a Better Way?' organised by the Cork Chamber of Commerce in May 1979. It is regrettable that the comprehensive report of the Commission of Inquiry on Industrial Relations, published in July 1981, has received so little attention.

### The Department of Finance
In this review of Dr Ronan Fanning's history of the Department, 1922-58, I give my own views on its constitution, functions and character.

### The Department of Economic Planning and Development
It was rather embarrassing that in one of my first speeches in Seanad Éireann to which I was first nominated by Jack Lynch as Taoiseach, I felt bound to oppose his government's creation of a new Economics Ministry. The grounds for my opposition are explained in that speech, which is reproduced here.

## The Central Bank, 1969-1976 – A Retrospect

These reflections, based on my own experience as Governor, attempt to rationalise the approach of a Central Bank to economic management and to describe the always delicate nature of the relationship between Central Bank and Government.

## Credit Creation for Government

A review, written for this volume, of the part played by credit creation in the financing of Government expenditure since 1972-73.

## Ireland: The Way Forward (mid-1981) with Postscript (early 1983)

The original article appeared in the July, 1981 edition of the Round Table Journal. I have restored to the text a qualifying phrase incorrectly deleted by the Editor of that Journal. I have also written a postscript summarising my present view of the situation.

## The Revival of Irish and Bilingualism in Ireland

My original notes on these topics have not hitherto been published. They are included in this volume to show, in the case of one lover of Irish, the combination of emotional engagement and critical analysis which has led to a sustained concern to keep the language alive – 'I have loved thee, Cynara, in my fashion'.

## Mise agus an Ghaeilge

A personal statement, with its humorous side, of my interest in and involvement with the Irish language. First published in An tUltach, Feabhra, 1978.

## Cultural Links

A broader view of the heritage transmitted to us largely through the Irish language but in other ways as well. Text of the John Snow Memorial Lecture delivered in September 1977 to a meeting of the Association of Anaesthetists of Great Britain and Ireland in the Royal College of Surgeons in Ireland.

*Third-level Education – Essential Public Safeguards*
Emphasises the importance in the public interest that legislation providing for independent universities and other third-
level institutions should expressly contain safeguards regarding standards of courses and degrees and excellence and impartiality in academic appointments.

*Commemoration: Seán S. Ó hÉigeartaigh; J. J. McElligott; J. P.
Beddy; J. H. Delargy*
These appreciations of departed friends are included as a
record of my indebtedness to them, which remains immense.

Ba dhuine de mo chomhleacaíthe sa Roinn Airgeadais é
Seán S. Ó hÉigeartaigh, fear díograsach, cumasach, a
chaith a dhuthracht ar son leas na Gaeilge agus leas na tíre.
Chnag an bás i dtoibinne é agus é i mbarr a éifeachta.
Foilsíodh an giota seo i gComhar, Meitheamh 1967.

J. J. McElligott's outstanding part in strengthening the
foundations of the new Irish Department of Finance and
establishing its reputation for integrity, impartiality and
commitment to economy is revealed in Dr Fanning's history
of the Department. On the personal plane, my feelings towards
him moved from awe to respect and then to admiration and
affection. He was a fearless and most able public servant. This
appreciation appeared in *The Irish Times* of 26 January 1974.

My close relationship with Jim Beddy, who died in September 1976, developed through my being officially concerned in
the Department of Finance with the affairs of the Industrial
Credit Company and then with those of An Foras Tionscail
and the Industrial Development Authority, all presided over
by him. I admired his patient and meticulous competence as
Chairman of the Commission on Population and Other Problems and of several major transport inquiries, his study of the
theory of profits and his papers on various subjects to the
Statistical and Social Inquiry Society of Ireland. He combined
the great qualities of scholarship, dedication to duty and
impartiality to a degree unusual in either the public or the
private sector. Amongst the greatest joys of my life are the
days we used spend together fishing for white trout on Lough
Inagh in Connemara. This appreciation was published in *The
Irish Times* of 1 October 1976.

Regrettably, I came to be a friend of J. H. Delargy's much too late in his life and mine. He died aged 81 on 25 June 1980. The address to the Glens of Antrim Historical Society in April 1981, which is reproduced here, is an extension of the appreciation published in *The Irish Times* on the day after his death. It will, I hope, show why I regard this man of vision and cultural concern as amongst the greatest Irishmen of my time.

## *My First Salmon*

I end with this little essay to show that one's interests are not all serious. Indeed, I believe that, for a reasonably balanced life, everyone needs to have one irresistible temptation, preferably not an immoral one. Mine is fishing. The incident occurred in Carrick, Co. Donegal in August 1964.

# Appendix 2

## Chronological List of Publications

Abbreviations

| | |
|---|---|
| *JSSISI:* | *Journal of the Statistical and Social Inquiry Society of Ireland* |
| *CBB:* | *Central Bank Bulletin* |
| *CBR:* | *Central Bank Report* |
| *Adm.:* | *Administration* |
| *IBR:* | *Irish Banking Review* |

1945 'The problem of full employment' *JSSISI* 1944-45

1947 *Financing by credit creation* Clonmore & Reynolds, Dublin

1949 'Ireland's external assets' *JSSISI* 1949

1953 Review of Nurkse 'Problems of capital formation in underdeveloped countries' and Frankel 'The economic impact on underdeveloped societies', *Studies* Winter 1953

1954 'The dollar problem reviewed' *Studies* Summer 1954

1955 'Why we need to export overseas' *Adm.* Spring 1955

1956 'Capital formation, saving and economic progress' *JSSISI* 1956; also in *Adm.* Summer 1956 and *Economic Development and Planning* IPA, Dublin 1969

1957 'Forbairt na Tíre Feasta' *Comhar* Nollaig 1957

1958 *Economic Development* (with collaborators), Stationery Office, November 1958

1960  'Staid na Tíre, Léacht an Oireachtais' *Adm.* Autumn 1960

1961  'The Civil Service and Development' *Adm.* Summer 1961

1962  'The Graduate in State Administration' *Adm.* Autumn 1962

1964  'Merits and problems of planning' *Adm.* Winter 1964

1966  'The new Ireland, its progress, problems and aspirations' Institut Royal des Relations Internationales, Bruxelles
'Economic planning in Ireland' *Adm.* Winter 1966

1969  'Productivity and full employment' *Adm.* Spring 1969
'An tÓr' *CBB* Fómhar 1969
'Monetary policy' *CBB* Geimhreadh 1969
'Banking and credit in Ireland today' *CBB* Geimhreadh 1969

1970  'The role of the Central Bank' *CBB* Earrach 1970
'Monetary developments at home and abroad' *CBR* 1969/70
'Inflation: are we doing enough to curb it?' *CBB* Geimhreadh 1970

1971  'Productivity and incomes' *CBB* Earrach 1971
'Todhchaí eacnamaíoch agus shóisialta na hÉireann' *CBB* Earrach 1971
'World poverty' *Adm.* Spring 1971

1973  'From protection to free trade – the Irish experience' *Adm.* Winter 1973

1976  'An Ceangal le Sterling – Ar Cheart é Bhriseadh?' *CBR* 1976; also in *Adm.* Spring 1976

1977  'An tSean-Chruach Fhéir' *An tUltach* Márta 1977
'Planning Irish development' *Adm.* Autumn 1977

1978  'Mise agus an Ghaeilge' *An tUltach* Feabhra 1978
'Cultural links' *Adm.* Autumn 1978

1979    'Industrial relations – is there a better way?' *Adm.*
        Autumn 1979
        'Ireland's external reserves' *Journal of the Institute of
        Bankers* January 1980

1980    'Economic retrospect' *Irish Independent* 8 January 1980
        Review of George O'Brien – Biographical memoir by
        James Meenan, *Sunday Independent* 21 September 1980
        'Instruments of financial policy' *Management* 1 January
        1981
        'The Irish pound – echoes from the past' *IBR* December
        1980
        'Who governs?' *Business and Finance* 18 December 1980

1981    'The economic need to adjust to technological change'
        *Science and Technology* February 1981
        'Ireland: the way forward' *The Round Table* July 1981
        'Future possibilities – Kilkenny Conference on Poverty'
        6-8 November 1981; Council for Social Welfare 1982
        'Sixty years on – achievement and disappointment' *Irish
        Times* 4 December 1981

1982    'Cora an tSaoil' *Comhar* Nollaig 1982

1983    'The Bank of Ireland, origins and consolidation,
        1783–1826' (the first of the essays included in the bicen-
        tenary commemorative volume, published May 1983)

# Index

Dates in brackets after an entry indicate the date of publication or foundation, or the years in office held.